ADVANCES IN HOSPITALITY
AND LEISURE

ADVANCES IN HOSPITALITY AND LEISURE

Series Editor: Joseph S. Chen

Volume 1: Advances in Hospitality and Leisure, edited by Joseph Chen

ADVANCES IN HOSPITALITY AND LEISURE

EDITED BY

JOSEPH S. CHEN

Indiana University, Bloomington, USA

ELSEVIER
JAI

Amsterdam – Boston – Heidelberg – London – New York – Oxford
Paris – San Diego – San Francisco – Singapore – Sydney – Tokyo

ELSEVIER B.V.
Radarweg 29
P.O. Box 211
1000 AE Amsterdam,
The Netherlands

ELSEVIER Inc.
525 B Street, Suite 1900
San Diego
CA 92101-4495
USA

ELSEVIER Ltd
The Boulevard, Langford
Lane, Kidlington
Oxford OX5 1GB
UK

ELSEVIER Ltd
84 Theobalds Road
London
WC1X 8RR
UK

First edition 2006

British Library Cataloguing in Publication Data
A catalogue record is available from the British Library.

ISBN-10:   0-7623-1284-x
ISBN-13:   978-0-7623-1284-9
ISSN: 1745-3542 (Series)

♾ The paper used in this publication meets the requirements of ANSI/NISO Z39.48-1992 (Permanence of Paper).
Printed in The Netherlands.

CONTENTS

RESEARCH NOTES

LIST OF CONTRIBUTORS

France Bélanger	Department of Accounting and Information Systems, Virginia Polytechnic Institute and State University, VA, USA
David Y. Chang	Department of Nutrition and Hospitality Management, East Carolina University, NC, USA
Joseph S. Chen	Department of Recreation and Park Administration, Indiana University at Bloomington, IN, USA
Hsin-You Chuo	Department of Hospitality Management, Tunghai University, Taichung, Taiwan
Jim Deegan	National Centre for Tourism Policy Studies, University of Limerick, Ireland.
Larry Dwyer	School of Economics, University of New South Wales, Sydney, Australia
Mainul Haque	Tourism Division, Department of Industry, Tourism and Resources, Canberra City, Australia
John L. Heywood	School of Natural Resources, The Ohio State University, OH, USA
Perry Hobson	School of Tourism & Hospitality Management, Southern Cross University, Lismore, Australia
Nan Hua	The School of Hospitality Management, The Pennsylvania State University, PA, USA
Tzung-Cheng Huan	College of Management, Graduate Institute of Leisure Industry Management, National Chia-yi University, Chia-yi, Taiwan

Henry G. Iroegbu	Hospitality and Tourism Management Program, School of Business and Public Administration, University of the District of Columbia, WA, USA
Colin Johnson	Department of Hospitality Management, San Jose State University, CA, USA
Nicole Katics	Management and Management Sciences Research Institute, University of Salford, Salford, UK
Brian King	Centre for Hospitality, Tourism & Marketing, Victoria University, Victoria, Australia
Thouraya Gherissi Labben	Lausanne Hospitality Research, Ecole hôtelière de Lausanne, Le Chalet-à-Gobet, Lausanne, Switzerland
Sangkwon Lee	Department of Recreation, Park, and Tourism Sciences, Texas A&M University, TX, USA
Willy Legrand	Department of Hospitality Management, International University of Applied Sciences Bad Honnef. Bonn, Bad Honnef, Germany
Joseph T. O'Leary	Department of Recreation, Park, and Tourism Sciences, Texas A&M University, TX, USA
Bruce Prideaux	School of Business, James Cook University, Queensland, Australia
Peter Schofield	Management and Management Sciences Research Institute, University of Salford, Salford, UK
Denver E. Severt	Rosen College of Hospitality Management, University of Central Florida, FL, USA
Lori B. Shelby	Department of Natural Resource Recreation and Tourism, Colorado State University, CO, USA
Philip Sloan	Department of Hospitality Management, International University of Applied Sciences Bad Honnef. Bonn, Bad Honnef, Germany

Hui Tak-Kee	Department of Decision Sciences, NUS Business School, National University of Singapore, Singapore
Chin-Fa Tsai	Department of Business Administration, National Chia-yi University, Chia-yi, Taiwan
Arun Upneja	The School of Hospitality Management, The Pennsylvania State University, PA, USA
Muzaffer Uysal	Department of Hospitality and Tourism Management, Virginia Polytechnic Institute and State University, VA, USA
David Wan	Department of Management and Organization, NUS Business School, National University of Singapore, Singapore
Suosheng Wang	Department of Tourism, Convention & Event Management, Indiana University Purdue University, Indianapolis, USA
Megan Woods	Swiss Hotel Management School, Leysin, Switzerland

AIMS AND SUBMISSION GUIDELINES

Advances in Hospitality and Leisure (*AHL*), a peer-review publication, aims to promote seminal and innovative research outputs pertaining to hospitality, leisure, tourism, and lifestyle. Specifically, the series will encourage researchers to investigate new research issues and problems that are critical but have been largely ignored while providing a forum that will disseminate singular thoughts advancing empirical undertakings both theoretically and methodologically.

The issue includes the articles on critical literature review that discuss the shortcomings of past research and provide the guidance for future research agendas in relation to hospitality, leisure, and tourism issues. In addition, empirical papers with a new investigative theme are included. In total the issue contains 10 full papers and 5 research notes.

For submission to future issues, please review the following guidelines.

Originality of Manuscript: The manuscript should represent an original work that has never been published elsewhere nor is being considering for publication elsewhere.

Style and Length of Manuscript: 12 pt Times Roman font; double spacing; APA; 7,000 words (Full Paper) or 4,000 words (Research Note).

Layout of Manuscript: First page: title of paper and author information; second page: title of paper, 100–120 word abstract, and keywords; third page and beyond: main text, appendix, references, figures, and tables.

Text of Manuscript: For literature review articles, please include introduction, critical literature review, problems in past research, and suggestions for future research. For empirical research papers, please include introduction, methods, findings and discussions, and conclusion.

AHL requires electronic submission. Please use an email attachment with Microsoft Word format to the editor Dr. Joseph Chen (joechen@indiana.edu) or send a diskette to Tourism Management Program, HPER Building #133, Indiana University, Bloomington, Indiana 47405, USA.

EDITORIAL BOARD

FULL PAPERS

A COMPARATIVE ANALYSIS OF MULTICULTURAL INVOLVEMENT IN CULTURE AND ART ACTIVITIES

Sangkwon Lee and Joseph T. O'Leary

ABSTRACT

The purpose of this research is to examine the characteristics and participation patterns in culture and art activities by multicultural groups through comparative examination using logistic regression analysis. Regarding the differences of participation patterns of cultural activities, the results show that there are meaningful changes of participation patterns by race. Income level seems to have dissipated as a barrier in attending cultural activities. In contrast, there is a meaningful change in the relationship between educational attainment and attendance in cultural activities. There are differences in art exhibition attendance by race. Income and educational attainment are also closely related to art exhibition attendance. The results of the analysis imply that it is necessary to segment the consumers of culture and art events specifically by race, income level, or educational attainment.

Advances in Hospitality and Leisure, Volume 2, 3–24
Copyright © 2006 by Elsevier Ltd.
All rights of reproduction in any form reserved
ISSN: 1745-3542/doi:10.1016/S1745-3542(05)02001-1

INTRODUCTION

It is imperative to recognize the meaning and significance of race and ethnicity in the US society where everyday life activities are becoming increasingly more impacted by ethnic and racial diversity (Hutchison, 2000). The population of Hispanics has already surpassed that of African Americans. The structure of race in the US is changing dramatically and diversity issues are one of the major issues in understanding the current American society. Therefore, more specific studies to help understand the relationship between multicultural groups and their participation patterns in cultural activities are needed. Most previous studies have assumed that the ethnic and racial groups will have different behaviors, preferences, or beliefs from the dominant white population. However, there have been only limited studies which have discovered systematic differences among groups (Hutchison, 2000).

A problem with conceptualizing the origins of the differential participation patterns among people of diverse cultural background is that, much of the cross-cultural research in leisure activity participation in the literature has tended to be concentrated in outdoor recreation, to the detriment of other areas. The realm of the 'expressive aspects of culture' (composed of the arts and entertainment), where minority populations tend to seek leisure diversion in greater numbers (Chick, 1998), tends to get less attention in such research. Even when research studies examine the relationship between cultural identity and cultural leisure activities, relatively few tend to focus on the arts (Filicko, 1996). Consequently, research that compares participation in the arts among people of different cultural backgrounds is not very common. With the changes taking place in the population because of the growth in certain racial and ethnic groups, understanding the patterns of involvement is critical for tourism planning, management, marketing, and product development.

The purpose of this research is to examine the characteristics and participation patterns in culture and art activities by ethnic groups and socioeconomic status through a comparative analysis in 1982, 1992, and 1997 using the Survey of Public Participation in the Arts (SPPA) sponsored by the National Endowment for the Arts (NEA). While individual surveys have been examined (NEA report #70, 1998; NEA report #71, 1999; NEA report #72, 1999; Schuster, 2000), there has been no research done comparing these surveys to look at changes from 1982 to 1997. These comparisons will provide meaningful new results and contribute to understanding societal diversity. In addition, by approaching consumer segmentation by race, this research will also provide useful information to event and festival managers at the various government levels in establishing festival planning and marketing. Owing to the sample, this study mainly will focus on the differences between whites and blacks.

LITERATURE REVIEW

Festivals and cultural activities are part of a thriving economic industry that continues to grow both domestically and internationally. Approximately 81 percent of US adults traveled to historic sites or to participate in arts and cultural activities in 2002 (Travel Industry Association of America, 2003). In this section, we summarize a variety of theories surrounding race issues and participation in culture and art activities. The relationship between race, class, and leisure behavior has long been a constant subject of interest for social scientists, and over the past 30 years, leisure scholars have produced a substantial amount of literature around the dynamics of race and ethnicity in leisure studies (Floyd, 1998). Many existing studies have focused on differences in whites and blacks (Hutchison, 2000). While research on the black–white differences has yet to produce any conclusive or cumulative results, much of the earlier race and ethnic literature developed around the marginality and ethnicity hypotheses.

Marginality and Ethnicity

The marginality and ethnicity hypotheses have been the two theoretical explanations that explicate the racial and ethnic variation in empirical leisure research (Hutchison, 1988; Floyd & Gramann, 1993; Bowker & Leeworthy, 1998). Researchers remain divided as to whether observed differences are due to race (Washburne, 1978), social class (Kelly, 1980), or to the combined factors of race and social class (Edwards, 1981). Dwyer and Hutchison (1990) examine participation differences between blacks and whites in an attempt to determine whether the differences were because of black ethnicity or class factors. The authors find that there is only a weak relationship between race and participation. The two perspectives, question whether differences in participation are due to the cultural characteristics of particular minority groups or to the social position they occupy in the dominant society (Hutchison, 1988). The marginality view suggests that black participation patterns result from limited socioeconomic resources, emphasizing minority social status in white majority society (Floyd, 1998;

Floyd, McGuire, Shinew, & Noe, 1994). Therefore, the marginality view suggests that differences in participation of recreational activities may be explained by differential access to recreation resources due to the income, occupation, and the inequitable distribution of recreation facilities and other public goods. Washburne (1978) argues that blacks have only limited access to leisure due to poverty and discrimination, and describes that the generally marginal position of blacks in society could have resulted in a lifestyle constrained by unmet needs and limited opportunities due to their social environment. In addition, Wilson (1980) suggests that social class is a more important determinant of economic and social opportunity than race.

Alternatively, the ethnicity hypothesis suggests that regardless of socio-economic standing, cultural processes are more important in influencing minority under-participation or variation between the two races. The ethnicity view explains differences in participation as reflecting divergent norms, value systems, and social organization between majority and minority populations (Floyd, 1998). According to Hutchison (1988), the ethnicity perspective is a cultural explanation that highlights leisure as an integral reflection of culture to explain the intergroup differences. These theoretical positions are important since they suggest different policies for meeting the needs of ethnic or racial groups. The fundamental problems for race and ethnicity research are the lack of theoretical and conceptual development and over reliance on the marginality and ethnicity hypotheses (Floyd, 1998). Some studies argue that the reason for the differences between ethnic groups might be more complex than just marginality and ethnicity. DiMaggio and Ostrower (1990) suggest the differences in art participation might come from economic status, familiarity, and even some discrimination and segregated networks. They find differences in arts participation between black and white Americans based on a cultural participation theory. Additionally, Shinew, Floyd, McGuire, and Noe (1995) suggest that there is class polarization among African Americans. Blacks within higher social classes might benefit from affirmative action and other programs, and have similar lifestyles and behaviors to white counterparts. On the other hand, poor blacks might become more differentiated from the higher classes of blacks. Gobster (1998) identifies some important themes relating to explanations for under-participation, including awareness and knowledge, marginality and opportunity, ethnicity and preference, and perceived discrimination and comfort. Floyd and Shinew (1999) suggest that the similarity of leisure preference between blacks and whites might be caused by their interracial contact, regardless of their socioeconomic background.

Convergence or Ethnic Assimilation

Yinger (1981) defines ethnic assimilation as a process of boundary reduction that can occur when members of two or more societies or of smaller cultural groups meet (Floyd & Gramann, 1993). Functionalist theories predict that ethnic cultural differences are eroded by modernization and intergroup contact and reduction of particularistic barriers (DiMaggio & Ostrower, 1990). It is assumed that interracial contact and increased interracial social interaction will increase the probability that, different ethnic groups will have a similar mode of life and access to cultural capital. Thus, greater similarity or convergence is expected among different ethnic groups (Floyd, 1999).

Structural Assimilation and Acculturation

Structural assimilation refers to the entry of a minority group into the social institutions of the majority, including the economic affordability, education, civic affairs, and government (Floyd & Gramann, 1993). Robert Park and the Chicago School suggest that differences between ethnic groups and the dominant (white) culture will disappear as these groups are assimilated into mainstream culture (Hutchison, 2000). That is, with the policy implication and cultural influence, the ethnic or racial minorities should behave the same as the dominant group (white). Floyd and Shinew (1999) find African Americans who with high interracial contact with whites had more similar leisure preferences with their white counterparts than with other blacks. The differences among race participation in cultural art events are due to differences in participants' competencies and to differences with respect to their social status position. The social status of participants in cultural events is related to the prestige of the activities (DiMaggio & Useem, 1978).

Acculturation is one dimension of ethnic assimilation. Acculturation assumes that an ethnic population may adapt and change some aspects of the dominant culture while rejecting others. The minority group only acquires cultural characteristics of the dominant group such as language, diet, and religion. Recent theoretical and empirical studies have challenged the assimilation perspective (Floyd, 1998). According to Hutchison (2000), the references to assimilation were replaced with acculturation more than two decades ago. Besides, the acculturation perspective had only been used in the studies of Hispanics (Floyd, 1998). It is not clear whether or how the assimilation or acculturation perspective applies to African Americans or other ethnic groups (Floyd, 1998; Hutchison, 2000).

Participation in Leisure Activities

With inter-group competitions, ethnic mobilization increases, minority economic advances, and institutional discrimination, assimilation will be prevented and the minority will maintain a distinctive unifying culture (DiMaggio & Ostrower, 1990). Woodard (1988) argues that social class is an effective determinant of participation in urban-oriented leisure such as visiting museums or libraries. McGuire, O'Leary, Alexander, and Dottavio (1987) compare the leisure preferences and constraints between senior white and black people. Their study indicates more similarities than differences in outdoor recreation preferences between different ethnic groups. Blacks preferred attending sporting events, picnicking and traveling, while whites preferred walking and other outdoor activities. In a study examining a correlation of participation pattern of blacks and whites, Stamps and Stamps (1985) find that there is greater similarity in leisure activities in the same race than among those of a similar social class. Hutchison (1988) points out that the differences between blacks and whites would not be explained by the simple influence of either social class or race, but by a more complex interaction between these two factors. Shinew et al. (1995) also find that the preference of leisure was influenced by an interaction of gender, race, and subjective social class. In addition, Johnson, Bowker, English, and Worthen (1998) examine the ethnicity and marginality theory of minority recreation participation by examining the differences in rural African Americans and whites visitation rates to national forest wildland areas. The authors test for black and white differences using logistic regression and the findings show that race, sex, age, and a race poverty interaction term are strong predictors of visitation. Overall, the results do not strongly support either ethnicity or marginality as a sole explanation of racial differences in recreation. Rather, they indicate that the two probably work in combination to explicate racial differences.

DiMaggio and Ostrower (1990) examine black and white patterns of arts participation. The authors find that black Americans in the arts participate at rates and in ways that are remarkably similar to that of white Americans, considering the degree of racial exclusion and oppression they have been subjected to. However, the effects of race on these activities are diminished by effects of educational attainment, and often less than those of income, gender, or place of residence. Thus, the authors conclude that the relationship between race and taste is differentiation without segmentation, meaning differing tastes, but not segregated or strongly bounded by subculture. The authors also argue that existing findings are intriguing but inconclusive, for they are based on geographically diverse samples with varying measures of participation or attendance, and also the absence of theory has impeded accumulation of knowledge just as much as incomparable data or methods have. Even if the tastes and behavior of blacks and whites are explainable in terms of a single theoretical framework, the specificity of the black American experience of discrimination and exclusion suggests that different dynamics may operate within the black and white populations.

METHOD

The 1982, 1992, and 1997 Surveys of Public Participation in the Arts (SPPA) sponsored by the National Endowment for the Arts provided the U.S. with data on a wide range of culture and art activities. Responses were weighted by age, gender, and race to represent all non-institutionalized Americans 18 years of age or older. This data contains the results of a set of questions on culture and arts consumption, parental background, and cultural socialization. The SPPA is unique in providing data on cultural socialization. Using the SPPA survey data, this research will conduct a longitudinal examination that allows for an understanding of changes of cultural participation structure and patterns of behavior.

This study employs two dependent variables: cultural arts participation activities and exhibition attendance activities. This study analyzes these two dependent variables separately to compare the differences in participation patterns of two activities over 15 years. Selected cultural activities include attending live jazz performance, live classical music performance, live opera performance, live musical play performance, live non-musical play performance, and live ballet performance. Exhibition attendance activities are examined including visiting an art museum or gallery, art and craft fair or festival, and historic park, monument, touring buildings or neighborhoods. Independent variables employed are race, gender, age, educational attainment, and household income. This research examines the relationships between cultural arts participation and socioeconomic variables. The relationships between exhibition attendance activities and socioeconomic variables are also investigated.

The racial groups in the survey are classified as white, black, Hispanic, American Indian, and Asian. However, the 1982 survey only includes white, blacks, and "other races" without specific classification. Household income is divided into the following four categories reflecting economic growth rate: poverty level (below $20,000 /below $19,999/below $9,999), low income

($20,001–$50,000/$20,000–$34,499/$10,000–$19,999), middle income ($50,001–$100,000/$35,000–$74,999/$20,000–$49,999), high income (over $100,000/over $75,000/over $50,000). Based on the general life cycle pattern, the adult population is classified into four groups in this paper. These are young people (18 through 29), early middle age (30 through 44), middle age (45 through 60), and mature individuals (61 and above). Generally educational attainment plays an important role as people acquire a taste for culture and the arts. This study uses three education categories: under-high school, post-high school, and college from the 1997 survey and two education categories: below high school and over college from the 1992 survey and 1982 survey.

Logistic regression analyses were used to predict participation in some culture and art activities, while considering the effects of racial groups, controlling for gender, educational attainment, household income, and age. Logistic regression has become commonly used to perform regression analysis on a dependent variable that represents two or more groups. Logistic regression estimates the probability of an event occurrence. We estimate the following logistic regression.

$$\text{Logit}(Y) = \beta_0 + \beta_1 RC + \beta_2 IN + \beta_3 ED + \beta_4 AG + \beta_5 GD \qquad (1)$$

$$\text{Odds}(Y) = e^{(\beta_0 + \beta_1 RC + \beta_2 IN + \beta_3 ED + \beta_4 AG + \beta_5 GD)} \qquad (2)$$

$$\text{Probability} = \text{odds}/(1 + \text{odds}) \qquad (3)$$

where Y is the cultural arts or exhibition attendance activities. RC, IN, ED, AG, and GD represent race, income, educational attainment, age, and gender, respectively. The model employed fits the application well based on statistical model criteria. The logistic regression coefficient can be interpreted as the change in the dependent variable, logit (Y), associated with a one-unit change in the independent variable. However, the change in $P(Y = 1)$ is not a linear function of the independent variables (Menard, 2001). By using the coefficients of variables, we can know the probability of an individual's participation in selected culture and art activities given his race, educational attainment, and income level. An estimate of odds ratio may be obtained from the estimated logistic regression coefficient. The relationship between the logistic regression coefficient and the odds ratio provides the foundation for the interpretation of all logistic regression results (Hosmer & Lemeshow, 2000).[1] Predictions for individual case can be obtained by replacing the variables in the equation with their values of specific cases. For instance, for a white male with early middle age and middle income levels in Table 4, logit (art museum) = −2.306−0.168(1) + 0.368(1) + 1.194(1) + 0.680(1) = −0.232.

Using this value, we can get a probability of art museum participation of $e - 0.232/(1 + e^{-0.232}) = 0.442$.

RESULTS

Cultural Arts Participation Activities

For purposes of reporting, we compare the difference in participation of cultural arts participation activities by race each year, and then examine the information across the three survey years. According to the 1982 survey, blacks are more likely than whites to participate in live jazz performance. In contrast, whites are more likely than blacks to attend a live classical music performance, live opera, musical or non-musical play, and a ballet performance. As one could predict, those with higher incomes are more likely than those with lower incomes to participate in all selected cultural arts activities. There is a large gap between the higher income and lower income groups in opera, musical or non-musical play participation. The effects of age are not statistically significant except for a live jazz performance. Young people (aged 18–29) and the early middle age group (aged 30–44) attend more frequently than other age groups. With regard to gender, the results show that females attend opera, musical or non-musical plays, and ballet at higher rates than males. Notably, the effects of education are statistically significant. People with a college education level attend more of the selected cultural arts activities than people who do not have a college education (Table 1).

The results of the 1992 survey show that whites are more likely than blacks to attend live jazz performance. This is a change of participation pattern from 1982 where blacks showed higher involvement in live jazz performance. Traditionally, as some studies (DiMaggio & Ostrower, 1992) indicated, blacks are more likely than whites to attend live jazz performance. In addition, blacks are less likely than whites to participate in non-musical performances. However, overall, the relationship between race and participation in cultural activities is not statistically significant. Therefore, we can conclude that there is no strong relationship between the two factors.

There is a strong relationship between income level and participation in all cultural arts activities except ballet performance. In other words, compared to those with lower income, those with a higher income participate more frequently. This result supports the marginality hypothesis.

Table 1. Cultural Arts Participation Activities in the 1982 SPPA.

	Live Jazz	Live Classical	Opera	Musical Play	Non-Musical Play	Ballet
Gender						
Male	0.013	−0.507	−0.405**	−0.488**	−0.419**	−0.994**
	(0.056)	(0.051)	(0.097)	(0.044)	(0.052)	(0.088)
Income						
Low	−0.051	−0.103	0.191	0.122	−0.200	−0.081
	(0.112)	(0.110)	(0.235)	(0.103)	(0.117)	(0.186)
Middle	0.084	0.151	0.355	0.695**	0.233*	0.216
	(0.110)	(0.107)	(0.230)	(0.100)	(0.111)	(0.179)
High	0.502**	0.752**	1.297**	1.452**	1.100**	0.793**
	(0.148)	(0.134)	(0.259)	(0.125)	(0.136)	(0.214)
Age						
Young	1.314**	−0.195*	−0.581**	0.018	−0.090	−0.053
	(0.100)	(0.083)	(0.161)	(0.072)	(0.086)	(0.133)
Early middle	0.680**	−0.057	−0.380**	−0.025	−0.042	0.085
	(0.100)	(0.074)	(0.135)	(0.065)	(0.077)	(0.119)
Middle	0.575**	−0.052	−0.263	0.005	−0.051	−0.185
	(0.100)	(0.075)	(0.135)	(0.066)	(0.079)	(0.126)
Education						
College	1.136**	1.649**	1.406**	1.340	1.568**	1.603**
	(0.061)	(0.056)	(0.109)	(0.046)	(0.057)	(0.095)
Race						
Black	0.811**	−0.562**	−0.542*	−0.530**	−0.582**	−0.747**
	(0.083)	(0.109)	(0.224)	(0.093)	(0.116)	(0.199)
Other	−0.381	−0.748**	−0.628	−0.861**	−0.851**	−0.543
	(0.203)	(0.188)	(0.365)	(0.168)	(0.202)	(0.291)
Constant	−3.656	−2.522	−4.081	−2.382	−2.687	−3.690
	(0.127)	(0.108)	(0.228)	(0.101)	(0.114)	(0.184)

Note: Estimates are logistic regression coefficients and standard errors.
*$p \leqslant 0.05$.
**$p \leqslant 0.01$.

Overall, the relationship between age and participation in cultural arts activities is not statistically significant. This implies there are no significant differences by age. However, the early middle age groups are less likely than mature individuals to attend live jazz, live classical music, opera, and a musical play performance. Like the 1982 survey result, females are more likely than males to participate in all selected cultural activities except ballet.

The effects of educational attainment are statistically significant. Compared to those with a lower education level, those with a college education level are more likely to participate in all selected cultural activities except for ballet performance.

In the 1997 survey, the most interesting result regarding race is that blacks are less likely than whites to attend a live jazz performance, a finding consistent with the 1992 result. In contrast and perhaps a bit of surprise, blacks are more likely than whites to attend live classical music and a live opera performance. Unlike the other survey results, there are no differences between income level and participation in selected cultural activities. However, people with higher incomes are less likely than people with lower incomes to attend the opera and musical play performances. Even though there are no differences between age groups in most cultural activity participation, young people and the early middle age group are more likely than other age groups to attend live jazz and live classical performances. In addition, males are more inclined to attend ballet performance than females. This result is different from the 1982 survey and suggests that there may be a change in the participation pattern. With regard to educational attainment, the effects of educational attainment are statistically significant. Unlike the previous two survey results, people who have a college education are less likely to participate in all selected cultural activities (Tables 2 and 3).

This study also examines differences in participation patterns of cultural activities among the selected variables by comparing the 1982, 1992, and 1997 surveys. The results show that there are meaningful changes in participation patterns by race. First, blacks were more likely to attend live jazz performances based on the 1982 survey. However, the 1992 and 1997 surveys show a shift, with whites more likely to go to in live jazz performances. This result is not consistent with the previous study (DiMaggio & Ostrower, 1990). Additionally, in the 1982 survey, blacks are less likely than whites to attend all selected cultural activities except live jazz performance, but the 1997 survey result shows that blacks are more likely to attend live classical music and opera performances. This is also a different result from the previous research (DiMaggio & Ostrower, 1990).

With regard to income, those with higher incomes are more likely than those with lower incomes to participate in most selected cultural activities in the 1982 and 1992 surveys. However, the results of the 1997 survey suggest that there are no differences between income and participation in cultural activities. Therefore, we could conclude that there is some evidence income level does not play a role as a barrier in attending cultural activities any longer. Although young people and those in early middle age are more likely

Table 2.   Cultural Arts Participation Activities in the 1992 SPPA.

	Live Jazz	Live Classical	Opera	Musical Play	Non-Musical Play	Ballet
Gender						
Male	−0.374**	−0.435**	−0.467**	−0.470**	−0.468**	−0.260
	(0.066)	(0.117)	(0.058)	(0.063)	(0.099)	(0.081)
Income						
Low	0.505**	0.166	0.669**	0.448**	0.404**	0.298
	(0.090)	(0.178)	(0.078)	(0.086)	(0.144)	(0.105)
Middle	0.688**	0.565**	1.019**	0.708**	0.697**	0.370
	(0.090)	(0.168)	(0.078)	(0.086)	(0.140)	(0.107)
High	1.089**	1.445**	1.653**	1.300**	1.281**	0.291
	(0.113)	(0.187)	(0.101)	(0.109)	(0.167)	(0.151)
Age						
Young	−0.540**	−0.294	−0.065	−0.168	0.256	−0.171
	(0.109)	(0.195)	(0.092)	(0.102)	(0.161)	(0.132)
Early middle	−0.490**	−0.465**	−0.265**	−0.270**	0.142	−0.031
	(0.081)	(0.150)	(0.072)	(0.079)	(0.130)	(0.101)
Middle	−0.152	−0.054	−0.027	−0.097	0.041	−0.075
	(0.082)	(0.146)	(0.074)	(0.081)	(0.137)	(0.107)
Education						
College	1.475**	1.478**	0.972**	1.132**	1.122**	0.972
	(0.071)	(0.142)	(0.057)	(0.065)	(0.110)	(0.083)
Race						
Black	−0.428**	−0.364	−0.021	0.054	−0.466*	0.223
	(0.126)	(0.238)	(0.095)	(0.103)	(0.198)	(0.124)
American	−0.117	−0.234	0.079	0.641	−0.798	1.409
Indian	(0.480)	(1.017)	(0.390)	(0.359)	(1.014)	(0.337)
Asian	−0.198	0.124	−0.774**	−0.852**	−0.270	−0.019
	(0.192)	(0.298)	(0.200)	(0.234)	(0.293)	(0.232)
Constant	−2.746	−4.233	−2.341	−2.547	−3.935	−3.139
	(0.089)	(0.172)	(0.077)	(0.084)	(0.147)	(0.107)

Note: Estimates are logistic regression coefficients and standard errors.
*$p \leqslant 0.05$.
**$p \leqslant 0.01$.

than middle and mature age groups to participate in live jazz performances in the 1982 survey, there are no significant differences in other cultural activities.

There is a meaningful change in the relationship between educational attainment and attendance in cultural activities. In the 1982 and 1992 surveys, people with a college education level participate more in all selected

Table 3. Cultural Arts Participation Activities in the 1997 SPPA.

	Live Jazz	Live Classical	Opera	Musical Play	Non-Musical Play	Ballet
Gender						
Male	−0.244*	0.166	0.145	0.131	−0.008	0.574**
	(0.113)	(0.111)	(0.158)	(0.107)	(0.108)	(0.150)
Income						
Low	0.223	0.064	−0.353	−0.131	−0.308	0.167
	(0.190)	(0.187)	(0.323)	(0.171)	(0.187)	(0.235)
Middle	−0.122	−0.259	−0.490	−0.335	−0.331	0.148
	(0.197)	(0.194)	(0.328)	(0.182)	(0.195)	(0.246)
High	0.036	−0.246	−1.065**	−0.685**	−0.409	−0.268
	(0.233)	(0.227)	(0.351)	(0.223)	(0.227)	(0.281)
Age						
Young	−0.810**	0.288	−0.243	0.238	0.147	−0.227
	(0.199)	(0.186)	(0.262)	(0.183)	(0.185)	(0.240)
Early middle	−0.516**	0.681**	0.304	0.251	0.184	0.051
	(0.181)	(0.166)	(0.243)	(0.163)	(0.163)	(0.217)
Middle	−0.173	0.088	0.263	0.318	0.148	0.162
	(0.192)	(0.170)	(0.252)	(0.171)	(0.171)	(0.230)
Education						
Post high	−0.233	−0.523**	−1.051**	−0.119	−0.568**	−0.149
	(0.163)	(0.161)	(0.310)	(0.143)	(0.157)	(0.212)
College	−0.479**	−0.963**	−1.478**	−0.332*	−0.968**	−0.544**
	(0.159)	(0.158)	(0.300)	(0.143)	(0.154)	(0.204)
Race						
Hispanic	0.224	0.312	0.399	0.267	0.340	0.155
	(0.201)	(0.204)	(0.325)	(0.182)	(0.197)	(0.262)
Black	−0.761**	0.606**	0.805*	0.181	0.149	0.383
	(0.189)	(0.213)	(0.380)	(0.186)	(0.194)	(0.281)
American Indian	0.434	0.169	−0.417	0.505	−0.025	−0.119
	(0.575)	(0.540)	(0.774)	(0.475)	(0.511)	(0.647)
Asian	0.515	0.027	−0.421	0.544*	0.565	0.464
	(0.305)	(0.275)	(0.330)	(0.267)	(0.289)	(0.394)
Constant	1.554	0.738	3.286	−0.276	1.153	1.610
	(0.233)	(0.215)	(0.411)	(0.201)	(0.219)	(0.275)

Note: Estimates are logistic regression coefficients and standard errors.
*$p \leqslant 0.05$.
**$p \leqslant 0.01$.

cultural activities than people who do not have a college degree. However, the analysis of the 1997 survey shows a very different outcome. People with lower education levels are more likely than other groups to participate in selected cultural activities. This outcome is also not consistent with the previous research. DiMaggio and Useem (1978) argue that educational attainment is an important factor in cultural activity participation.

Exhibition Attendance Activities

Whites show a greater likelihood for participation than blacks in exhibition attendance activities in the 1982 and 1992 surveys. However, the participation of blacks is higher than that of whites in the 1997 survey. In particular, American Indian attendance is higher than other races' attendance in the 1992 survey. Overall, the effects of race are statistically significant in the 1982 and 1992 surveys. However, in the analysis of the 1997 survey, the differences among race groups disappear. Even though art museum participation rises with education in the 1982 and 1992 surveys, it decreases with income and education in the 1997 survey.

The effects of income are statistically significant except in the 1997 survey. There is a proportionally positive relationship between income level and visit to art museum in the 1982 and 1992 surveys. In contrast, the 1997 survey results show those with lower incomes are more likely to attend than those with higher incomes.

The effects of education are also statistically significant. This analysis points toward a similar result as those discovered with income. In the 1982 and 1992 surveys, people with a college education level participate more in art museums than people who do not have a college degree. Unlike the previous results, analysis of the 1997 survey shows that each one-unit increase in college and post-high school measure is associated with a decrease of 1.585 and 0.907 in an art museum visit. This implies that people with a post-high degree are more likely to visit art museums than people who have a college degree.

Since the effects of age are statistically significant, we can conclude that there is a difference among age groups in art museum participation. Young people and the early middle age group visit more frequently than other age groups except in the 1997 survey. With regard to gender, the result with the 1982 and 1992 surveys shows that females participate at art museums at higher rates than males.

Whites visit art fairs or festivals more frequently than blacks in the 1982 and 1992 surveys. However, blacks attend art fairs or festivals more frequently than whites in the 1997 survey. In addition, American Indians also show high participation. Like participation rates for art museums, income and education are positively associated with art fair or festival attendance in the 1982 and 1992 surveys. People with higher income and education levels were more likely to visit art fairs or festivals. In the 1997 survey, however, there is a distinct change and the relationship reversed and people with higher income and education levels were less likely to visit art fairs or festivals (Table 4).

There is also a significant relationship between age and attendance at art fairs or festivals in the 1982 and 1992 surveys. Young people and those in their early middle age have a relatively high participation rate at art fairs or festivals compared with other age groups. In the 1997 survey, however, young people and those in the middle age group are more likely to participate than those in the early middle age group. Males visit less frequently than females (Table 5).

Whites visit historic parks or monuments more frequently than blacks in the 1982 and 1992 surveys although the differences between race groups in the 1982 survey are not statistically significant while the 1992 survey shows the difference among the race variables clearly. Black attendance is higher than that of whites in 1997. In the 1982 and 1992 surveys, there is a strong positive relationship between income and attendance at historic parks or monuments. The education variables also show similar results. People with higher income and education tend to be involved more extensively in visits to historic parks or monuments (Table 6).

The analysis of the 1982 and 1992 survey shows that young and early middle age people more frequently visit historic parks or monuments than the middle age group. However, the results of the 1997 survey are statistically insignificant. We conclude that there are no age differences for historic park or monument visits. Like participation at art museums and art fairs or festivals, males are less inclined to visit historic parks or monuments.

CONCLUSION AND DISCUSSIONS

The purpose of this research was to examine the characteristics and participation patterns in culture and art activities by ethnic groups and socioeconomic status. The results show that there are meaningful changes of participation patterns by race for cultural activities. Blacks are more likely to attend a live jazz performance based on the 1982 survey. However, the 1992 and 1997 surveys show that whites are more likely to participate in live jazz performances. In the 1982 survey, blacks are less likely than whites to attend all selected cultural activities except a live jazz performance, but the 1997 survey result shows that blacks are more likely to attend live classical

Table 4. Exhibition Attendance Activities (Art Museum).

	1982	1992	1997
Gender			
Male	−0.336**	−0.168**	0.227
	(0.042)	(0.046)	(0.117)
Income			
Low	0.165	0.411**	−0.177
	(0.094)	(0.054)	(0.180)
Middle	0.494**	0.680**	−0.354
	(0.091)	(0.056)	(0.193)
High	1.186**	0.710**	−0.461
	(0.118)	(0.086)	(0.240)
Age			
Young	0.423**	0.304**	−0.438
	(0.068)	(0.070)	(0.199)
Early middle	0.242**	0.368**	−0.039*
	(0.063)	(0.054)	(0.172)
Middle	0.009	0.222**	−0.197
	(0.129)	(0.058)	(0.300)
Education			
Post high	−	−	−0.907**
			(0.147)
College	1.492**	0.796**	−1.585**
	(0.044)	(0.043)	(0.153)
Race			
White	0.009	1.194**	−0.197
	(0.129)	(0.146)	(0.300)
Black	−0.538**	0.297	−0.086
	(0.152)	(0.163)	(0.347)
Hispanic	−	−	−0.379
			(0.346)
American Indian	−	1.745**	0.434
		(0.312)	(0.582)
Constant	−2.396	−2.306	0.700
	(0.159)	(0.155)	(0.361)

Note: Estimates are logistic regression coefficients and standard errors.
*$p \leqslant 0.05$.
**$p \leqslant 0.01$.

Table 5. Exhibition Attendance Activities (Art Fair or Festival).

	1982	1992	1997
Gender			
Male	−0.798**	0.020	0.707
	(0.074)	(0.048)	(0.123)
Income			
Low	0.816**	0.503**	−0.207
	(0.154)	(0.058)	(0.190)
Middle	1.234**	0.680**	−0.503
	(0.151)	(0.059)	(0.207)
High	1.017**	1.004**	−0.261
	(0.212)	(0.088)	(0.247)
Age			
Young	0.643**	0.378**	0.301
	(0.114)	(0.073)	(0.197)
Early middle	0.436**	0.318**	−0.412*
	(0.108)	(0.058)	(0.184)
Middle	0.264	0.271**	−0.278
	(0.106)	(0.061)	(0.193)
Education			
Post high	−	−	−0.705**
			(0.163)
College	0.999**	0.976**	−0.579**
	(0.076)	(0.044)	(0.159)
Race			
White	0.370	1.115	−0.823**
	(0.242)	(0.156)	(0.285)
Black	−0.817**	0.223	−0.334
	(0.278)	(0.175)	(0.334)
Hispanic	−	−	−0.316
			(0.328)
American	−	0.721*	−1.643*
Indian		(0.347)	(0.707)
Constant	−2.068	−2.829	0.221
	(0.286)	(0.166)	(0.353)

Note: Estimates are logistic regression coefficients and standard errors.
*$p \leqslant 0.05$.
**$p \leqslant 0.01$.

Table 6. Exhibition Attendance Activities (Historic Park or
Monument).

	1982	1992	1997
Gender			
Male	−0.181*	−0.326**	−0.095
	(0.073)	(0.046)	(0.119)
Income			
Low	0.709	0.436**	−0.296
	(0.157)	(0.052)	(0.178)
Middle	1.120	0.711**	−0.588**
	(0.154)	(0.056)	(0.194)
High	1.354	1.200**	−0.443
	(0.214)	(0.105)	(0.237)
Age			
Young	0.486**	0.098	−0.257
	(0.115)	(0.069)	(0.196)
Early middle	0.427**	0.177**	−0.311
	(0.109)	(0.054)	(0.173)
Middle	0.163	0.026	−0.167
	(0.108)	(0.057)	(0.182)
Education			
Post high	–	–	−0.541**
			(0.152)
College	1.137**	1.306**	−0.657**
	(0.075)	(0.045)	(0.152)
Race			
White	0.303	0.652**	−0.412
	(0.243)	(0.126)	(0.288)
Black	−0.383	0.497**	0.228
	(0.274)	(0.140)	(0.331)
Hispanic	–	–	−0.227
			(0.333)
American Indian	–	0.779**	−0.715
		(0.312)	(0.601)
Constant	−2.349	−0.855	0.450
	(0.289)	(0.134)	(0.350)

Note: Estimates are logistic regression coefficients and standard errors.
*$p \leqslant 0.05$.
**$p \leqslant 0.01$.

music and opera performances. The ethnicity perspective is supported by our findings.

Income variables are closely related to cultural attendance activities based on the 1982 and 1992 surveys. However, the results of 1997 survey suggest that there are no differences between income level and cultural activity participation. Therefore, we could cautiously conclude that income level seems to have dissipated as a barrier in attending cultural activities. This result also points out that the younger groups are less likely to attend live jazz performances. In relation to other cultural activities, there are no significant differences by age groups. The relationship between educational attainment and participation in cultural activities is ambiguous and not consistent with the result of previous studies. There is also gender difference in participating cultural activities.

There are differences in art exhibition attendance by race. Whites were more likely than blacks to visit art museums, art fairs or festivals, and historic parks or monuments in the 1982 and 1992 surveys. However, the analysis of the 1997 survey shows a very different result. In spite of the weak statistical significance, blacks, Hispanics, and American Indians are more likely than whites to participate in art exhibition activities. Income and education variables are closely related to art exhibition participation. In other words, people with higher income levels and education attainment are more likely than other groups to visit art exhibition activities. Additionally, there are differences among gender, age, and art exhibition attendance activities.

The results of this paper demonstrate the need to segment the consumers of culture and art events specifically based on race, income level, and educational attainment. The results of this study show that there are differences in level of participation in cultural activities or exhibition activities dependent on socioeconomic attributes. Understanding characteristics of participants in culture and art activities is a key ingredient for enhancing the quality of events or festivals and providing a customized service. This also enables leisure and tourism practitioners to better develop specific events or festivals to meet the needs of target groups.

Increasingly multi-ethnic and multi-racial populations urge policy makers to consider diversity in policy making for cultural events or festivals. Emerging diversity issues in American society also requires new approaches to embrace various cultural characteristics of different races. For example, the Hispanic population has been growing dramatically during the last decade and is now the second largest population in the U.S. This structural change of population could affect participation patterns of cultural events or festivals in various ways. From a marketing perspective, it is necessary to understand cultural preferences and participation patterns of each race for establishing effective marketing strategies of cultural events or festivals. In addition to race, other socioeconomic variables such as income, educational attainment, and age should be considered for segmenting consumers of cultural events or festivals.

Some limitations of this paper should be considered in future research. First of all, this study focuses on just the relationship between race and the participation patterns of culture and art exhibition activities. Thus, since this study does not cover the causes of varying relationship between ethnicity and participation patterns, issues such as acculturation, assimilation, convergence, and culture resistance, more specific studies of culture and art activity attendance are needed. For example, the patterns of cultural convergence and resistance can be obtained by testing for interactions between race, age, and educational attainment. Second, due to the different data collection approaches between the 1997 survey and the 1982 and 1992 surveys, additional examination of methodological versus substantive differences are needed. Finally, for profound understanding of cultural participation activities, more in-depth culture and art related analyses are needed. These analyses would explain the causes of cultural participation differences by race, income, educational attainment, and so forth.

NOTES

1. For more detailed information about interpretation, see Menard (2001, pp. 48–50).

REFERENCES

Bowker, J. M., & Leeworthy, V. R. (1998). Accounting for ethnicity in recreation demand: A flexible count data approach. *Journal of Leisure Research, 30*(1), 64–78.
Chick, G. (1998). Leisure and culture: Issues for an anthropology of leisure. *Leisure Sciences, 20*, 111–133.
DiMaggio, P., & Useem, M. (1978). Social class and arts consumption: The origins and consequences of class differences in exposure to the arts in America. *Theory and Society, 5*, 141–161.
DiMaggio, P., & Ostrower, F. (1990). Participation in the arts by Black and White Americans. *Social Forces, 68*(3), 753–778.

Dwyer, J., & Hutchison, R. (1990). Outdoor recreation participation and preferences by black and white Chicago households. In: J. Vinning (Ed.), *Social science and resource management*. Boulder, CO: Westview Press.

DiMaggio, P., & Ostrower, F. (1992). *Race, ethnicity and participation in the arts: Patterns of participation by Hispanics, whites, and African-Americans in selected activities from the 1982 and1985 surveys of public participation in the arts*. Washington, DC: Seven Locks Press.

Edwards, P. K. (1981). Race, residence, and leisure style: Some policy implications. *Leisure Sciences, 4*, 95–112.

Filicko, T. (1996). In what spirit do Americans cultivate the arts? A review of survey questions on the arts. *Journal of Arts Management, Law and Society, 26*(3), 221–246.

Floyd, M. F., & Gramann, J. H. (1993). Effects of acculturation and structural assimilation in resource based Recreation: The case of Mexican Americans. *Journal of Leisure Research, 25*(1), 6–21.

Floyd, M. F., McGuire, F. A., Shinew, K. J., & Noe, F. P. (1994). Race, class, and leisure activity references: Marginality and ethnicity revisited. *Journal of Leisure Research, 26*(2), 158–173.

Floyd, M. F. (1998). Getting beyond marginality and ethnicity: The challenge for race and ethnic studies in leisure research. *Journal of Leisure Research, 30*, 3–22.

Floyd, M. F. (1999). Race, ethnicity and use of the national park system. *Social Science Research Review, 1*(2), 1–24.

Floyd, M. F., & Shinew, K. J. (1999). Convergence and divergence in leisure style among Whites and African Americans: Toward an interacial contact hypothesis. *Journal of Leisure Research, 31*(4), 359–384.

Gobster, P. H. (1998). Explanations for minority under-participation in outdoor recreation: A look at golf. *Journal of Park and Recreation Administration, 16*, 46–64.

Hosmer, D. W., & Lemeshow, S. (2000). *Applied logistic regression* (2nd ed.). New York: Wiley.

Hutchison, R. (1988). A critique of race, ethnicity, and social class in recent leisure-recreation research. *Journal of Leisure Research, 20*, 10–30.

Hutchison, R. (2000). Race and ethnicity in leisure studies. In: W. C. Gartner & D. W. Lime (Eds), *Trends in outdoor recreation, leisure and tourism* (pp. 63–71). London: CAB International.

Johnson, C. Y., Bowker, J. M., English, D. B. K., & Worthen, D. (1998). Wildland recreation in the rural south: An examination of marginality and ethnicity theory. *Journal of Leisure Research, 30*(1), 101–120.

Kelly, J. R. (1980). Outdoor recreation participation: A comparative analysis. *Leisure Sciences, 3*, 129–154.

McGuire, F. A., O'Leary, J. T., Alexander, P. B., & Dottavio, F. D. (1987). A comparison of outdoor recreation preferences and constraints of black and white elderly. *Activities, Adaptation and Aging, 9*(4), 95–104.

Menard, S. W. (2001). *Applied logistic regression analysis* (2nd ed.). Thousand Oaks: Sage.

National Endowment for the Arts (NEA). (1998). *1997 Survey of public participation in the arts: Half of US adults attended arts performances or exhibitions*. Research division note #70. Washington, DC: National Endowment for the Arts.

National Endowment for the Arts (NEA). (1999). *Demographic characteristics of arts attendance: 1997*. Research division note #71. Washington, DC: National Endowment for the Arts.

National Endowment for the Arts (NEA). (1999). *Arts participation by region, state, and metropolitan area*. Research division note #72. Washington, DC: National Endowment for the Arts.

Schuster, J. M. (2000). *The geography of participation in the arts and culture*. Research Division Report #41. Washington, DC: National Endowment for the Arts.

Shinew, K. J., Floyd, M. F., McGuire, F. A., & Noe, F. P. (1995). Gender, race, and subjective social class and their association with leisure preferences. *Leisure Sciences, 17*, 75–89.

Stamps, S. M., & Stamps, M. B. (1985). Race, class and leisure activities of urban residents. *Journal of Leisure Research, 17*, 40–56.

Travel Industry Association of America. (2003). *The historic/cultural traveler*. Washington, DC.

Washburne, R. (1978). Black under-participation in wildland recreation: Alternative explanations. *Leisure Sciences, 1*, 175–189.

Wilson, W. J. (1980). *The declining significance of race: Blacks and changing American institutions* (2nd ed.). Chicago: University of Chicago Press.

Woodard, M. D. (1988). Class, regionality, and leisure among urban Black Americans: The post-civil rights era. *Journal of Leisure Research, 20*(2), 87–105.

Yinger, J. M. (1981). Toward a theory of assimilation and dissimilation. *Ethnic and Racial Studies, 4*, 249–264.

THE IMPACT OF TRAINING ON INTERFIRM DYNAMICS WITHIN A DESTINATION QUALITY NETWORK: THE CASE OF THE FUCHSIA BRAND, IRELAND

Megan Woods and Jim Deegan

ABSTRACT

Quality has been widely recognised as an important source of competitive edge in the tourism industry. Much of the focus of research to date has been on the individual firm. However, there has been a shift from interfirm competition to interdestination competition, resulting in a lacuna in the research and a need for more attention to be afforded to management of quality at the destination level. Given the fragmented and diverse nature of the tourism destination, many researchers have underlined the need for co-operation in any effort to improve quality at the destination. However, there is often a reluctance among tourism businesses, particularly small- and medium-sized tourism enterprises (SMTEs) to cooperate. This paper sheds light on the impact of training on interfirm dynamics within a destination quality management network. The findings revealed that training of network members influenced the development of a referral system, which in turn helped to create a tourism quality value chain for the visitor.

Advances in Hospitality and Leisure, Volume 2, 25–50
ISSN: 1745-3542/doi:10.1016/S1745-3542(05)02002-3

INTRODUCTION

Quality is widely acknowledged to be a critical factor of competitiveness in the tourism industry. Indeed, according to Poon (1993, p. 254), 'quality is perhaps the most important principle for competitiveness in the travel and tourism industry.' Many authors (Callan, 1994; Gouirand, 1994; Fayos-Solá, 1996; Lewis, 1997; Lenehan & Harrington, 1998; Netter, 1999) echo Poon's verdict. Indeed, Soriano (1999, p. 59) believes that, at present, quality is a source of competitive advantage, 'but as clients' demands continue to increase, quality will become essential simply for survival in the tourist business.' By 2010 Europe will have a total of 140 million people aged 50-plus, growing to 160 million by 2020. These consumers are experienced travellers, who demand high standards of quality (Klein, 2001; Smeral, 2004). As Howie (2003, p. 1) sums up, 'the tourist of today is a more experienced traveller – therefore more demanding, more informed of his or her rights and less passive in the quest for things to do – than the tourist of a previous generation.' Thus, effective quality management represents a significant source of competitive advantage in the travel and tourism industry.

However, what materialises from a literature review of quality management in the tourism and hospitality industry is that most often the focus has been on the agency level, i.e. on the individual organisation as opposed to the domain level, i.e. the level of the tourism destination. Furthermore, the emphasis has often been on large businesses, especially hotels, such as Accor North America, Four Seasons and Regent Hotels and Resorts, Hyatt Regency, Marriott International (Dubé & Renaghan, 1999; Dubé, Enz, Renaghan, & Siguaw, 2000; Enz & Siguaw, 2000), Hilton (Hirst, 1991; Huckestein & Duboff, 1999; Maxwell & Quail, 2002) and the Ritz Carlton, twice winner of the Malcolm Baldrige National Quality Award (Partlow, 1993; Haywood, 1997). Airlines also predominate (Ostrowski, O'Brien, & Gordon, 1993; Chan 2000a, b) along with tourist attractions such as Disney (Schueler, 2000; Kandampully, 2000). Yet tourism is essentially a place-based phenomenon (Urry, 1990; Dredge & Jenkins, 2003). It is the tourism destination as a whole which appeals to potential tourists; tourists go on holiday first to a destination, and then to an accommodation unit (Lenehan & Harrington, 1998). Since the fundamental product in tourism is the destination experience, 'competition therefore centres on the destination' (Ritchie & Crouch, 2000, p. 1).

While there has been a shift from interfirm competition to interdestination competition (Go & Govers, 2000), there has not been, however, a corresponding shift in emphasis in the tourism quality literature (Postma & Jenkins, 1997). Because tourism belongs to the service sector, many ideas from service marketing and quality management have been put into practice in tourism organisations and companies, especially the larger ones, but with regard to the tourism destination per se, 'only a few articles on the subject exist and there is little empirical experience to draw upon' (Postma & Jenkins, 1997, p. 184). Yet Lenehan and Harrington (1998, p. 264) comment, 'the quality philosophy must be seen to be active throughout the destination; no company or organisation can act alone in a resort or city. While commentators have considered intra-organisational quality issues, the time is ripe for inter-organisational, destination-wide issues to be addressed.' Thus, the purpose of this paper is to address this gap in the literature by focusing on the issue of quality at a destination or domain level as opposed to solely concentrating on the individual or agency level. The particular emphasis is on interfirm co-operation at the destination as a means to quality improvement in light of the fragmentary nature of the tourism destination, and the specific role that training plays in fostering this.

This paper presents the findings from a case study, which examined the interactive dynamics behind a multi-sectoral destination quality brand based in the region of West Cork in Ireland, called the Fuchsia Brand. The case study was one element of a much larger study, which also examined two other destination quality management (DQM) initiatives in France. The findings presented here relate to the specific aspect of interfirm dynamics within one such DQM system. It is argued that a greater insight into this area will allow destination quality managers to more fully exploit the synergy of a DQM network with a view to ensuring a destination quality experience. It was found that there were three phases of involvement and co-operation within the network, each categorised by different determinants. The first phase, the pre-application phase, was characterised by applicants' motivations for joining a network; the second phase, the application phase, was governed by the criterion of compulsory participation in training courses; and the third phase, the full membership phase, was determined by the members' confidence in the brand as a quality system and their perception of brand membership benefits. The focus of this paper is on the impact of the second phase, namely that of compulsory training, on the third phase, where the level of involvement and networking was more at the discretion of the brand members. Findings reveal that the training courses helped instill a sense of confidence in the brand in addition to playing a pivotal role in fostering an active system of networking and a 'destination mentality,' crucial to the competitiveness of the destination.

LITERATURE REVIEW

The tourism system is frequently described as highly fragmented (Shaw & Williams, 1994). This fragmentation derives from the number and diversity of service providers, which make up the tourism destination product. This characteristic represents a significant challenge for destination managers in light of the consumer's demand for a quality of experience. Indeed, according to Baum and Henderson (1998, p. 4):

> One of the biggest challenges facing the delivery of quality in the service sector is represented by the concept of the service delivery chain within which consumers' total experience consists of an amalgam of purchases and non-tariff encounters which may be the delivery management responsibility of a diversity of service providers.

According to Murphy, Pritchard, and Smith (2000, p. 44), 'a destination may be viewed as an amalgam of individual products and experience opportunities that combine to form a total experience of the area visited.' This definition underlines how, despite the fragmentation on the supply side, the experience at the destination is perceived as a *gestalt* by the visitor, and that there is a demand on the part of the consumer for a total quality of experience (QOE) (Otto & Ritchie, 1995). This need for coordination and consistency on the supply side is the result of an expectation for such on the demand side. Essentially, today's tourists expect satisfaction with their entire tourist experience at a given local tourism destination rather than merely with the individual components of the total tourism product (e.g., accommodation, catering and activities) that they consume within the destination at different times and places (Ryan, 1997). This has implications for the interdependency of the various components. The concept of a tourism value chain is a useful concept for discussing this interdependency. The tourism value chain illustrates that the sum of these various components (such as restaurants, accommodation and attractions) go to make up the holistic tourist experience. Each component represents a link in the value chain.

Thus, whereas an individual supplier may view the service they provide from the 'link level' i.e. as an individual and isolated component, the tourist may evaluate their holiday at a destination from a *gestalt* perspective, i.e. as a total experience or aggregate of links and therefore on the 'chain level.' Each link of the chain represents a 'moment of truth,' which can influence the quality of the visitor's experience. Ultimately, therefore, all links are interdependent. One weak link or failure point in the chain may contribute to an overall lower level of satisfaction perceived by the tourist.

Compounding the complexity and increasing the unpredictability of the 'moments of truth' is the fact that the very diversity of the tourism destination offering allows for a multiple of individual and unique products as each tourist decides the service providers with whom they will interact (Ashworth & Voogd, 1990; Postma & Jenkins, 1997). The tourist destination is actually the core product of the tourist experience, but it is the tourist who puts together several secondary and additional sub-products. Thus, there can be innumerable permutations of any tourism value chain. This underlines the highly individual character of such an aggregated product (Dietvorst, 1993). The consequences of this fragmentation at the destination level for quality are spelled out by Augustyn (2001, p. 7):

> When confronting the expectations of contemporary tourists with the fragmented nature of the local tourism destination product, one can easily realise that a tourism business that operates in isolation from other tourism/tourism-related businesses/organisations within a given local tourism destination will hardly be able to meet the widespread expectations of today's tourists.

A well-managed and quality conscious tourism establishment will, in most cases, succeed in meeting the specific requirements of its customers, i.e. those requirements relating purely to the scope of the establishment's activities, and thus only to a fraction of the total tourism product that the tourist consumes at the destination. Hence, while commitment to quality within an individual tourism establishment will undoubtedly increase the customer loyalty towards that particular establishment, it will not necessarily increase customer loyalty towards the entire local tourism destination within which that individual tourist establishment is situated (Augustyn, 2001). This suggests that a more macro approach must be taken with regard to tourism quality management, namely adopting a destination level approach (Woods, 2003).

The Call for Co-operation

The fragmentary nature of the tourism destination implies the need for co-operation. The value of strategic relationships in the tourism industry is widely acknowledged (Telfer, 2000; Crotts, Buhalis, & March, 2000). Consequently, over the last decade, there has been a proliferation of collaborative alliances in tourism, and the benefits of these have been widely reported in the literature (Palmer & Bejou, 1995; Jamal & Getz, 1995; Komppula, 1998; Bramwell & Sharman, 1999). As a result, from local to international levels, tourism planners and operators are now moving away

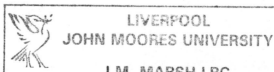

from adversarial models of operation, discovering the power of collaborative action (Selin, 1993; Palmer & Bejou, 1995; Crotts, Aziz, & Raschid,
1998; Bramwell & Sharman, 1999; Fyall, Leask, & Garrod, 2001; Telfer,
2000, 2001). Crouch and Ritchie (1999, p. 139) consider such co-operation
to be pivotal to a quality tourism product.

> There is...an emerging shift taking place in the global paradigm that demands greater
> co-operation and collaboration at the local and regional levels to ensure a quality tour-
> ism product that can compete effectively at the global level – what some authors refer to
> as co-opetition.

Telfer's (2001) study of the Niagara wine region, shows how co-operation at
the destination reaped rewards with regard to marketing, product development and product quality, which helped transform the wine route into
a highly marketable and identifiable entity as a tourism destination. As
Augustyn (2001, p. 9) concludes: 'The economies of scale associated with
such an approach together with the potential ability of a destination to meet
the expectations of contemporary tourists constitute the major incentives for
taking a formal collaborative approach towards managing quality at the
local tourism destination.'

Thus, a review of the literature reveals how collaboration and co-
operation can lead to many benefits in a variety of areas, such as marketing,
training, quality and adding value to the tourism destination product for
both the individual tourism enterprise as well as the tourism destination. In
short, many firms have discovered that more value can be created and
shared through co-operative alliances than through adversarial relationships
(Crotts, Aziz, & Raschid, 1998). As De Keyser and Vanhove (1997, p. 33)
plainly state, the complex and fragmented nature of tourism obliges the
various participants 'to learn to work together and enter agreements with
each other.' Echoing this, Postma and Jenkins (1997, p. 190) categorically
conclude that the improvement of both the quality of separate service organisations and the total perceived quality of the aggregated product 'pre-
supposes co-operation.' Thus, it is not only an improvement in the quality of
the individual services that is vital to a reinforcement of the total perceived
quality but their interconnection (Braithwaite, 1992). This concept is re-
iterated by Augustyn and Knowles (2000, p. 341): 'The fragmented nature of
tourism supply at the destination, combined with the need for the provision
of total tourism products that satisfy the visitor's needs calls for co-
operation within tourism regions'. According to Ashworth and Voogd
(1990) and Dietvorst (1993), only through co-operation will it be possible to
give a proper response to individual interests as consumers construct their

own tailored experience from the multiple services and products available at the destination. Furthermore, from the viewpoint of quality control, it is important that forms of co-operation focusing on the consumer be developed (Postma & Jenkins, 1997). In addition, co-operation is necessary, since due to fragmentation at the destination level, quality and its management becomes a broadly based and collective responsibility (Baum & Henderson, 1998). This arises from the assumption that 'no single organisation or individual can exert direct control over the destination's development process' (Jamal & Getz, 1995, p. 184). Thus, a destination can only be successful if the tourist organisations realise that they are part of a system (Postma & Jenkins, 1997).

For the benefits of co-operation at a destination to be reaped, it necessitates that tourism enterprises are willing to cooperate. Indeed, tourism models generally describe an ideal system characterised by close communication between each of the components (Selin, 1993). This has often proven not to be the case, particularly with regard to small independent firms (Sablerie, 1996; Luciani, 1999), despite the fact that their isolation (Poon, 1990; Luciani, 1999; Netter, 1999) often adds to their other constraints (Hjalager, 1996; Buhalis & Cooper, 1998; Telfer, 2001; Morrison, 2002). Travel and Tourism Intelligence (2001) defines small enterprises as having between 10 and 49, and medium, between 50 and 249 employees. Companies employing less than 10 individuals are often embraced under the term 'small,' but are also sometimes referred to as micro enterprises. The difficulty of getting small tourism businesses involved in training, and other initiatives such as quality certification and environmental tourism initiatives has been documented (Gouirand, 1994; Synergy, 2000). This is significant given that many tourism destinations are composed primarily of small and micro tourism enterprises (Gouirand, 1994; Baum, 1999; Middleton, 2001). Despite this acknowledged reticence among many tourism businesses to cooperate, it has been acknowledged that the area of collective business networks between tourism firms, particularly small ones, has largely been neglected by hospitality and tourism researchers (Crotts, Buhalis, & March, 2000; Telfer, 2000; Tinsley & Lynch, 2001). Thus, any greater understanding of the factors which encourage tourism enterprises to cooperate within a network is valuable.

In order to gain a deeper insight into the factors which encourage tourism firms to cooperate and network at a destination, attention was given to a destination quality network in West Cork, Ireland called Fuchsia Brands, where there was evidence of successful networking among brand members. The findings revealed that the criterion of participation in training courses during the application phase played a crucial role in the level of networking in the full membership stage.

METHODOLOGY

To arrive at a greater understanding of the interactive dynamics behind a multi-sectoral destination-wide quality initiative, a realist case study approach was used. A criteria-based procedure was used to select the case study. The criteria included the following attributes: recognition as a successful destination quality initiative; a certain number of brand members representing different tourism activities; a composition of mostly small tourism enterprises; and the potential for networking among its members. Fuchsia Brands Ltd. was considered to fulfil these criteria, insofar as it was Ireland's first local destination quality brand, and since its inception has gained widespread recognition as a successful tourism marketing, training and networking initiative. Established following the success of a similar food network, the tourism network encompasses a wide variety of tourism service enterprises from the accommodation, restaurant, transport, activity and visitor attraction sectors, and had a total of 64 brand members at the time of investigation. The businesses are mostly micro in size, and often family run. With regard to the destination itself, West Cork is situated in the south western corner of Ireland. The area is famed for the richness and diversity of its heritage, culture and landscape. The region's attractions range from the town of Kinsale in the east, which is known as the gourmet capital of Ireland, to a series of rugged peninsulas in the west jutting into the Atlantic Ocean. Other attractions include bustling market towns, heritage and archaeological sites, stretches of sandy beach, and opportunities for golfing, sailing, diving and hiking.

The main methodology employed was a series of in-depth face-to-face interviews with brand managers and brand members. The total number of tourism service providers willing and available to be interviewed totalled 46 out of 64, accounting for 58 of the 78 establishments which belong to the brand. In order to 'include those which represent rival propositions' (Yin, 1994, p. 150), the 46 interviews covered the heterogeneous range of business establishments in the following categories: hotels, guesthouses, self-catering accommodation, bed and breakfasts, hostels, caravan and camp-sites, restaurants, activities (such as diving, sailing and walking), attractions (such as a model railway village, heritage centre, parks and gardens) and transport (island ferry), and as such included every enterprise type represented in the brand. The interviews were carried out during the winter of 2002, and were conducted on the premises of each interviewee.

In order to gain an insight into the dynamics behind participation and interaction in a quality initiative, particularly among small and micro enterprises, respondents were asked to discuss different aspects of brand membership during the in-depth interviews. These included *inter alia* motivations for joining, the advantages and drawbacks of brand membership, the relevance and fruitfulness of the membership criteria and the nature of any links each enterprise had with other tourism enterprises, be they brand members or not. In all cases, the person within each enterprise who was most directly involved with the Fuchsia quality network was interviewed. These were the owners/managers of the businesses and/or those who had participated in the training courses (the completion of which is an important prerequisite for attaining brand membership). Both roles necessitated regular communication with the Fuchsia organisation.

Yin (1994) proposes four tests for ensuring the quality of any research. Healy and Perry (2000) have adapted these tests to the context of the realist case study approach. These tests of construct validity, contingent validity, analytic generalisation and reliability or 'methodological trustworthiness' were used to ensure the quality of the research. To meet the criterion of construct validity, prior theory was used from quality management, destination management and co-operation and network theory to define the constructs of this study. Further efforts to ensure construct validity included the maintenance of a case study database and the use of multiple sources of data and triangulation. One of the most important sources of case study information is the interview (Yin, 1994). In addition to the 46 interviews conducted, documentation was also used to corroborate and augment evidence. Different sources were the quality documents themselves, for instance, codes of practice, quality charters, customer response cards and lists of quality criteria. Market research reports, brand management reports on customer satisfaction feedback and consumer brand awareness, brand newsletters, websites and press-cuttings were also consulted. Given that all interviews were conducted on-site, direct observation provided an additional form of triangulation.

The second quality criterion for realist research is 'contingent validity,' i.e. validity about generative mechanisms and the contexts that make them contingent. This criterion was met by concentrating on why things happened and not just describing them, namely in this case study, understanding the impact of the dynamics of the second phase of brand membership on those of the third phase. To do this successfully, the context of cases like the size of firms and type of tourism enterprises in question were described.

In keeping with the third criterion of external validity or 'analytic generalisation' the focus of the research was on theory development as opposed to theory testing. Lastly, efforts to increase the reliability or 'methodological trustworthiness' of the case study involved the design of a semi-structured interview schedule and the tape-recording of all interviews, thus keeping evidence of the raw data. Word-for-word transcription of interviews facilitated the building of a case study database. This database was crucial to the consideration of alternative propositions (Yin, 1994). While concepts derived from the literature were used to guide the researcher, and particular issues were of interest, data reduction was achieved through the application of an inductive approach. This proved useful in ensuring that analysis was not confined to predetermined categories, which would bias an interpretation towards confirmation of the tentative theoretical framework.

FINDINGS AND DISCUSSION

Findings revealed that there were three significant phases with regard to brand membership, i.e. the pre-application phase, the application phase and the full membership phase. Each phase was characterised by a set of factors, which determined association with the brand. Of interest during the *pre-application phase* were those factors, which determined the decision of the tourism enterprises to apply for membership of the quality network. The *application phase* revolved around the process of satisfying a number of criteria, including most importantly, compulsory participation in a number of training courses. This participation in training courses marked the application phase. During the last phase, i.e. that of *full membership*, the determinants of continued involvement with the quality brand network appeared to be confidence in the brand as a quality system and the perceived benefits from brand membership. The major focus of the following discussion concerns the impact of the compulsory participation during the application phase (second phase) on the level of networking during the full-membership phase (third phase).

Briefly, in the *pre-application phase* or first phase, of interest are those motives, incentives and other reasons, which propelled the tourism service providers to associate themselves with a destination-based quality network. It emerged from the interviews that the motivations to become a member of Fuchsia Brands Ltd ranged from the pragmatic, such as a desire to acquire recognition for quality, to the altruistic, such as a desire to participate in a community project. Supporting the work of Selin and Chavez (1995), incentives appeared to play a major role in encouraging tourism providers to apply for membership in a network. The main factors were: the use of a quality seal, access to funding, marketing, training and advice and a sentiment of goodwill towards a community initiative.

The Application Phase: Compulsory Participation in Training

The application phase involved the fulfilment of a number of criteria. These were: membership and approval of the Irish National Tourism Development Authority (known as 'Bord Fáilte' at the time of the study), membership of the Regional Tourism Authority, an on-site inspection and compulsory attendance at a series of training courses. Of the above, participation in the training courses was the criterion which involved the most effort and commitment from the brand applicants. The focus here is on those characteristics of the compulsory training, which were to prove significant factors in encouraging networking and co-operation at a later stage of brand membership when levels of participation would be more voluntary. These characteristics are now discussed.

1. The brand's support infrastructure: facilitating businesses to raise levels of quality. Barriers to further training for small tourism businesses include 'the cost of training and inflexibility of hours and place of delivery' (Becton & Graetz, 2001, p. 113). Each of these barriers was reduced as a result of Fuchsia Brands membership, thus facilitating tourism operators' participation in training. With regards to place of delivery, training courses were held in a variety of locations throughout the region so as to share the onus of travelling among the applicants. Although some interviewees found that the journey time and distance to the training venue was prohibitive, others appreciated that the alternative would have been to travel to the major cities of Cork or Dublin. The latter situation was seen to be a major deterrent, and the difference made, especially to small and family businesses, in having training courses that were 'local' and 'convenient' was judged critical by many applicants.

Similarly, brand membership helped overcome time and financial restraints. With regard to the convenience of timing of the training courses, expressions like 'they didn't take too long' and 'they're run over winter' were commonly used. In light of Fyall et al.'s (2001) observation that the urge to collaborate appears more pressing in the shoulder and off-peak periods of the tourist season, when visitor numbers are at their lowest, it was fitting that training was organised for these periods, lessening the inconvenience for tourism service providers. Other comments concerned the heavily subsidised nature of the courses. Several operators mentioned that if an operator wanted to undertake the training independently without the support of the brand, the cost would be prohibitive.

In addition to the training courses being made more widely accessible in a temporal, geographical and financial sense, the course content was delivered in a manner which was accessible to many of the small business operators involved. Almost all the operators expressed their appreciation of this. For over half of the applicants, it had been a number of decades since they had been in an educational institution and, indeed, few had had previous industry training, some admitting that they had entered the tourism and hospitality business with little or no experience. To them, the simple and straightforward way in which the course content was delivered by the trainers had played a role in facilitating their attainment of the standard.

Moreover, in addition to the course content delivery, the course content itself appeared, for the most part, to be tailored to the needs of the small tourism business operators, which constituted the majority of the total number of brand applicants. Some of the things with which they were most impressed on the training courses were matters which had almost appeared inconsequential to them at first, i.e. 'the very simple things,' such as 'greeting people at the door, opening the door, how to deal with people.' In contrast to the general consensus that the training was useful, there was a number of isolated comments that some aspects of the training were too targeted towards larger businesses. Several operators advocated the segregation of larger businesses from smaller ones for the purpose of training in order to ensure that the respective business types' training needs were appropriately and effectively met. This sentiment serves to highlight the difference between the training needs of small businesses and those of larger businesses. Too often, however, the provision of training programmes belongs more to the domain of tourism corporations and is in tune with large firm business models, which contributes to market failure from the perspective of small- and medium-sized enterprises (SMEs) (Morrison, 2003). The above findings underline the importance of adapting course content to small firms. Moreover, they support Morrison's (2003, p. 806) call for SME development programmes 'to be driven by SME needs and preferred models, styles and delivery of learning.' In addition to this, they show Friel's (1999) and Morrison and Thomas' (1999) argument that small enterprises cannot be treated as scaled down versions of the larger firm to be applicable to a destination quality management context.

The general feedback concerning the training was, nevertheless, that most of the courses were tailored to the small tourism business in terms of timing, venue, required investment, content style and delivery. The mere inclusion of small operators in the quality process was seen as an important preliminary measure. Out of the 46 members interviewed, 35 ran enterprises with less than 10 employees. Of these micro enterprises, 19 conveyed how the respondents were impressed by the way in which it was emphasised by the trainers that quality was not just the prerogative of the larger firm.

Thus, within the destination quality network framework, a training support infrastructure was provided to overcome the typical obstacles common to tourism businesses, particularly small ones, and to encourage involvement in a quality network. Without this support, the criterion of mandatory training might well have been a deterrent to involvement instead of a facilitating factor for co-operation at the destination.

2. Facilitated training, yet an investment nevertheless. While much was done to facilitate the uptake of training and to make the course content and delivery appropriate for the brand applicants, the training was, nonetheless, considered by the applicants to represent a challenge and an investment of resources. Although training was 'brought to them' (i.e. held in the region of West Cork), many still had to travel a considerable distance, given the remote location of some of the establishments. Interviews also highlighted that although the courses were subsidised, 'an investment' was, however, required from the individual enterprises, since the subvention was based on a system of matched funding. A further factor which contributed to the challenge of training was the lack of previous formal training. In addition, many respondents felt that their age was a handicap. Thus, while every opportunity was provided to the brand applicants to participate in and complete the training, lack of previous training, age and length of time away from formal education, in addition to the considerable amount of travelling to the training courses, the concentration required and the financial investment involved, meant that attendance was still onerous. This resulted in a sense of achievement and triumph that many experienced on completion of the training courses despite the hurdles. These sentiments would play a role in the dynamics behind networking and interaction during the full membership phase.

3. The ways in which the training was seen to raise quality. The primary purpose of training was to guarantee a certain level of quality among all of the applicant enterprises (who originally had diverse approaches to, and standards of quality). The perception that this purpose was realised

would later play a role in the level of networking. The training component ranged from courses on hygiene and safety to customer care and various principles of quality through to an emphasis on what was special and distinctive about the destination. In general, there was much positive feedback about the training. Interviewees spoke of a new 'awareness' as a result of the training courses. This awareness related to 'new ideas' that they had been given and that they had subsequently put into place as well as awareness about what was 'expected of you.'

The newly acquired ideas, knowledge and skills appeared to lead not just to the implementation of quality measures in their businesses, but also to something less tangible, and equally important to them. Namely, over a third of interviewees spoke of the newfound confidence which the training had given them. For those concerned about the many eventualities of host–guest interaction, the case histories of the training courses gave the trainees access to the lessons of experience that they could not have otherwise gained, and with it came this new confidence, and in turn, it was felt, a new professionalism. The training courses were successful in instilling in the trainees a philosophy of quality. Indeed, some felt they were already reaping the results of this quality policy, in the form of positive testimonials, a strong reputation and repeat business. Thus, a variety of tourism enterprises, including B&Bs, hostels, self-catering and caravan and camp-sites, felt that the training had been beneficial. Once again this was to have a bearing on the level of networking and co-operation at a later stage of brand membership.

4. Fragmentation and diversity: a challenge for training. Despite the positive general consensus, however, the challenge of diversity and fragmentation of the tourism destination product was reflected in the fact that not all sectors felt as positively with regard to the training courses as others did. Most often the non-food tourism providers appeared to experience a sense of frustration and annoyance in light of the apparent focus on food which characterised the training courses, and which was of more relevance to those tourism business operators who provided food to their guests. This element of dissatisfaction was significant insofar as it related to perceived benefits of brand membership, which as discussed later, were found to be a factor determining continued association with the brand.
5. Training as a forum for interaction and networking. While there existed negative sentiment with regard to the above aspect of training, i.e. its perceived bias towards food serving operators, one aspect appeared to compensate for this and make the investment worthwhile, namely the

advantage of networking. Due to the informal nature of the training, there was much scope for networking between the applicants. Regardless of sector, many businesses, in particular the SMTEs and the newly established firms, commented that they had learned as much from talking to other brand applicants as from listening to the trainers. This supports Morrison's (2003) emphasis on the effectiveness of peer-learning, acknowledging that owner-managers may have a certain respect for each other (Wyer, Mason, & Theodorakopoulos, 2000). The fruits of this networking were to be seen to their full effect in the next phase of membership, i.e. that of full membership, and are discussed shortly in more detail.

In summary, as a mandatory criterion for brand membership, participation in training was compulsory and as such was not left to the discretion of the tourism businesses. However, the dynamics during this phase were to have knock-on effects in the third phase, i.e. that of full membership, where levels of network involvement were more voluntary. The most significant aspects of this second phase are presented in Fig. 1.

The characteristics of the brand's training system are outlined in the boxes 1–4 on the inner circle and the consequences of these characteristics, in the boxes A–D on the outer circles. Firstly, the positive benefits of the support infrastructure for SMTEs were felt, insofar as training was subsidised, relatively convenient and generally tailored to the needs of small businesses (Box 1). Thus, the usual obstacles to participation in training, especially for small firms, were overcome to varying degrees, hence facilitating participation (Box A). Secondly, the fact that the applicants felt that they had, nevertheless, made an investment in time, money and effort (Box 2), despite the presence of the support infrastructure, generated a feeling that the completion of training was indeed an achievement (Box B). Moreover, the general consensus with respect to the training courses was that they were useful, leading to new skills, a quality philosophy, a newfound confidence and professionalism and, in some cases, profitability (Box 3), which in turn resulted in the perception among brand applicants that the standards of participating enterprises were raised (Box C). Lastly, the fact that training was not specifically tailored to different sectors (Box 4) had both negative and positive consequences. Already in this application phase, sentiments of dissatisfaction appeared to arise, as some sectors, especially the non-food tourism providers, felt that the training modules were unfairly weighted in favour of the food tourism providers, given the emphasis on food preparation and hygiene. On a more positive note, training constituted a forum

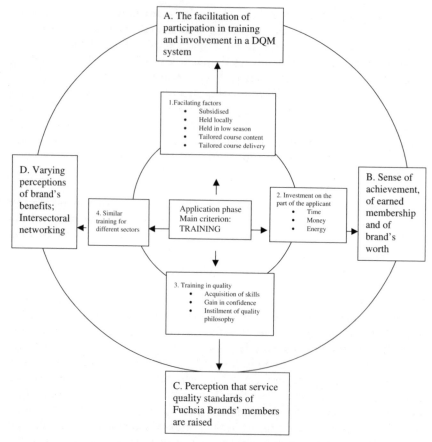

Fig. 1. Characteristics and Consequences of the 'Application Phase.'

for social interaction between all the brand members, regardless of sector (Box D). All of these factors appeared to have an impact on the degree of participation and involvement during the phase of full membership.

Full Membership Phase: Reaping the Rewards of the Training Phase

While the 'application' phase was characterised by the stipulation of mandatory participation in training, the fulfilment of which was facilitated in various ways, during the third phase of membership, i.e. 'full membership,' levels of involvement were more voluntary. It appeared that the determinants of long-term involvement were confidence that the brand network was functioning as a quality system and a perception that there were benefits to brand membership. This section examines the impact the training phase had on these determinants of involvement during that third phase.

Confidence in the Quality System

Reflecting the original motivations of a number of brand applicants, it emerged from the interviews that the tourism providers, once full members, attributed great importance to the fact that the Fuchsia brand act as a quality seal and function as a quality system. Crucial to this was that the other members uphold the quality standards which were expected of them, and were thus worthy of the brand. The ways in which this concern about other members was articulated ranged from hesitant comments to open expressions of distrust and resentment. What helped reassure the members and counter the distrust was the fact that, having been through the rigorous application process themselves and made the investment described earlier (Box 2), they felt a sense of the brand's worth as a quality standard (Box B). Thus, there was a common sentiment that brand membership could not be bought but had to be 'earned.' The implication for many members was that any operator who had undergone this rigorous process would be genuinely concerned with offering a quality service. This underlines how the sense of investment and achievement experienced during the application phase played an important part in building 'faith in the system.' It is clear from the findings that training and the other screening criteria resulted in a perception by most of the brand members that brand membership ensured a certain standard of quality, at least in the initial stages. For more lasting confidence, it was found that there was a need for an effective monitoring system, which is in keeping with most quality models, e.g., EFQM, SERVQUAL, Deming and Baldrige models and ISO 9000.

Perceived Benefits

Just as *expected* benefits had played a major role in encouraging tourism providers to join the network in the pre-application phase, *perceived* benefits appeared to be a significant factor in determining continued association with and participation in the brand network. This supports Jamal and Getz

(1995), Selin and Chavez (1995), Haywood (1997) and Bramwell and Sharman (1999), who maintain that the recognition of individual and/or mutual benefits is a prerequisite for the successful collaborative management of the destination. The benefits for the members of Fuchsia Brands included the use of a quality seal, marketing, a source of competitive edge and networking. The benefit upon which training had the most impact during the third phase was the level of networking.

Although interaction with other operators was alluded to by a small number of tourism service providers as an original motivation to join the network, having become members, the aspect of being part of a network was considered by a majority of members to be a significant advantage. Indeed, many found this to be the most rewarding aspect of belonging to the association. Thus, while Palmer (1998) notes that many members do not join local associations primarily for the tangible economic benefits, but instead for the social benefits of networking with other people in their business sector, the findings of this case study revealed that although many joined in the hope of reaping tangible economic benefits, the social benefits were significant in keeping them involved in a local association. Much of the foundation for networking during the third phase had been laid during the training phase. The findings of this case study suggest that the compulsory training courses, as a major forum for networking, played a pivotal role in fostering an informal referral system among its members, encouraging a rich exchange of ideas and information and creating a 'destination mentality' among brand members, whereby members thought beyond the agency level to the destination level.

Earlier it was discussed how the major concern of members with respect to the brand was that other members were maintaining quality standards. It emerged from the interviews that a more general concern of the members was the ability to make confident referrals, when they were unable to accommodate guests. Unprompted, many interviewees, particularly those working in accommodation or restaurant units, raised the issue of referrals and spoke of the importance of being able to make a good one. If they made a bad recommendation, as some of them had experienced, it could lead to the guests' disappointment, for which they felt partly responsible. The importance of approval was highlighted by accommodation providers' responses that they would send guests that they could not accommodate to either Bord Fáilte or Fuchsia Brand approved accommodation. Because members were aware that Fuchsia branded businesses had, like themselves, been through the courses and satisfied all the criteria, members felt that they could count on fellow members to provide quality service (Boxes B and C).

This, in turn, would ensure a satisfied customer, which meant a clear conscience and the possibility of business from them at another point in the future.

Although the knowledge that other people had completed the training was important, the findings reveal that knowing them as acquaintances or friends was equally crucial in making a confident referral. Many respondents would make referrals to those with whom they had struck up a friendship during the training courses. This finding supports Axelrod (1984), Cooke (1998) and Rainnie (2002) who stress the importance of direct physical interaction for the creation of trust and the success of networks. Since the training courses were considered to be the most important opportunity for meeting people, they not only played a role in guaranteeing a standard, they were equally significant in acting as a forum for networking (Box 4). The significance of personal acquaintance with fellow members highlights the importance of actual physical networking among members, which the training courses afforded, and suggests that a simple listing of Fuchsia Brand tourism suppliers (such as on the organisation's map, brochure and other literature) alone would not suffice to encourage this referral system.

An additional factor to the above determinants of recommendations was a basic knowledge of the products and services available under the brand that came from networking with the different operators. Once again this 'awareness' often arose from direct physical interaction with other tourism providers. In summary, for many brand members, referrals seemed to be made on the basis of a number of factors: most importantly, knowledge that members had done the courses, satisfied the criteria and were approved; personal acquaintance; and an awareness of what services and products were available to recommend. One respondent's comment highlights the interplay of these different factors.

> Where the Fuchsia comes into it is, the more you know somebody, the more you'll be inclined to recommend them...it's like, I didn't know Casey's of Baltimore until I did that course with Nicky who was chef there at the time. Now I've often sent people there since, purely, I feel they should be similar to us, since they've done all this stuff. There's the Baltimore sailing centre or the one in Adrigole, they are places I wouldn't have been aware of and would quite happily refer people to now...

Analysing her comments, one can identify the personal acquaintance between the respondent, the marketing manager of an hotel and Nicky, who was a chef at 'Casey's of Baltimore,' was important, because 'the more you know somebody, the more you'll be inclined to recommend them.' The fact that she had met him at the training course and knew that he had participated in the training, and that Casey's of Baltimore has satisfied the criteria, i.e. 'done all this stuff,' further increased her confidence. In addition to this, having met him and others, she was made aware of the existence of the amenities, which meant that she was in a position to recommend them. In short, the training provided the forum for the acquisition of skills, the physical interaction between network members, and awareness-raising about member establishments. Thus, the brand appeared to function as a signal among the brand members. This corresponds to the role of a 'brand of faith' (*une marque de confiance*) as described by Blangy and Kouchner (1999) in the case of the National Park of Guadeloupe: member tourism establishments, such as rural tourism accommodation, a traditional plantation, a floral park and activities are recommended by the National Park and each other.

A leitmotiv of the research findings for this case study was the sentiment on the part of some of the non-food tourism service providers, such as the activities and attractions, that the brand was of greater relevance to the food providers (Box D). According to the former, the accommodation and food providing sectors profited more from brand membership than they did, in particular with regard to training, customer satisfaction measurement and the emphasis on high quality foods. In short, the perceived advantages were less for the activities and attractions. Since perceived advantages were revealed to be a determinant of continued association with the brand and thus the long term well-being of the brand, this finding is significant. However, discussions about referrals revealed that attractions and activities were most often the object of these referrals. Having gained an increased awareness about the attractions and activities throughout the region, many accommodation enterprises considered the passing on of this knowledge and information as a value-adding component to the service which they offered to their guests. Most B&B operators spoke of the routine of post-breakfast itinerary planning sessions, while several hotels had systematically incorporated it into their checking-in procedure. Thus, although the activities' and attractions' managers found the training and the brand's source of distinction of less relevance to them, brand membership appeared to be advantageous to them in terms of the referrals and recommendations which they received from other members of the 'alumni.' Therefore, even though course content might have varied in its relevance for the different sectors, a physical presence at the courses appeared to reap rewards given that training was pivotal to the degree of networking and referring. This is an important finding insofar as it offers an incentive to those sectors, which might perceive lack of benefits, particularly in comparison to the food and accommodation sectors, to become involved in a destination quality network. The inclusion of activities and attractions into DQM initiatives is vital as it increases the breadth of the network's tourism value chain.

As was shown, the fragmentation and diversity of the tourism destination product was often reflected in the divided attitudes of the different tourism sectors with respect to various aspects of the training. Thus, the diversity of the West Cork tourism destination product presented a challenge to the destination quality managers. However, it was found that the brand offered a forum for exchanges which helped overcome, and indeed, appeared to profit from the multi-dimensional and diverse nature of the destination product. A number of tourism service providers admitted their own surprise at the fruitful exchanges, which resulted from interaction between such 'a cross-section' of operators. Interviewees spoke about a rich cross-sectoral exchange of ideas and solutions which arose from networking between business types, which 'would be, on the face of it, totally different.'

The exchanges and personal benefits reaped from network membership seemed to foster a general spirit of co-operation among these members, many of whom were theoretically in competition with each other. Many spoke unprompted of the benefits of networking and felt that there was a real ethos of co-operation and indeed, at this tourism destination, a spirit of 'community.' The function of the network as a 'social glue' (Porter, 1998) was expressed by one respondent: ' ...and I think what it's done is to have made a community that are working *together* as opposed to *against* each other.'

In short, the fruits of interaction on the training courses in the application phase came to full fruition in the full membership phase, where an informal referral system developed, a rich 'knowledge spillover' was facilitated and a domain mentality was fostered. Largely as a result of the training, the brand appeared to function as a quality signal to other enterprises, and thus, once the customer engaged with one brand member, there appeared to be a strong likelihood that the customer would be referred to other member establishments and hence, kept within a quality value chain in the region of West Cork.

CONCLUSION

The challenge for destination quality managers is to present a highly fragmented value chain which constitutes the tourism destination product as one seamless interface and quality experience for the visitor. The findings of this case study suggest that the network membership criterion of compulsory participation in training played a crucial role in fostering networking and guaranteeing the success of the DQM initiative. While other findings from this case study revealed that this destination quality brand did not constitute a successful direct marketing communication to the potential visitor, the findings discussed here indicate that the brand did function as an assurance of quality to the network members themselves. The facilitation of training for tourism enterprises, their own sense of investment and achievement and their perception that training did raise standards ensured that they used the brand to be an effective signal of quality to each other. This combined with the forum for interaction and exchange, which the tourism courses constituted, led to the development of an informal referral system and a 'destination mentality' among its members. Consequently, once visitors were within the network, there appeared to be a strong propensity for brand members to refer them to other brand members. The potential benefits of this is that the visitor's service encounters at the destination are of a high quality, and – given the representation of a wide range of activities and attractions – that they are encouraged to stay longer, increasing the destination's competitiveness. The findings of the case study suggest that destination managers wishing to establish a DQM initiative include participation in training as a condition for its network members, given the impact this can exercise on the creation of a tourism quality value chain at the destination.

ACKNOWLEDGEMENT

The authors would like to acknowledge the Irish Research Council for Humanities and the Social Sciences for the scholarship funding received during this study.

REFERENCES

Ashworth, G. J., & Voogd, H. (1990). *Selling the city: Marketing approaches in public sector urban planning.* London: Belhaven Press.

Augustyn, M. M. (2001). Can local tourism destinations benefit from employing the ISO 9000:2000 quality management system? In: *Tourism, innovation and regional development: Proceedings of the ATLAS 10th anniversary conference,* Dublin, October 4–6. Dublin: ATLAS.

Augustyn, M. M., & Knowles, T. (2000). Performance of tourism partnerships: A focus on York. *Tourism Management, 21*(4), 341–351.

Axelrod, R. (1984). *The evolution of co-operation.* New York: Basic Books.

Baum, T. (1999). Human resource management in tourism's small business sector: Policy dimensions. In: D. Lee-Ross (Ed.), *HRM in tourism and hospitality: International perspectives on small to medium-sized firms* (pp. 3–16).

Baum, T., & Henderson, J. (1998). Quality enhancement as a key to competitiveness – the case of Singapore. *Proceedings of the EuroCHRIE Conference on Competitiveness in the International Hospitality Industry*, Lausanne, Switzerland, November 5–6.

Becton, S., & Graetz, B. (2001). Small business – small minded? Training attitudes and needs of the tourism and hospitality industry. *International Journal of Tourism Research, 3*, 105–113.

Blangy, S., & Kouchner, F. (1999). La marque de confiance du parc national de la Guadeloupe. *Cahier Espaces, 61*, 94–103.

Braithwaite, R. (1992). Value chain assessment of the travel experience. *Cornell Quarterly, 33*(5), 41–49.

Bramwell, B., & Sharman, A. (1999). Collaboration in local tourism policymaking. *Annals of Tourism Research, 26*(2), 392–415.

Buhalis, D., & Cooper, C. (1998). Competition or co-operation? Small and medium-sized tourism enterprises at the destination. In: E. Laws, H. W. Faulkner & G. Moscardo (Eds), *Embracing and managing change in tourism international case studies* (pp. 324–346).

Callan, R. J. (1994). Quality assurance certification for hospitality marketing, sales and customer services. *Service Industries Journal, 14*, 482–498.

Chan, D. (2000a). Beyond Singapore girl: Brand and product/service differentiation strategies in the new millennium. *Journal of Management Development, 19*(6), 515–542.

Chan, D. (2000b). The story of Singapore airlines and the Singapore girl. *Journal of Management Development, 19*(6), 456–472.

Cooke, P. (1998). *Unpublished report for the Irish marine tourism industry*.

Crotts, J., Aziz, A., & Raschid, A. (1998). Antecedents of suppliers' commitment to wholesale buyers in the international travel trade. *Tourism Management, 19*(2), 127–134.

Crotts, J. C., Buhalis, D., & March, R. (2000). *Global alliances in tourism and hospitality management*. New York: The Haworth Hospitality Press.

Crouch, G. I., & Ritchie, J. R. B. (1999). Tourism, competitiveness, and societal prosperity. *Journal of Business Research, 44*, 137–152.

De Keyser, R., & Vanhove, N. (1997). Tourism quality plan: An effective tourism policy tool. *The Tourism Review, 3*, 32–37.

Dietvorst, A. (1993). *Tourist recreation development and spatial transformations*. Wageningen, Netherlands: Agricultural University.

Dredge, D., & Jenkins, J. (2003). Destination place identity and regional tourism policy. *Tourism Geographies, 5*(4), 383–407.

Dubé, L., Enz, C. A., Renaghan, L. M., & Siguaw, J. A. (2000). Managing for excellence. *Cornell Hotel and Restaurant Administration Quarterly, 41*(5), 30–39.

Dubé, L., & Renaghan, L. M. (1999). Strategic approaches to lodging excellence. *Cornell Hotel and Restaurant Administration Quarterly, 40*(6), 16–29.

Enz, C. A., & Siguaw, J. A. (2000). Best practice in human resources. *Cornell Hotel and Restaurant Administration Quarterly, 41*(1), 48–62.

Fayos-Solá, E. (1996). Tourism policy: A midsummer night's dream? *Tourism Management, 17*(6), 405–412.

Friel, M. (1999). Marketing practice in small tourism and hospitality firms. *International Journal of Tourism Research, 1*(2), 97–109.

Fyall, A., Leask, A., & Garrod, B. (2001). Scottish visitor attractions: A collaborative future? *International Journal of Tourism Research, 3*, 211–228.

Go, F. S., & Govers, R. (2000). Integrated quality management for tourist destinations: A European perspective on achieving competitiveness. *Tourism Management, 21*(1), 79–88.

Gouirand, P. (1994). La formation à la gestion et à la Qqualité dans l'hôtellerie familiale et indépendante. In: *WTO seminar on quality – A challenge for tourism*, Madrid, 18–19 April, (pp. 91–95), Madrid: WTO.

Haywood, K. M. (1997). Creating value for visitors to urban destinations. In: P. Murphy (Ed.), *Quality management in urban tourism* (pp. 169–182).

Healy, M., & Perry, C. (2000). Comprehensive criteria to judge validity and reliability of qualitative research within the realism paradigm. *Qualitative Market Research, 3*(3), 118–126.

Hirst, M. (1991). Newer and better ways. *Managing Service Quality, 1*(5), 247–251.

Hjalager, A. (1996). Agricultural diversification into tourism: Evidence of a European community development program. *Tourism Management, 17*(2), 103–111.

Howie, F. (2003). *Managing the tourist destination*. London: Continuum.

Huckestein, D., & Duboff, R. (1999). Hilton hotels: A comprehensive approach to delivering value to all stakeholders. *Cornell Hotel and Restaurant Administration Quarterly, 40*(4), 28–38.

Jamal, T. B., & Getz, D. (1995). Collaboration theory and community tourism planning. *Annals of Tourism Research, 22*(1), 186–204.

Kandampully, J. (2000). The impact of demand fluctuation on the quality of service: A tourism industry example. *Managing Service Quality, 10*(1), 10–18.

Klein, R. (2001). Public policies and cultural tourism: EU activities. *Proceedings of the 1st Conference on Cultural Tourism Economy and Values in the XXI Century*, Fira de Barcelona, March 29–31.

Komppula, R. (1998). Factors affecting SME's commitment to an issue-based network-case, North Karelia tourism strategy. *Proceedings of the Conference on Growth and Job Creation in SMEs*, Helsinki, January, (pp. 474–497).

Lenehan, T., & Harrington, D. (1998). *Managing quality in tourism: Theory and practice*. Dublin: Oak Tree Press.

Lewis, R. C. (1997). *Cases in hospitality marketing and management*. New York: Wiley.

Luciani, S. (1999). Implementing yield management in small and medium-sized hotels: An investigation of obstacles and success factors in Florence hotels. *International Journal of Hospitality Management, 18*(2), 129–142.

Maxwell, G. A., & Quail, S. (2002). Human resource strategy and development for quality service in the international hotel sector. In: N. D'Annunzio-Green, G. A. Maxwell & S. Watson (Eds), *Human resource management: International perspectives in hospitality and tourism* (pp. 90–103).

Middleton, V. (2001). *Marketing in travel and tourism*. Oxford: Butterworth-Heinemann.

Morrison, A. J. (2002). The small hospitality business: Enduring or endangered? *Journal of Hospitality and Tourism Management, 9*(1), 1–11.

Morrison, A. J. (2003). SME management & leadership development: Market reorientation. *Journal of Management Development, 22*(9), 796–808.

Morrison, A. J., & Thomas, R. (1999). The future of small firms in the hospitality industry. *International Journal of Contemporary Hospitality Management, 11*(4), 148–154.

Murphy, P., Pritchard, M. P., & Smith, B. (2000). The destination product and its impact on traveller perceptions. *Tourism Management, 21*(1), 43–52.

Netter, L. N. (1999). Tourisme et qualité: Hier, aujourd'hui et demain. *Cahier Espaces, 61*, 8–15.

Ostrowski, P. L., O'Brien, T. V., & Gordon, G. L. (1993). Service quality and customer loyalty in the commercial airline industry. *Journal of Travel Research, 32*(2), 16–25.

Otto, J. E., & Ritchie, J. R. B. (1995). Exploring the quality of the service experience: A theoretical and empirical analysis. *Advances in Services Marketing and Management, 5,* 37–63.

Palmer, A. (1998). Evaluating the governance style of marketing groups. *Annals of Tourism Research, 25*(1), 185–201.

Palmer, A., & Bejou, D. (1995). Tourism destination alliances. *Annals of Tourism Research, 22*(3), 616–629.

Partlow, C. G. (1993). How Ritz-Carlton applies 'TQM'. *Cornell Hotel and Restaurant Administration Quarterly, 30*(4), 16–24.

Poon, A. (1990). Flexible specialisation and small size: The case of Caribbean tourism. *World Development, 18*(1), 109–123.

Poon, A. (1993). *Tourism, technology and competitive strategies.* Wallingford, UK: CAB International.

Porter, M. E. (1998). Clusters and the new economics of competition. *Harvard Business School Press,* (November-December), 77–90.

Postma, A., & Jenkins, A. K. (1997). Improving the tourist's experience: Quality management applied to tourist destinations. In: P. Murphy (Ed.), *Quality management in urban tourism* (pp. 183–197).

Rainnie, A. (2002). New regionalism in Australia – limits and possibilities. *Social inclusion and new regionalism workshop,* University of Queensland, 11 October.

Ritchie, J. R. B., & Crouch, G. I. (2000). The Competitive destination: A sustainability perspective. *Tourism Management, 21*(1), 1–7.

Ryan, C. (1997). *The tourist experience: A new introduction.* London: Cassell.

Sablerie, C. (1996). Donner les clés du pays pour retenir et faire revenir: L'expérience de Calvados accueil. *Cahier Espaces, 48,* 183–188.

Schueler, J. (2000). Customer service through leadership: The Disney way. *Training and Development, 54*(10), 26–31.

Selin, S. (1993). Collaborative alliances: New interorganisational forms in tourism. *Journal of Travel and Tourism Marketing, 2*(2/3), 217–227.

Selin, S., & Chavez, D. (1995). Developing an evolutionary tourism partnership model. *Annals of Tourism Research, 22*(4), 844–856.

Shaw, G., & Williams, A. M. (1994). *Critical issues in tourism: A geographical perspective.* Oxford: Blackwell.

Smeral, E. (2004). Tracking the future: Europe 2010. *Proceedings of the 'Charting Tourism Success' Conference,* Dublin, Ireland, April, 5.

Soriano, D. R. (1999). Total quality management: Applying the European model to Spain's urban hotels. *Cornell Hotel and Restaurant Administration Quarterly, 40*(1), 54–59.

Synergy. (2000). *Tourism certification: An analysis of Green Globe 21 and other tourism certification programmes.* London: Synergy.

Telfer, D. J. (2000). Tastes of Niagara: Building strategic alliances between tourism and agriculture. *International Journal of Hospitality and Tourism Administration, 1*(1), 71–88.

Telfer, D. J. (2001). Strategic alliances along the Niagara wine route. *Tourism Management, 22*(1), 21–30.

Tinsley, R., & Lynch, P. (2001). Small tourism business networks and destination development. *International Journal of Hospitality Management, 20*(4), 367–378.

Travel and Tourism Intelligence. (2001). Improving performance in small and medium-sized hotels: The Swiss experience. *TTI Country Reports, 5,* 43–60.

Urry, J. (1990). *The tourist gaze.* London: Sage.

Woods, M. (2003). A warm welcome for destination quality brands: The example of the Pays Cathare Region. *International Journal of Tourism Research, 5,* 269–282.

Wyer, P., Mason, J., & Theodorakopoulos, N. (2000). Small business development and the 'learning organisation'. *International Journal of Entrepreneurial Behaviour and Research, 6*(4), 239–259.

Yin, R. K. (1994). *Case study research: Design and methods* (2nd ed.). Beverly Hills, CA: Sage.

THE HIDDEN COSTS OF CHEAP GROUP TOURS – A CASE STUDY OF BUSINESS PRACTICES IN AUSTRALIA

Bruce Prideaux, Brian King, Larry Dwyer and Perry Hobson

ABSTRACT

This paper deals with an issue that has been identified in many markets where there are large numbers of package tourists. In Australia, there have been a number of studies undertaken into the use of a range of dubious business practices employed by Inbound Tour Operators (ITOs), particularly in the Korean market. The cause for this problem is identified as the minimization of the retail price of package tour by transferring part of the cost of the tour to ITOs in the destination country. Under this system, ITOs are paid a daily tour rate below their real costs and are forced to recover losses by employing a range of dubious business practices including forced shopping and kickbacks from shops. The paper models the normal operation of the package tour cycle where no business practices are used and compares this to the Korean package inbound market in Australia where the use of business practices of this nature is widespread.

Advances in Hospitality and Leisure, Volume 2, 51–71
Copyright © 2006 by Elsevier Ltd.
All rights of reproduction in any form reserved
ISSN: 1745-3542/doi:10.1016/S1745-3542(05)02003-5

INTRODUCTION

There is an old saying that states 'There is no such thing as a free lunch.' In tourism, as in any other business, profitability depends on the ability to develop a product or service that appeals to customers while minimizing costs and maximizing price followed by successfully selling that product or service in a competitive marketplace. Products or services cannot be sustained if they do not yield a profit and in the tourism industry this maxim must also be applied to all the members of the distribution and supply channels that are involved in providing products and services. In the package tour sector, profits on individual packages are usually very small and firms trading in this sector rely on volume to derive a profit. In markets where customers place price ahead of other considerations of service delivery, in pursuit of the illusory 'free lunch', firms may implement strategies to minimize the purchase price at the point of sale and recover any losses incurred in subsequent business transactions undertaken by the tour purchaser later in the tour. In the auto industry, for example, a loss made from a low initial sale price of a vehicle may be recovered through subsequent inflated costs in the sale of parts or after sales servicing of the vehicle. In the tourism industry similar types of practices may be used to attract customers by offering a low initial price then recovering losses later in the package tour cycle. The package tour cycle describes the range of actions that occur from the time when a package travel purchase is made, includes the delivery of the tour product in the destination and concludes when the customer returns to their point of origin.

Package tours are defined as tours where members travel in a group, pay for a bundle of travel services including airfares, accommodation, meals and transport and are escorted by a guide for the duration of the tour. This paper examines a range of dubious 'business practices' that may be used by tour operators and other members of the supply chain to entice customers to purchase a low price package tour product and then recover any losses made from the initial low sale price by using a range of business practices later in the package tour cycle. To illustrate the type of practices that are used, the South Korean inbound tourism into Australia is presented as a case study. The business practices discussed in this case study are similar to those found in many other inbound tourism markets, either to a greater or lesser extent. The research reported in this paper is based on a report to the Tourism Ministers Council (Prideaux, Dwyer, King, & Hobson, 2005) that investigated the economic impact of a range of business practices on Australia's inbound markets from parts of Asia including Korea.

In the Australian tourism industry, there has been an ongoing debate about the impact of the problems that arise from business practices used by members of the inbound sector to maintain profitability in a market that has a reputation for very thin profit margins and where volume is a key strategy to achieve profitability. The issue has arisen in a number of inbound markets including Korea, China, Japan and Taiwan, and has been the subject of ongoing media reporting, academic research, government reports and legislative action. This paper commences with a review of a number of government reports and the academic literature before discussing the issues that have arisen in the Korean inbound market.

Research has identified that income and price are the important economic variables that influence international tourism demand (Anastasopoulos, 1989; Crouch, Schultz, & Valerio, 1992; Jud & Joseph, 1974; Uysal & Crompton, 1984; Dwyer, Forsyth, & Rao, 2002). Allied with creating demand for a specific destination is the ability of that destination to sustain demand over the long run. One key factor sustaining demand is maintaining positive consumer satisfaction (Cadotte & Turgeon, 1988). This paper will focus on the role of price and consumer demand as key elements in sustaining demand for package tours while treating income as a given for outbound markets that are growing. While not considered in this paper, previous research has established that per capita incomes in source countries constitute an important factor affecting outbound flows of tourists. Rapid economic growth in Korea and other Asian nations is a key factor underlying the high growth rate in these outbound markets.

Consumer satisfaction is a key indicator of the ability of a destination to deliver a product that appeals to the tourist, and an indicator of the ability of a destination to deliver on the promise that is made through the marketing image that is developed in the mind of the tourist. Numerous research articles (Peter & Olsen, 1987; Pizam & Milman, 1993) have examined the issue of consumer satisfaction and there is almost unanimous agreement that knowledge of customer expectations and requirements provides an understanding of how customers perceive the quality of a good or service. The tourism marketing literature currently reflects two major approaches to consumer research (Kozak & Rimmington, 2000). The American School led by Parasuraman, Zeithaml, and Berry (1985) views consumer satisfaction as a negative or positive outcome resulting from the consumer's propensity of comparing initial expectations and perceived performance of products and services. The second major approach, championed by Gronroos (1990), views consumer satisfaction as the customers perceptions of the outcome of actual performance. These approaches have been extensively debated in literature but a consensus has not yet emerged.

A danger for destinations is that tourists will not be able to distinguish between measuring consumer satisfaction with a particular product (e.g. tour operator) and the destination. As a consequence, one unpleasant experience may not have a significant impact on the tourist's overall level of satisfaction but a series of experiences, particularly where they are linked, may result in overall destination dissatisfaction. Kozak and Rimmington (2000) state that it is important to identify and measure consumer satisfaction with each component of the destination because of the potential for consumer satisfaction/dissatisfaction with one part of the destination may grow into consumer satisfaction/dissatisfaction with all components of the destination.

Consumer satisfaction and its measurement is an important process for destinations. Sustained growth is more likely to occur in markets that have positive consumer satisfaction (Heung & Qu, 2000). The implications of this discussion are apparent in the context of business practices having an adverse impact on consumer satisfaction with a destination. If consumer discontent occurs as a result of business practices, the destination may suffer a decline in reputation leading to a fall in visitor numbers.

A number of reports (Tourism Queensland (TQ), 1999; Centre for International Economics (CIE), 2000; Australian Tourist Commission (ATC), 2003; Bureau of Tourism Research (BTR), 2004) funded by various government agencies in Australia have examined the impact of business practices that operate in the nation's inbound package tour market and found that there were serious grounds for concern that these practices were having a negative effect on customer satisfaction. Unfortunately, these reports failed to look beyond the Australian element of the package tour and ignored the impact of price in the origin markets. The first major report to discuss these issues was produced for the Queensland Government in 1999. The aim of the report (TQ, 1999) was to provide an impact assessment study, which would be used for a later review to satisfy the requirements of the National Competition Policy (NCP), a Federal government policy designed to promote competition in the business sector. The discussion paper identified but did not quantify issues that appear to have arisen as a result of business practices in the inbound sector.

While these issues were not investigated in detail, the report (TQ, 1999, p. 44) noted that 'the current lack of industry cohesion and coverage and the disparate nature of the industry make voluntary self-regulation less viable. A voluntary accreditation system and other industry voluntary initiatives currently would not achieve increased compliance, without legislative back-up.'

In a subsequent report prepared by CIE (2000) and commissioned by the Tourism Ministers Council, the authors identified three broad categories of business practices:

- Uncompetitive shopping arrangements – whereby the choice of the tourist is limited to those shops favoured by the tour operator, for example, those that pay the tour operator a commission or that are part of the same vertically integrated firm.
- False or misleading practices – aimed at deceiving the tourist over the nature of the tour package or the true value of the package.
- Low service quality – tours that do not feature the 'best' attractions in a region or the service on the tour is of low standard.

The report noted that two practices (lack of choice of stores and lack of access to Australian products) are generally viewed as outcomes rather than instruments by which shopping is made uncompetitive. According to the report, the capacity to control the behaviour of tour groups is a key factor in facilitating the emergence of the alleged business practices to emerge. The report also noted that as the number of fully independent travellers (FIT) increases, the incidence of controlling behaviour will decline. The report did not investigate any element of visitor satisfaction that would confirm or dispute these arguments.

The report (CIE, 2000) noted that there was very little information on how the practices occurring in the Inbound Tour Operator (ITO) sector feed back to visitor satisfaction, arrivals and expenditure. The report (CIE, 2000, p. 6) further noted that '… ..just whether a practice is damaging and undesirable depends on the circumstances and is not clear cut. For example, commissions are an essential feature of much of the travel industry and judging what is excessive is no simple matter. Similarly, packages that offer low service quality may be an efficient way of extending the range of the market'. However, the report did state that false or misleading representations of the quality of elements of the tour is a practice likely to reduce repeat business and can be classed as a damaging practice.

The report identified a number of revenue losses including: the loss to the economy of consumers going home 'with money in their pockets', a greater share of expenditure is being captured by foreign-owned shops, revenue losses due to adverse word of mouth and losses incurred by upstream businesses.

The CIE report outlined a range of possible initiatives that could be used to control various arrangements currently operating. These are illustrated in Fig. 1. It should be noted that most of the recommendations have yet to be implemented despite their apparent usefulness.

Issue	Possible prescription
Uncompetitive shopping	▪ Disclosure of commissions
Arrangements	▪ Use of tour guides with appropriate minimum competencies
	▪ Industry acceptable, minimum itinerary standards
False or misleading	▪ Disclosure of commissions
Representations	▪ Use of tour guides with appropriate minimum competencies
	▪ Industry acceptable, minimum itinerary standards
Low service quality	▪ Financial viability risk profiles
	▪ Compulsory insurance (public liability, PI)
	▪ Use of accredited product suppliers
	▪ Use of tour guides with appropriate minimum competencies
	▪ Industry acceptable, minimum itinerary standards

Fig. 1. Possible Prescriptions for Legislation. *Source*: CIE (2000).

The Bureau of Tourism Research (BTR, 2004) published a report on visitor dissatisfaction with aspects of guided tours during the period 2001–2002 and found that there was a degree of dissatisfaction from some respondents with various aspects of package tourism including: the overall tour, accommodation quality, tour activities, shopping time, tour guide service, tour value for money and 'forced' shopping. A report by The Australian Taxation Office (2003) indicated that there were identifiable losses in taxation revenue as a result of cash dealings associated with package tourism to Australia. While not extensively debated in the literature a number of authors (Prideaux & Kim, 1999; Kim & Sohn, 2002; Tse, 2003) have identified problems that have arisen in inbound markets as a result of the type of business practices that are used particularly by the ITO sector.

While providing a useful context to the operations of business practices in this sector, these reports did not consider visitor satisfaction data or undertake economic modelling into the business practices under investigation. The current paper extends the scope of the discussion to incorporate a number of additional aspects including the operation of the distribution channels and conditions in the retail travel market in Korea that underpins the need for many of these practices.

For the nation, adverse impacts were identified as:

- Adverse impacts on the image of Australia as a tourist destination and hence on future visitation.
- Adverse economic impacts.
- Criminal offences arising from breaches of consumer, taxation and immigration laws.
- Consumer dissatisfaction with tours associated with business practices leading to bad publicity as a result of negative word-of-mouth communication with adverse impacts on visitation.
- Reduced repeat visitation as a consequence of dissatisfaction with the business practices.
- Reduced expenditure within Australia as a result of dissatisfaction with the business practices used.
- The incurring of losses by suppliers as a result of ITO business failures.
- Taxation revenue foregone as a result of cash-in-hand dealings.

In this paper these issues are discussed in the context of the Korean inbound sector in Australia but have a wider application to other inbound sectors.

METHOD AND ANALYSES

The aims of this research are to: develop a package tour model that illustrates the relationships between the various participants in the inbound market and from this model create a second model that illustrates the operations of the Korean inbound package tour market; and to identify the types of business practices that are used in both Korea and Australia. To identify the range of business practices used and from that knowledge build a model to illustrate the type of relationships involved, the research team undertook a review of previous reports on the issue and conducted semi-structured interviews with government officials, tour guides involved in the Korean inbound market, inbound operators and representatives of companies involved in supplying goods and services to inbound operators in the Korean market. Interviews were also conducted in Korea with representatives of firms and organizations conversant with the operations of the Korean outbound sector.

The authors identified several limitations to the ability of the research to be generalized to other inbound markets, including the fluidity of specific inbound markets, which may change with little notice and the model that illustrates the structure of the Korean inbound market to Australia may not apply in other destinations where Koreans constitute a significant inbound sector. The paper's finding that the use of business practices is strongly influenced by the relationship between the retail and wholesale sectors in Korea and the emphasis on price rather than quality by the current cohort of Korean tourists applies to the contemporary market structure and may not apply in the future as the Korean outbound market matures. Changes either to the importance placed on price by Korean consumers or to the level of competition in the outbound travel market in Korea may invalidate the model illustrated as Fig. 3 in the future.

Significance of Package Tourism to Australia

In a number of the nation's major Asian markets, package tours are a popular form of travel and during 2002, international visitors on package holiday tours accounted for around 14 per cent (624,500 visitors) of all international visitors. Selected figures of the share of international package tourists from the major Asian source countries are displayed in Table 1.

Expenditure by tourists travelling on package tours is significant and in 2002 Korean package tour members spent an estimated AUD$62.6 million

Table 1.   International Visitors on Guided Group Holiday Tours from Japan, Korea, China, Taiwan and the Rest of the World in 2002[a].

	Visitors on Guided Group Holiday Tours				
	Number (in 000s)	Share of all visitors on group tours (per cent)	Share of all international visitors	All Group Tour Visitors (in 000s)	Total International Visitors[b] (in 000s)
Japan	410.1	85.8	61.4	477.8	667.8
Korea	51.3	92.7	29.7	55.3	172.4
China	36.8	63.8	20.5	57.6	179.6
Taiwan	35.6	97.4	40.0	36.6	89.1
Other countries	90.7	59.0	2.7	153.8	3 353.8
Total	624.5	80.0	14.0	781.0	4 462.8

Source: BTR, 2004.
[a]Includes visitors on guided group holiday tours, sporting group tours, special interest group tours other than a sporting tours and business or convention group tours.
[b]Total visitors include group tour and non-group tour visitors.

Table 2. Estimates of Expenditure in Australia Associated with Package Tourism from Identified Markets.

Origin	2002	2004	Per cent	2008	Per cent	2012	Per cent
China	46.804	67.814	9.3	135.054	10.2	232.021	20.5
Korea	62.617	78.973	10.8	115.078	13.3	162.153	14.3
Taiwan	33.668	36.678	5.0	41.995	4.8	43.843	3.8
Japan	506.252	545.588	74.9	620.108	71.7	696.451	61.4
Total	649.341	729.053	100	866.708	100	1134.468	100

Source: Table prepared by the authors. Expenditure data in Table 2 is multiplied by Tourism Forecasting Council estimated annual average growth rate of holiday tourism of each market (TFC, 2002, December).

(BTR, 2004). Table 2 illustrates estimates of expenditure in Australia by package tourists from China, Korea, Taiwan and Japan for the years 2004, 2008 and 2012 and was developed to indicate the significance of spending by this market. Providing the assumptions that underlie this table are plausible, the significance of package tourist in overall economic terms will continue to grow and any factors that impact on this market sector will have serious consequences for the national tourism industry.

Key assumptions underpinning Table 2 are as follows.

Future growth in package tourism numbers from the identified markets increases at the same rate of growth as holiday tourism from each of those markets. Expenditure levels of visitors from the identified markets increase at the same rate as numbers of visitors. The forecast numbers take no account of the influence of the business practices on tourism flows or expenditure from the identified markets.

The estimates in Table 2 are indicative only of the potential expenditure that will accrue to Australia from each market. In the absence of other information, it is assumed that expenditure related to package tourism will, Ceteris paribus, increase at an equivalent rate to that of expenditure from holiday tourists. If the pattern of tourism flows changes this assumption may prove unrealistic. On this basis, it is estimated that package tourism expenditure from the identified markets is worth $729 million to Australia in 2004 and this will rise to $1134 million in the year 2012.

Given the various assumptions explained earlier, Table 2 indicates that the relative market shares of revenues for both China and Korea are increasing, primarily due to the decreasing market share of Japan. The expenditure estimates in Table 2 are based on TFC forecasts of visitor numbers, which take no account of possible reductions in visitors from the identified markets due to dissatisfied package tourists. If the cumulative impact of the business practices is negative and consumer dissatisfaction rises over time, the potential for the projections illustrated in Table 2 will be substantially reduced.

Structure of the Package Tour Market

A package tour typically includes airfares, accommodation, guides, sightseeing, tour escorts and transfers. In many cases, the package will also include meals, sightseeing and entrances to attractions in the destination country. It is also common practice to offer optional extras such as supplementary attractions, cultural shows and visits to superior restaurants. Such elements are priced outside the standard tour inclusions to minimize the initial purchase price.

Fig. 2 illustrates the general structure of the inbound package tour market and highlights the roles undertaken by different types of firms. Note that this model does not include the forms of relationships between sectors of the package tour cycle that occur when various forms of business practices are used to boost the revenue of the ITO sector.

The model illustrated in Fig. 2 was developed on the findings of interviews undertaken by the research team with informants in Australia, China and Korea and is used as a benchmark to illustrate operational relationships between firms within the inbound market. Unavoidably, the model involves an element of oversimplification. A range of business relationships exists within individual source markets linking ITOs, Tourist Specialist Shops and tour guides. For the purposes of this research the term 'tourist specialist shop' is used to describe a variety of shops that specialize in tourist retailing. These shops are providing services and products tailored specifically to a particular source market. The various retail establishments that operate in this specialist environment are also known as Duty Free Shops, Tax Free Shops and Souvenir Shops. A number of factors determine the structure of inbound tour operations, which prevails at the destination. These include: ownership, degree of vertical integration, nationality of markets serviced and cultural aspects.

To develop a tour programme based on the sale of package tours, ITOs are contracted by outbound or wholesale travel agents (WTAs) in the origin country to undertake the destination-based ground component. This relationship is characterized in Fig. 2. In this model the WTA in the origin country takes the responsibility for purchasing airline tickets and contracts a destination-based ITO to operate the advertised itinerary. These services include accommodation, guide, services, transport, meals, attractions and a range of optional activities such as entry into attractions.

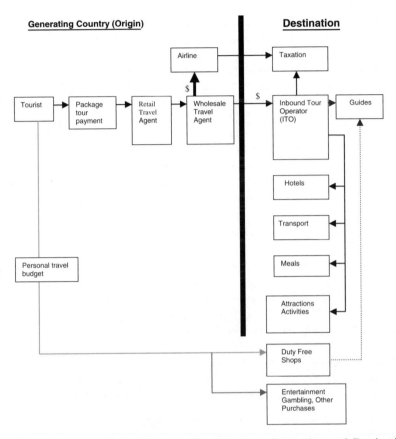

Fig. 2. The Structure of the Package Tour Cycle in Generating and Destination Countries.

The disbursement of funds to pay for the various elements of the tour such as airfares, accommodation, taxes, meals and transport is also illustrated in Fig. 2. In principle, the funds paid by the wholesale travel agent in the country of origin to the ITO should cover the ground component of the tour, while yielding an adequate profit for the ITO. The retail travel agent, and (where one is involved) wholesale travel agent in the origin country, will also expect a profit that is usually collected as commission.

As illustrated in Fig. 2, tourists have two travel budgets. The first budget is used to pay for the cost of travel that in the case of package tours includes hotels, attractions, meals, transport and attractions. The second budget is used to pay for holiday destination expenses including shopping, entertainment, recreation, gambling and other services. In a number of Asian cultures including Korea, Japan, China and Taiwan, the visitor's shopping budget is used primarily to fund expenditure on obligatory gifts with a more modest amount used for personal purchases. In the package structure there is usually minimal intersection between the visitor's two travel budgets, except in cases where tour guides take tourists to specific shops (or other businesses) and receive a small commission. The major beneficiaries of any payment by shops or other businesses are tour guides and drivers. In the industry model illustrated in Fig. 2, there are generally no kickback or payments beyond the level of the guide. As is the case in many destinations, this is the standard model of package tour operations in Australia.

Underlying Causes of the Business Practices

The emergence of the business practices identified in this research can be linked to changes in the nature of the relationship between consumers, retailers, tour operators, ITOs, wholesale companies and government regulations that are identified in Fig. 2. Moreover, while the nature of the relationships in the travel supply chain that occur in the generating country may impact on the destination country, the destination country has little ability to demand changes to these relationships in the generating country. Based on the findings of previous reports and the research conduced for this research, the major factors that cause the development of business practices include:

- The nature of the market power relationships that exist between Wholesale Travel Agents, Retail Travel Agents and ITOs.
- In nations where competition among retail travel agents is high, WTAs may be forced to lower their prices to capture business. In these circumstances the WTA may either lower the overall quality of the package tour product or they may pass the price cuts down the supply chain by reducing the daily rates paid to ITOs.
- Profit-taking by WTAs at the expense of ITOs.
- Market conditions in origin countries and within Australia.
- Short-term profit horizons of many product suppliers.
- The degree of intervention in the package tour market by government. In Australia, for example, there is no requirement for tour guides to hold a licence as a condition of employment.
- The total number of organized group and package travellers in a specific inbound market is high.

- Where inbound markets are new and where travellers have little experience of Australia as a destination.
- Travellers have little experience in travel and limited access to independent advice on the destination (CIE, 2000).

The problem of low tour prices and the use of business practices are not unique to Australia. In a recent paper on Chinese Inbound Tourism Tse (2003) noted similar problems in Hong Kong to those found in Australia. The driving forces behind the problems experienced in Hong Kong were identified as low tour prices and the culturally determined need to undertake shopping. Kim and Sohn (2002) identified similar problems in many destinations visited by Koreans.

How the Business Practices Operate

Based on the evidence uncovered by this research, the major causes of the business practices used in some inbound markets are: the structure of the package tour cycle in the origin country as well as the destination country; and the balance of market power between the members of the package tour cycle in the origin and destination nations. In origin markets where price, rather than quality, is the key selling point of package tours, the supply chain will respond in a manner that minimizes the initial price of package tour and pushes the revenue shortfall to the destination country where the remaining elements of the supply chain will attempt to recover these losses. ITOs are the key elements in the supply chain in the destination country and are the group that will usually attempt to generate additional revenue through using a range of business practices. The losses incurred by the initial low package sale price are pushed onto the destination country through the payment by WTOs of daily tour fees that are below the daily costs incurred by ITOs. Where the balance of market power lies in origin countries the operators in the package tour cycle in the destination country may become price takers rather than price makers. If market power does not favour the origin nation, operators in the destination country are much more likely to command commercially profitable rates.

The methods used by ITOs to recoup losses from low tour fees include negotiating lower room rates with hotels, using hotels of a lower standard than advertised, shopping commissions, forcing guides to cover their wages through tips and on-selling the right to direct customers to tourist specialist shops by tour guides. Shopping commissions are the most common business practice and involve the ITO negotiating with specific shops to pay a commission for each sale to a tour member and/or negotiating with tourist specialist shops to provide a range of services including guides and coach transfers at no cost to the ITO. Where shopping commissions are used as the main means of recovering outlays, package tour members are normally given no choice in the shops to where they are taken to and accommodation is usually arranged at hotels that are at some distance from tourist shopping precincts. In Asian cultures where the purchase of gifts for relatives and associates is a cultural requirement (Hobson, 1996), the ability of ITOs to gain substantial commissions is higher than in markets where there is no cultural requirement to purchase gifts. Another practice that is sometimes used is to combine the roles of guide and driver. This practice is uncommon in the lower cost destinations, which characterize Asia but occur in a number of Australian inbound markets because of the significantly higher level of wages, which prevail within Australia.

When shopping is controlled by ITOs, the practice of 'over-shopping' can emerge and generate negative impacts on the visitor experience. In some cases, the combined self-interest of the tour operator and retailers will create pressure to increase the amount of shopping within the tour. By reducing the range of other activities previously promised to tourists, they may hope to maximize the revenue from tourist purchases. This could result in a negative overall tourist experience. Pan and Laws (2003) have investigated this situation in Australia and found that it is imperative to establish benchmarks for the standard of services offered to Chinese visitors to retain Australia's competitive advantage.

According to industry sources, duty-free shops have developed a pivotal role in the operation of inbound tours to Australia. In some cases, duty-free shops (tourist specialist shops) have evolved into *de facto* ITOs, arranging many elements of the itinerary. In a development that is not found in other inbound markets, some wholesale agents in Taiwan are paid on a per-head basis for shopping rights to visitors while in Australia. This practice has the potential to generate higher leakages of tourism expenditure from Australia since the money is sent directly to firms in the origin country.

Another reported practice involves specialist shops paying a predetermined price (poll tax). This practice gives shops exclusive rights over the travel itinerary. In such situations, the tourist specialist shop may assume responsibility for providing the guide in the destination country and for arranging coach transfers. The shop pays the guide a fixed daily amount or, more commonly, a commission. In these circumstances the guide is acting as a *de facto* salesperson for the tourist specialist shop. A number of difficulties arise when the traditional role of guides changes and they are required to represent the interests of a third party rather than the tour group members. These include the possibility of unethical advice being provided to tour members with a view to encouraging them to purchase goods thereby leading to greater commission payments for the guide. Some of these issues were highlighted by Yu and Weiler (2001). The extent of the system of paying poll taxes to ITOs is highlighted in the Taiwanese inbound market where the poll tax payment according to one informant, fell from $120 per person in late 2001 to $80–90 per person by early 2003, reflective of the weakening Taiwanese economy and the associated drop in visitation.

The payment of commissions is an acceptable business practice worldwide. Nevertheless, in the context of the present research, commissions cannot be separated from business practices that appear to erode the quality of the Australian tour package product from the perspective of visitors. Commissions received by individual ITOs are used to pay for the shortfall between the amount paid by the country of origin outbound tour operator to the ITO, and the actual daily costs associated with transporting, accommodating and feeding their clients. Any funds remaining after the shortfall has been paid may be classified as profit. As many of the ITOs are Australian residents or citizens only a small percentage of any profits are likely to be remitted overseas to the country of origin of the ITO, leaving some portion of the profit if any, to be re-invested locally.

Market Overview of Korea

Following the liberalization of outbound travel by the Korean government in 1989 the demand for outbound travel by Koreans expanded substantially. In 2002, 14.2 per cent of all Koreans travelled overseas compared to 17.4 per cent of all Australians who travelled overseas in the same year. Koreans have become significant travel consumers, although their preference remains for low-cost package tours. Evidence is only beginning to emerge of Korea wholesalers developing packages that offer differentiated price level based on the standard of hotel used for members of the same tour group. A number of firms are beginning to offer tours that are at the quality end of the price spectrum.

During the 1980s the Korean outbound market was progressively deregulated and increasing numbers of Koreans were able to travel abroad without government approval (Iverson, 1997). At the same time the Korean government also deregulated the retail travel industry attracting many small investors keen to establish their own travel business. Between 1995 and 2001, the number of overseas retail travel agents increased from 1,502 to 3,185. As a consequence of increased competition in the retail sector, retail travel agents commenced discounting. Retail travel agents then applied pressure on tour wholesalers to either pay higher commissions or reduce the wholesale cost of tours. In turn, the wholesalers applied pressure on ITOs in destinations to reduce their prices, partly explaining the problems that are currently encountered in the ITO sector in many countries including Australia.

The explanation for continued support of low-cost package tours is, to a large extent, found in the nature of Korean society, which is quite different from Western society. Perhaps of more importance is the collective nature of Korean society (Prideaux & Kim, 1999), which underpins the continued popularity of group tours.

Tourist specialist shops operating in the Korean sector of international tourism usually employ staff who speak fluent Korean. Aside from the importance of being able to communicate in their own language, the ability of the staff to explain the benefits of particular items, particularly when purchased as gifts, is important. The purchaser is expected to be able to explain the quality and purpose of the item to the person to whom the item is later given as a gift. Additionally, informants in the Korean travel industry indicate that in general, Korean consumers have little confidence in non-Korean speakers in supplying them with the information they require to make a purchase, particularly when it is a health product.

Realizing that there were problems in the retail travel industry, but conscious that Korea wished to be an open economy with reducing levels of government regulation, the Korean government responded to this problem by developing accreditation policies rather than attempting to reduce competition in the retail travel agent sector through regulation. Accreditation systems used in the travel sector are the 'Quality Enterprise for Service in Korea' scheme sponsored by the Ministry of Industry and Resources and the 'Quality of Tourism Products' scheme sponsored by the Ministry of Culture and Tourism and administrated by the Korean Association of Travel Agents (KATA). The 'Quality Enterprise for Service in Korea' scheme is based on accreditation of participating firms but does not have a complaints mechanism. The 'Quality of Tourism Products' scheme has a complaints mechanism; however, the numbers of complaints are generally low, totalling 93 in 2002 for all outbound markets. These schemes do not appear to have had any noticeable impact on reducing the pressure on the Korean tour industry to reduce prices below cost and push the problem onto the destination.

Operation of the Korean Inbound Markets in Australia

Fig. 3 outlines the structure of the relationships between the various sectors of the Korean inbound market and illustrates the convergence of tourist's

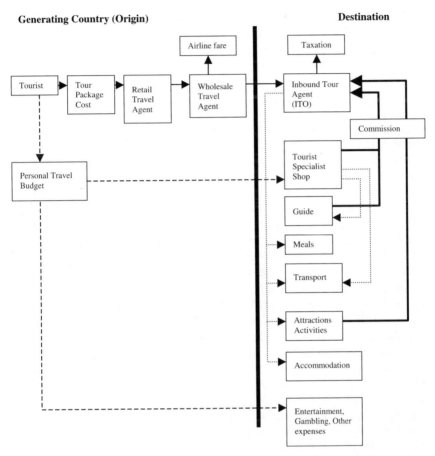

Fig. 3. Operation of the Korean Inbound Industry in Australia.

travel and shopping budgets. This has occurred as the retail cost of an Australian package has fallen to near or below cost, with the losses being carried by the ITO sector. To offset these losses, ITOs have developed business arrangements with tourist specialist shops based on a monopoly on package tour group members' shopping opportunities in exchange for an agreed payment and in some cases provision of a guide and transport. The relationship between tourist specialist shops and ITOs is fluid and subject to regular change. In effect, the customer is paying higher prices for goods purchased at tourist specialist shops to offset the low tour package prices paid in Korea. In the long term, visitors derive no benefit from low retail package tour prices and, because of the inefficiencies inherent in this system, ultimately pay a higher price.

Effects of Business Practices on Visitor Satisfaction

Existing data sets were reviewed with a view to evaluating the extent of visitor satisfaction with elements of package tourism to Australia. Some differences were evident between the results of these surveys. Given the nature of the subject this was not unexpected. Satisfaction and dissatisfaction measures provide a strong indication of the capacity of a destination to deliver a tourism experience that will continue to attract visitors into the future. If the destination meets expectations, the tourist is satisfied, while if the destination falls short of expectations, the tourist is dissatisfied. As a consequence, future visitation can be affected. However, the measurement of satisfaction and dissatisfaction is a complex matter that continues to pose many problems for researchers (Whipple & Mach, 1988).

The BTR (2004) investigated the level of dissatisfaction using results of the annual International Visitor Survey (IVS) of 2001 and 2002. Questions were designed to assess the satisfaction/dissatisfaction levels of international visitors with various aspects of guided group holiday tours in Australia. The report found that in 2001, Korea had the highest proportion of visitors on guided group holiday tours who were dissatisfied with at least one aspect of their group holiday trip (13,100 or 26.5 per cent). This was much higher than was the case for all international group holiday visitors (16.1 per cent). In the case of Japan, 47,300 (12.8 per cent) of the 370, 100 visitors on guided group holiday tours travelling to Australia in 2001 were dissatisfied with at least one aspect of the tour.

Despite some differences in specific results, the studies of satisfaction with package tourism to Australia from a number of countries including Korea indicate an identifiable degree of dissatisfaction with the products offered. The BTR study on dissatisfaction with package tours to Australia supports earlier findings by Prideaux and Kim (1999) on dissatisfaction/satisfaction of Korean package tourists. One significant finding of the BTR report was that group tour members have a lower intention to return than individual travellers.

It is concluded that, overall, Australia is not performing as well as it could in the package tour market and this may have a substantial impact on visitor satisfaction, from Korea. This dissatisfaction does not appear to relate to Australia as a destination but will inevitably impact adversely on consumer perceptions of Australia and the willingness of its regulatory authorities to remedy the situation. Although the survey questions did not specifically mention unethical business practices, it may be concluded that these underpin much of the dissatisfaction experienced. It is concluded that to increase visitor satisfaction, tour design needs to change.

CONCLUSION

The association between dissatisfaction, business practices and visitation is complex. It is rendered even more complex by the possible inability of many tourists to distinguish between unsatisfactory experiences arising from the type of tour offered, as opposed to the experience of Australia as a destination. Levels of dissatisfaction with Australian tourism products may be related to items that are independent of, or only tenuously linked to, the business practices discussed. Where tourists are aware that they are paying for part of their tour price through commissions they may factor this into their travel decisions. In these circumstances, it is unlikely that visitor flows would increase as a consequence of the elimination of business practices, particularly if the elimination of these practices resulted in the additional amounts paid to ITOs by the WTAs being recovered from tourists at the time of original tour purchase. If the tour package price remained unchanged at the point of sale overseas after the business practices were eliminated, perhaps as a result of legislation (that is prices to WTA and ITO are unchanged), ITOs would experience revenue losses from the removal of the shopping commissions system. This would in turn affect operating viability and many firms would exit the industry. The upshot of these considerations is that shopping commissions do not increase expenditure by travel package visitors to Australia since the shopping commissions may be regarded as replacing otherwise higher priced ground content.

While these practices are common in many destinations visited by Koreans, and also occur domestically in Korea, it would appear that Australia is in danger of losing international competitiveness in the package tour market. Moreover, Australia is a high cost long haul destination, which is at the 'luxury' end of the purchasing spectrum. While there may be an element of 'conspicuous consumption' associated with travel to Australia, it is also likely that travellers will be value conscious. In practice, they may be unwilling to tolerate practices, which they have experienced in short-haul destinations such as Thailand, with a shopping product such as Australia (placing Thailand in the 'convenience shopping' category). The same may apply in the case of Korea, albeit in a context where there are wider ranges of long-haul alternatives available to consumers.

Restoration of the balance between the members of the package tour cycle outlined in Fig. 2 will eliminate the need for ITOs in the destination country to resort to business practices to boost revenue to make up for the cost-push from the origin market. While not addressed in this paper, the issues involved here will undoubtedly require government intervention including the licensing of tour guides and penalizing guides and ITOs who participate in these practices. While the current situation in the Korean inbound market can be directly related back to the retail practices of travel agents in Korea, the willingness of ITOs in Australia to accept below cost ground fees is also a contributing factor. If ITOs were able to resist pressure to accept loss making ground fees the need for business practices would disappear.

ACKNOWLEDGMENT

This research was funded by the Sustainable Tourism Cooperative Research Centre whom the authors wish to thank for their support.

REFERENCES

Anastasopoulos, P. (1989). The US travel account: The impact of fluctuations of the US dollar. *Hospitality Education and Research Journal, 13*, 469–481.

Australian Tourist Commission (ATC). (2003). Assessing the quality of the Chinese visitor experience in Australia, visitor satisfaction modelling: *Teleconference Presentation to ATC Asia*, 9 May 2003, ATC, Sydney.

Bureau of Tourism Research (BTR). (2004). *Report on dissatisfied visitors on guided group holiday tours: Responses by visitors from Japan, Korea, China and Taiwan.* Canberra, Australia: Author.

Cadotte, E. R., & Turgeon, N. (1988). Satisfiers and dissatisfiers: Suggestions from consumer complaints and compliments. *Journal of Consumer Satisfaction, Dissatisfaction and Complaining Behavior, 1*, 74–79.

Centre for International Economics (CIE). (2000). *Regulatory options for inbound tour operators.* Sydney: Author.

Crouch, G. I., Schultz, L., & Valerio, P. (1992). Marketing international tourism to Australia. *Tourism Management, 13*(2), 196–208.

Dwyer, L., Forsyth, P., & Rao, P. (2002). The price competitiveness of travel and tourism: A comparison of nineteen destinations. *Tourism Management, 21*(1), 9–22.

Gronroos, C. (1990). *Service management and marketing: Managing the moments of truth in service competition.* Lexington, MA: Lexington Books.

Heung, V. C. S., & Qu, H. (2000). Hong Kong as a travel destination: An analysis of Japanese tourists' satisfaction levels and the likelihood of them recommending Hong Kong to others. *Journal of Travel and Tourism Marketing, 9*(1/2), 57–80.

Hobson, J. S. P. (1996). Leisure shopping and tourism: The case of the South Korean market to Australia. *Turizam, 44*(9–10), 228–244.

Iverson, T. J. (1997). Decision timing: A comparison of Korean and Japanese travellers. *International Journal of Hospitality Management, 16*(2), 209–219.

Jud, G. D., & Joseph, H. (1974). International demand for Latin American tourism. *Growth and Change, 5*(1), 25–31.

Kim, B. S., & Sohn, D. (2002). Price competition in the Korean group package travel industry and consumer damage: A triangulation approach. *Proceedings of the First Asia Pacific Forum for Graduate Students Research* (pp. 592–601), Hong Kong SRA, China, The Hong Kong Polytechnic University.

Kozak, M., & Rimmington, M. (2000). Tourist satisfaction with Mallorca, Spain, as an off-season holiday destination. *Journal of Travel Research, 38*, 260–269.

Pan, G., & Laws, E. (2003). Tourism development of Australia as a sustained preferred destination for Chinese visitors. *Asia Pacific Journal of Tourism Research, 8*(1), 37–47.

Parasuraman, A., Zeithaml, V. A., & Berry, L. L. (1985). A conceptual model of service quality and its implications for the future. *Journal of Marketing, 49*(Fall), 41–50.

Peter, L., & Olsen, J. L. (1987). *Consumer behaviour: Marketing strategy perspectives.* Burr Ridge, IL: Irwain.

Pizam, A., & Milman, A. (1993). Predicting satisfaction among first-time visitors to a destination by using expectancy disconfirmation theory. *International Journal of Hospitality Management, 12*(2), 197–209.

Prideaux, B., Dwyer, L., King, B., & Hobson, P. (2005). *Study into inbound practices affecting product quality in Australia's tourism industry.* Gold Coast, Australia: Sustainable Tourism Cooperative Research Centre.

Prideaux, B., & Kim, S. M. (1999). Bilateral tourism imbalance – is there a cause for concern? The case of Australia and Korea. *Tourism Management, 20*(4), 523–532.

The Australian Taxation Office. (2003). *The cash economy under the new tax system.* Canberra, Australia: Author.

Tse, W. (2003). An analysis of industry response to the influx of visitors from China to Hong Kong. *Proceedings of the first APAC-CHRIE Conference*, Richmond, VA, I-CHRIE.

Tourism Forecasting Council (TFC). (2002). *Forecast.* Canberra, Australia: Author.

Tourism Queensland (TQ). (1999). *Inbound tourism: An integrated approach to future regulation.* Brisbane: Author.

Uysal, M., & Crompton, J. L. (1984). Determinants of demand for international tourist flows to Turkey. *Tourism Management, 5*(4), 288–297.

Whipple, T., & Mach, T. S. (1988). Group tour management: Does good service produce satisfied customers? *Journal of Travel Research, 27*, 16–21.

Yu, X., & Weiler, B. (2001). Mainland Chinese pleasure travellers to Australia: A leisure behaviour analysis. *Tourism, Culture & Communication, 3*, 81–91.

THEME PARK VISITORS' DYNAMIC MOTIVATIONS

Hsin-You Chuo and John L. Heywood

ABSTRACT

In addition to individual differences, variations in visitors' motivations may result from temporal variance. The leisure ladder model (LLM) is one of the most representative motivation models, which proposes patterns for an individual's temporal dynamic nature. This study attempts to examine empirically the ageing and experiential variations of the theme park visitors' motivations, which underlie the model. Using stratified and systematic sampling techniques, survey data were collected from visitors to four leading theme parks in Taiwan – an Asian island nation. Limited support for the ageing variation was found and its changing pattern was also recognized in this study. A relatively more discriminating scale to measure the extent of visitor's experience was also suggested.

INTRODUCTION

Theme parks are one of the most typical commercial products that are collectively supported and constituted by various facets of the tourism industry, since theme parks are classified and located in the domain where three main components (i.e., travel, hospitality, and local commercial recreation) of the commercial recreation and tourism industry converge

Advances in Hospitality and Leisure, Volume 2, 73–90
Copyright © 2006 by Elsevier Ltd.
All rights of reproduction in any form reserved
ISSN: 1745-3542/doi:10.1016/S1745-3542(05)02004-7

(Crossley, Jamieson, & Brayley, 2001). Several studies and reports (Geddes, 1994; Jones & Robinett, 1993; Wong & Cheung, 1999) have indicated that Asia has been identified as the world's next leading international theme park market. Lavery and Stevens (1990) indicated that the North American theme park market reached maturity when the Disney parks in Orlando were developed in 1971, but that the demand for theme parks is still growing worldwide. Evidence for this worldwide demand can be observed from the fact that Disneyland Paris and Tokyo Disneyland were subsequently opened in April 1983 and April 1992, respectively, after the North American theme park market reached maturity. Hong Kong Disneyland opened in April 2005 and Shanghai Disneyland is scheduled to open in 2008 to satisfy the increasing recreation demand emerging in China and neighboring Asian countries. New challenges to the global theme park market undoubtedly will arise from these new theme parks and in the Asian theme park industry. In connection with this growing phenomenon, visitors' motivations to visit theme parks in the geographic area of Asia are definitely one of the most significant issues, which need to be investigated.

Tourist Motivation

Significant efforts have been devoted to understanding and conceptualizing tourist motivations. Based on different aspects of the underlying thought, Kozak (2002) indicates that there are two major streams of motivation studies in the literature. Accordingly, some researchers (e.g., Cohen, 1972; Plog, 1974; Dann, 1977) emphasize the heterogeneous nature of tourist motivation (multiple motivations) while others (e.g., Pearce, 1993) believe that individuals have limited motives and are likely to change their motivation in ascending stages over time (Kozak, 2002).

In the former stream of motivation literature, Crompton's (1979) push-pull model provides one of the most representative conceptual frameworks (Bansal & Eiselt, 2004). In the model, tourist motivations are shaped by two forces. The first force pushes a tourist away from home and the second force pulls the individual toward a destination. Factors constituting the 'push' force are origin-related and refer to the intangible, intrinsic desires of a tourist such as the desire for escape, while 'pull' factors refer to the tangible features, e.g., recreation facilities and the unique scenic, cultural, or historical resources, of a given destination (Uysal & Hagan, 1993). Since tourists' multiple motivations were found to differ among individuals (Witt & Wright, 1992; Uysal & Hagan, 1993), the concept of market segmentation has often been used both to reveal and address the heterogeneous natures of tourists' motivations. Segmentation studies (e.g., Ahmed, Barber, & d'Astous, 1998; Andereck & Caldwell, 1994; Chen, 2003b; Donnelly, Vaske, DeRuiter, & King, 1996; Loker-Murphy, 1996; Loker & Perdue, 1992; McCool & Reilly, 1993; Shoemaker, 1994, 2000; Weaver, McCleary, Lepisto, & Damonte, 1994) divide some specific travel markets into distinct subsets of consumers with common motivations, and this has been one of the most prevalent issues in the field of hospitality and tourism research. However, Williams (2002, p. 163) points out that in recent years a discernible shift has been recognized by a number of marketing researchers leading to a groundswell of criticism against the marketing concept. In response to the criticism, on the one hand, some recent studies have proposed new approaches involving more advanced analytical techniques (e.g., Bloom, 2005; Chen & Hsu, 1999) and introduced new segmentation concepts to the literature (e.g., Chen, 2003a,b) in order to enhance the usefulness of segmentation applications. On the other, Littler (1995) and Thomas (1997) (as cited by Williams, 2002) indicate the limitation of the segmentation concept by explaining that the unpredictability and instability of consumers in market segments may be due to their inconsistent motivations. This instability and unpredictability shows that in addition to their heterogeneous natures, tourists' motivations might also reflect a temporal dynamic tendency. Coincidentally, it is interesting that the temporal dynamic tendency of tourist motivations also reflects the underlying thought of the other stream of motivation studies in the literature.

Leisure Ladder Model

In the latter stream of motivation literature, Pearce's (1993) leisure ladder model (LLM) is one of the most accepted conceptual theories (Cook, Yale, & Marqua, 2002). The leisure ladder is a specific form of the travel career ladder (TCL), which was developed by Pearce (1988). Pearce developed the TCL model based on Maslow's (1970) suggestions and Mills' (1985) findings. Later on, Pearce (1991), developed the leisure ladder as a specific form of TCL for their theme park research. Pearce (1993) further diagrammatized the LLM especially to reflect the motivations of domestic visitors to theme park settings.

In Pearce's LLM for theme park settings, theme park visitors' motivations to visit theme parks change over time. Five ascending levels of motivations to visit theme parks – relaxation/bodily needs, stimulation, relationship, self-esteem/development, and fulfillment – are used to illustrate the varying motivations of a particular theme park visitor. People tend to ascend levels of the ladder as they become older or more experienced visitors in theme park settings. Accordingly, variations in visitors' motivations to visit theme parks that are caused by ageing and by increasing experience with theme park visitation are respectively called *ageing variation* and *experiential variation* in this study.

Examinations of LLM

Generally speaking, the temporal dynamic nature of theme park visitor's motivations is one of the most critical hypotheses of the LLM. Although three studies – those by Pearce (1991), Loker-Murphy (1996) and Wong and Cheung (1999) – have been devoted to the examination of the ageing and experiential variations of visitors' motivations to visit theme parks, the temporal dynamic nature has not been properly examined and successfully verified.

Pearce's (1991) study revealed motivation patterns of three demographic segments, i.e., 13- to 16-year-old children, single adults, and families, taken from the research sample. The three segments were predominantly motivated by different motivations. Based on the findings, Pearce claimed that the temporal dynamic nature of the travel career system was evident in the data, with the shift in dominant motivation level moving in the direction from "relaxing" to "part of place." However, the conclusion was based on a premise that the members of the family segment had to be older and more experienced visitors in theme park settings than single adults. This premise does not seem to be necessarily true. Therefore, Pearce's (1991) findings do not sufficiently support the temporal dynamic nature of the LLM.

Loker-Murphy (1996) generally verified that the underlying structure of backpackers' travel motivations is consistent with the five categories proposed by Pearce (1991). She asserted that the results generally supported the theory because most motivations representing the same level of the ladder appeared together in the results. In fact, the results of the study did support the underlying motivation structure of the TCL model; however, the dynamic nature of individuals' motivations was not investigated.

Wong and Cheung's (1999) findings did not sufficiently support the dynamic nature of the LLM since the conclusions reached from their findings seem unconvincing. They adopted the five levels of motivation proposed in the LLM as a framework to evaluate respondents' motivations to visit theme parks. Seven theme types were examined to determine which was most preferred by respondents. By looking at the percentage of the respondents who ranked a theme as one of their top three preferences, they found that "nature" (66.7%) was the most preferred theme. It was followed by themes of "fantasy" (46.7%) and "adventure" (44.8%). The researchers then arbitrarily assumed that all the respondents in their study were "relatively inexperienced" theme park visitors. Based on the two findings, i.e., that "adventure" was one of the respondents' top three preferred themes and that all the respondents in the study were assumed to be "relatively inexperienced," they concluded that the dynamic nature proposed in the LLM for theme park settings had been reinforced because all the respondents in their study were seeking to satisfy a lower-level motivation (i.e., stimulation).

Wong and Cheung's (1999) conclusion seems somewhat overstated and is not well supported. A substantial proportion (22%) of their respondents visited theme parks ranging from three times or more a year to once every six months. Even if the respondents really were relatively inexperienced, there was still insufficient evidence to conclude that the finding reinforces the dynamic nature proposed in the LLM for theme park settings, since "nature" and "fantasy" were ranked even higher than "adventure" as the respondents' most preferred theme.

Hypotheses to be Examined in This Study

The lack of support for the primary hypotheses underlying Pearce's (1993) LLM, i.e., which assume that visitors' motivations to visit theme parks will vary by age and experience, led to this study. The purpose of this study was to examine the influences, if any, of age and experience on visitors' motivations to visit theme parks. In order to examine the temporal dynamic nature – ageing variation and experiential variation – of theme park visitor's motivations underlying the LLM, Hypotheses 1 and 2 were formulated. Subsequently, the assumption that people ascend the levels of the LLM as they become older and more experienced led to the formulation of Hypotheses 3 and 4, respectively:

H1. On each of the five motivation levels of the LLM, there will be a significant difference in motivations to visit theme parks among visitors in different age groups.

H2. On each of the five motivation levels of the LLM, there will be a significant difference in motivations to visit theme parks among visitors in different experiential groups.

H3. Among the five motivation levels of the LLM, the higher the level observed, the stronger the older visitors will be motivated.

H4. Among the five motivation levels of the LLM, the higher the level observed, the stronger the more experienced visitors will be motivated.

METHODS

Pilot Study

A pilot study was conducted to identify the theme park motivations to be investigated in this study. A convenience sample for the pilot study was contacted from August 1998 to March 1999. The sample consisted of 80 theme park visitors who were interviewed as they were leaving two of the four leading theme parks in Taiwan, Leofoo and Window on China. By asking respondents about their reasons for visiting the theme parks, a list of theme park attributes was generated. As the list contained many descriptors that were similar, the descriptors were merged and organized into different theme park attributes. Six experienced professionals from the top five Taiwan theme parks then reviewed these attributes for meaning and validity. Fourteen theme park attributes, underlying visitors' motivations to visit theme parks, were elicited from the results of the pilot study including: animated characters, educational function, escape, family, friendship, health, making new friends, mood improvement, pressure relief, shows, themes, thematic restaurants, thrill rides, and unique facilities. Based on the motivation framework and content description proposed in the LLM, each of the five motivation levels may be represented in terms of respondents' desires for related theme park attributes (as shown in Table 1). Two attributes, animated characters and shows, were not positioned in any of the LLM's motivation levels. All of the other elicited attributes were used in the data analyses.

Research Instrument

A structured-undisguised questionnaire was subsequently developed for obtaining related information from respondents. In addition to eliciting the degree to which each of the 14 theme parks' attributes motivated respondents' theme park visitations, the questionnaire requested respondents'

Table 1. Each of the Five Motivation Levels in the LLM for Theme Park Settings is Represented in Terms of Visitors' Motivations to Related Theme Park Attributes.

Motivation Level	Components/Theme Park Attributes
V. Fulfillment	Theme
IV. Self-esteem and development	Educational function
III. Relationship	Family, friendship maintenance, and making new friends
II. Stimulation	Thrill rides and unique facilities
I. Relaxation/Bodily needs	Escape, pressure relief, thematic restaurant, health, and Mood improvement

demographic information. Respondents were asked to rate each of the statements in the questionnaire on a five-level Likert scale from "strongly disagree" (coded as one) to "strongly agree" (coded as five). It was assumed that the data collected through the scales were distributed normally and that a response on one scale, say of "strongly agree," was exactly the same as a similar response on any other scale in the research instrument. Besides, a list of the eight amusement/theme parks was provided in the questionnaire to avoid misunderstanding or ambiguous explanation. In addition, respondents were asked to indicate how many times they had visited each of the eight amusement/theme parks, among the top five most popular parks in Taiwan since 1990, within the past three years.

A test run of the questionnaire was conducted prior to the start of the fieldwork. Wording and sequencing of questions in the questionnaire were refined, based on the suggestions of 60 test-run respondents. The questionnaire was designed to be completed within 10 min.

Sampling Design and Data Collection

Most theme/amusement park researchers have collected data from individuals in shopping areas or from households listed in commercial databases rather than from visitors to particular theme/amusement parks (e.g., McClung, 1991; Moutinho, 1988; Stemerding, Oppewal, & Timmermans, 1999; Thach & Axinn, 1994; Wong & Cheung, 1999). In comparison, onsite random sampling of theme park visitors at multiple theme parks may provide more empirically convincing and representative results. Accordingly, this study was designed to collect primary data directly from domestic visitors to the four leading theme parks in Taiwan. On the one hand, Taiwan is a relatively integrated market, which is separated geographically from the other Asian markets. On the other, an empirical study with a nation-wide field of vision can be implemented with less difficulty in such an Asian island nation.

Visitors to the top four theme parks in Taiwan were the target population for this study. The top four theme parks are: Leofoo, Jenfusan Fancyland, Window on China, and Formosan Aboriginal Culture Village. According to the official report on annual theme park attendance in Taiwan (Tourism Bureau, 2002), these four leading parks shared 67.7% (4,563,127 visitors) of the annual theme park market in 2001 (6,735,571 visitors). A stratified sampling technique was used to select potential respondents on randomly chosen dates in 2001. Two days – one weekday and one weekend day – were randomly selected between October 10 and November 18, 2001 for sampling at each of the four parks. Considering the numbers of daily visitors, every 20th individual was selected and invited to participate in the study when leaving the theme park. Sixty junior students from a local university were trained as data collectors. The questionnaire was distributed in person to each visitor who agreed to participate in the study and was completed on site.

Subsampling of nonrespondents was conducted to adjust for nonresponse bias. This was done to reduce the nonresponse rate and to estimate the differences between respondents and nonrespondents. All subjects were in-formed of the nature and scope of the research without identification of the specific research goals. They were also told that participation was voluntary and that their responses were confidential and anonymous. In other words, subjects were selected based on their willingness to volunteer their personal information on site. If a visitor refused the first contact, a second contact would be made and an incentive – a coupon for free parking at the theme park – offered for participation in the study. Data from respondents and non-respondents were examined for differences by using a t-test and χ^2test. It was assumed that the subsample of nonrespondents represented all non-respondents.

Data Analysis

The average ratings of theme park attributes were used to represent the extent of the five motivation levels underlying the purposes of the respondents' theme park visits. All respondents were divided into segments by age and visit frequency to determine whether the segments differed by motivation levels. Several equal size age-based segments were grouped by dividing the respondents based on their self-reported age information. On the other hand, respondents were also divided into experiential-based segments based on the magnitude of their experiences with theme park visitation. For each of the five motivation levels of the LLM, within each set of the age- and experiential-based segments, inter-segment differences in motivations were examined by one-way ANOVAs.

Based on Thach and Axinn's (1994) suggestion, respondents were segmented by experience into breadth of experience (BOE) and depth of experience (DOE) categories, respectively. BOE is evaluated by the number of different parks a person has visited. DOE is assessed by the number of times a person has visited available parks. In this study, both the scales used to measure experience were employed and only the listed theme parks, which respondents visited within the past three years (including the current visit), were taken into account. Accordingly, respondents were divided into BOE- and DOE-based experiential segments based on the magnitude of their BOE and DOE, respectively.

RESULTS

A usable sample of 778 respondents was obtained from visitors to the top four theme parks in Taiwan. On the eight sampling dates, 19,360 visitors departed from the four sampled parks – Leofoo (6,812 visitors), Jenfusan Fancyland (6,779 visitors), Formosan Aboriginal Village (2,744 visitors), and Window on China (3,025 visitors). From this sample 966 visitors were contacted, with 703 agreeing to participate in the study and 263 refusing to participate. However, 75 of the 263 who declined the first contact agreed to participate after a second contact when an incentive was offered. As a result, a response rate of 80.4% was achieved. Table 2 profiles respondents in the research sample in terms of demographics.

Estimation of the Effect of Nonresponse

To estimate the possible effects of nonresponse, data from first-time respondents and nonrespondents (first-time refusers who completed the questionnaire after being offered an incentive in a second contact) were compared. The values obtained from the subsample were projected to all nonrespondents. Differences between subsamples of the 703 first-time respondents

Table 2. Demographic Profile of the Research Sample.

Variable	Frequency	Valid Percentage	Variable	Frequency	Valid Percentage
Age			Temporal distance (min)		
Under 16	69	8.9	d ⩽ 60	465	60.5
16–24	546	70.3	60 < d ⩽ 120	78	10.1
Over 24	162	20.8	120 < d ⩽1 80	83	10.8
Total	777	100	d > 180	143	18.6
Gender			Occupation		
Male	351	45.1	Student	520	66.8
Female	427	54.9	Non-student	258	33.2
Total	778	100	Total	778	100
Marital status					
Single	655	84.5			
Married	120	15.5			
Total	775	100			$N = 778$

and the 75 first-time refusers were examined. No significant differences were found between the responses of the two subsamples. As a result, it could be assumed that there was no significant effect of nonresponse.

Variation in Respondents' Motivations by Age

Three equal-size age segments were successfully identified from the total sample (Table 3). These consisted of 34.7% *youths* (17 and under), 34% *young adults* (18–21), and 31.3% *adults* (22 and older). Table 4 shows the results of one-way ANOVAs across the three age segments based on the segment members' motivations to visit theme parks. Significant differences across the three age segments were found in motivation levels of "stimulation" ($F = 4.20$, $p = 0.02$), "relationship" ($F = 6.85$, $p = 0.00$) and "development" ($F = 6.01$, $p = 0.00$). Using Tuckey's honestly significant difference (HSD) test for post hoc comparisons, significant differences were found between *youths* (3.99) and *adults* (3.78) in their level of "stimulation"; between *young adults* (3.64) and *youths* (3.43) in their level of "relationship"; and between *adults* (3.49) and *youths* (3.20) in their level of "development."

The changing pattern of respondents' ageing variation across the middle three levels of the leisure ladder demonstrates that the older the members were, the stronger they were motivated by higher levels of motivation; conversely, the younger the members were, the stronger they were motivated

Table 3. Results of ANOVA and Tuckey's HSD Tests on Means of Age Across Three Age Segments.

Age Segment	N	Mean of Age	S.D.	F value	p
Youths	270	15.71 ab	1.79		
Young adults	264	19.34 ac	1.12	688.014	0.000
Adults	243	32.28 bc	9.16		
Total	777	22.13	8.77		

Note: Means within a motivation level with the same alphabet are significantly different from each other using Tuckey's HSD test.

Table 4. Results of ANOVA on Members' Motivations to Visit Theme Parks Across the Three Age Segments.

Motivation Level	Age Segment	n	Mean	S.D.	F	p
Fulfillment	Youths	241	3.50	1.11		
	Young adults	244	3.48	1.01	0.045	0.956
	Adults	201	3.48	1.11		
Development	Youths	270	3.20a	1.06		
	Young adults	260	3.32	0.83	6.008	0.003
	Adults	243	3.49a	0.94		
Relationship	Youths	270	3.43a	0.80		
	Young adults	264	3.64a	0.62	6.847	0.001
	Adults	243	3.51	0.60		
Stimulation	Youths	270	3.99a	0.86		
	Young adults	264	3.84	0.81	4.203	0.015
	Adults	242	3.78a	0.86		
Relaxation	Youths	270	3.58	0.70		
	Young adults	264	3.58	0.58	0.770	0.463
	Adults	240	3.51	0.63		

See Note of Table 3.

by lower levels of motivation. Fig. 1 illustrates the changing pattern of respondents' ageing variation across the five motivation levels on the leisure ladder based on the results shown in Table 4. Therefore, evidence supports the ageing variation in respondents' motivations to visit theme parks – but only for the middle three levels of the LLM. In other words, Hypotheses 1 and 3, which jointly represent the ageing variation of theme park visitor's motivations underlying the LLM, are both only partially supported by the empirical evidence in this study.

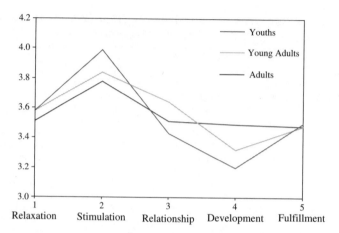

Fig. 1. The Changing Patterns of Sub-Groups' Ageing Variations Across Motivation Levels.

Variations in Respondents' Motivations by Experience

Respondents were classified in terms of their "breadth of experience" and "depth of experience," respectively. By using one-way ANOVAs, differences in motivation magnitude among respondents in the three BOE and three DOE segments in each of the five LLM motivation levels were correspondingly examined. In other words, the second and the fourth hypotheses were tested in terms of the two experiential measurements.

Breadth of Experience
Using the first measurement, respondents were successfully classified into the three BOE segments, including 300 (38.6%) *focused visitors* (visited 1–2 parks), 299 (38.4%) *selective explorers* (visited 3–4 parks), and 354 (23.0%) *variety seekers* (visited 5–8 parks). Table 5 shows that significant differences in BOE (i.e., members' average number of park visits) were found across the three BOE segments ($F = 2793.37$, $p = 0.00$). Tuckey's HSD tests showed that *focused visitors* visited fewer parks (1.45) than *selective explorers* (3.51) and *variety seekers* (5.72), and that *selective explorers'* 3.51 mean parks visited were significantly fewer than *variety seekers'* 5.72 mean parks visited.

Analysis of the BOE segments by motivation levels found significant differences for the motivation levels of "relationship" ($F = 3.34$, $p = 0.04$) and "development" ($F = 4.51$, $p = 0.01$) (Table 6). Significant differences were found between *variety seekers* (3.62) and *focused visitors* (3.46) in the

Table 5. ANOVA and Tuckey's HSD Tests on Members' Average Number of Park Visits (i.e., BOE) Across Three BOE Segments.

BOE Segment	n	Mean (No. of Park Visits)	S.D.	F	p
Focused visitors	300	1.45 ab	0.50		
Selective explorers	299	3.51 ac	0.50	2793.375	0.000
Variety seekers	179	5.72 bc	0.89		
Total	778	3.22	1.75		

See Note of Table 3.

Table 6. ANOVA on Members' Motivations Across the Three BOE-Segments.

Motivation Level	BOE Segment	n	Mean	S.D.	F	p
Fulfillment	Focused visitors	266	3.48	1.02		
	Selective explorers	260	3.47	1.05	0.095	0.910
	Variety seekers	161	3.52	1.19		
Development	Focused visitors	300	3.32	0.90		
	Selective explorers	297	3.25a	0.94	4.509	0.011
	Variety seekers	177	3.51a	1.05		
Relationship	Focused visitors	300	3.46a	0.65		
	Selective explorers	299	3.54	0.68	3.343	0.036
	Variety seekers	179	3.62a	0.75		
Stimulation	Focused visitors	300	3.81	0.81		
	Selective explorers	298	3.91	0.85	1.513	0.221
	Variety seekers	179	3.93	0.89		
Relaxation	Focused visitors	299	3.55	0.60		
	Selective explorers	297	3.55	0.64	0.119	0.888
	Variety seekers	179	3.58	0.72		

See Note of Table 3.

motivation level of "relationship," and between *variety seekers* (3.49) and *selective explorers* (3.25) in the motivation level of "development." Since significant differences between the three BOE segments were only found in two (i.e., relationship and development) of the five LLM motivation levels, neither Hypothesis 2 nor Hypothesis 4 was significantly supported in terms of BOE measurement.

Depth of Experience
Similarly, respondents were also successfully classified into the three DOE segments. Significant differences in DOE (i.e., members' average number of

park visits) were found across the three DOE segments (Table 7). The results of Tuckey's HSD tests showed that *novices* visited parks fewer times (1.42) than *juniors* (3.86) and *veterans* (8.59). The 3.86 mean number of visits by *juniors* was also significantly lower than the 8.59 mean number of visits by *veterans*. However, the analysis of motivations to visit theme parks across the three DOE segments revealed no significant differences (Table 8). As a result, there was no evidence to support Hypothesis 2 by the approach of DOE measurement. Consequently, Hypothesis 4 was not supported in terms of DOE measurement either.

Table 7. ANOVA and Tuckey's HSD Tests on Members' Average Times of Park Visits (i.e., DOE) Across Three DOE Segments.

DOE Segment	n	Mean (Times of Park Visits)	S.D.	F	p
Novices	242	1.42 ab	0.49		
Juniors	295	3.86 ac	0.80	1075.088	0.000
Veterans	241	8.59 bc	2.94		
Total	778	4.57	3.36		

See Note of Table 3.

Table 8. ANOVA on Members' Motivations Across the Three DOE Segments.

Motivation Level	DOE Segment	n	Mean	S.D.	F	p
Fulfillment	Novices	218	3.49	1.02		
	Juniors	254	3.50	1.00	0.035	0.965
	Veterans	215	3.47	1.21		
Development	Novices	242	3.37	0.89		
	Juniors	295	3.31	0.95	0.299	0.742
	Veterans	237	3.33	1.03		
Relationship	Novices	242	3.47	0.67		
	Juniors	295	3.55	0.68	1.051	0.350
	Veterans	241	3.55	0.72		
Stimulation	Novices	242	3.80	0.80		
	Juniors	295	3.86	0.81	2.833	0.059
	Veterans	240	3.98	0.93		
Relaxation	Novices	241	3.54	0.59		
	Juniors	293	3.60	0.63	1.262	0.284
	Veterans	241	3.51	0.70		

Although the experiential variation proposed in the LLM was not verified in this study by using either BOE or DOE measurement, results of this study do reflect the discriminating ability of the two experiential scales. Results of this study (Tables 6 and 8) suggest that BOE may serve as a better discriminating scale than DOE to explore variation in theme park visitors' motivations caused by increasing experiences with theme park visitation. In other words, it can be stated that increasing BOE rather than DOE may induce changes in theme park visitors' motivations.

STUDY LIMITATIONS

The findings of this study are inevitably subject to several limitations. First, the research sample drawn from visitors to the top four leading theme parks in Taiwan limits the ability of the researcher to generalize results of this study to other populations. However, it should also be noted that the practical applications of the findings to the market domain in China are still significant since it is also true that the ethnic dissimilarity between populations in Taiwan and China is almost negligible. Second, the sampled theme parks in this study are relatively small in comparison with theme parks such as Disney parks in terms of both operation scale and volume of attendance. In fact, it is very possible that small-scale theme parks might tend to focus their facilities on meeting particular visitor motivations rather than full-range motivations in order to establish relative advantages over their competitors with fairly limited resources. The limited supporting findings of this study might result from the possibility that full-range variation of visitor's motivations is relatively difficult to observe on the basis of relatively small-scale theme parks. The last limitation refers to the nature of the research purpose. The research purpose of this study was to examine the dynamic nature of visitors' motivations proposed in the LLM. In order to be consistent with the model, this study had to omit from the pilot study two of the elicited theme park attributes, which underlie visitors' motivations to visit theme parks because they did not fit in with the content description in LLM's motivation framework. However, the two omitted attributes, animated characters, and shows, certainly play significant roles in visitors' experiences of theme park visitation from the view of practical operation. In other words, the full range of motivations elicited from the pilot study of this research were partially adopted in the following process of examination due to the limited scope of the LLM's proposition.

CONCLUSION

The significance of this study for the current body of knowledge is the examination of the temporal dynamic nature of theme park visitors' motivations. Findings of this study provide limited support for the dynamic tendency and the shifting pattern of ageing variation proposed in the LLM. On the other hand, no empirical evidence regarding the dynamic tendency of the experiential variation was found in this study. Besides, this study suggests that increasing the number of different parks a person has visited rather than increasing the number of times a person has visited particular parks tends to induce changes in their statuses across the motivation levels in the LLM. Finally, this study also emphasizes that only selected rather than integral theme park attributes underlying visitors' motivations to visit theme parks are considered in Pearce's (1993) LLM for theme park settings.

   Based on the findings and limitations of this study, several recommendations for further research can be drawn. First, both the theoretical and empirical efforts of future research can attempt to further refine or extend the LLM's content exhaustiveness by embracing all the significant theme park attributes that constitute visitors' motivations to visit theme parks, especially on the basis of ageing variation. Second, the measurements and the consequences of visitors' theme park visitation experiences might be interesting issues for future research. Visitors' theme park visitation experiences can be measured based on different aspects of conceptual constructs. Accordingly, more scales for measuring visitors' theme park visitation experiences might be developed for various research purposes. Besides, in addition to visitors' shifting motivations, some behavioral, perceptual, or attitudinal changes that are also consequences of visitors' increasing experience of theme park visitation might be explored further. Finally, on a more practical level, further systematic research on various issues in connection with the increasing recreation demand emerging in the geographic area of Asia is highly recommended because global theme park management's new challenges will mainly arise there.

ACKNOWLEDGMENTS

The authors would like to express their appreciation to the National Science Council in Taiwan, which provides a grant (NSC-91-2415-H-029-005) supporting the current research.

REFERENCES

Ahmed, S. A., Barber, M., & d'Astous, A. (1998). Segmentation of the Nordic winter sun seekers market. *Journal of Travel and Tourism Marketing, 7*(1), 39–63.

Andereck, K. L., & Caldwell, L. L. (1994). Motive-based segmentation of a public zoological park market. *Journal of Park and Recreation Administration, 12*(2), 19–31.

Bansal, H., & Eiselt, H. A. (2004). Exploratory research of tourist motivations and planning. *Tourism Management, 25*(3), 387–396.

Bloom, J. Z. (2005). Market segmentation: A neural network application. *Annals of Tourism Research, 32*(1), 93–111.

Chen, J. S. (2003a). Market segmentation by tourists' sentiments. *Annals of Tourism Research, 30*(1), 178–193.

Chen, J. S. (2003b). Developing a travel segmentation methodology: A criterion-based approach. *Journal of Hospitality and Tourism Research, 27*(3), 310–327.

Chen, J. S., & Hsu, C. H. C. (1999). The use of logit analysis to enhance the market segmentation study. *Journal of Hospitality and Tourism Research, 23*(3), 268–283.

Cohen, E. (1972). Toward a sociology of international tourism. *Social Research, 39,164–182.*

Cook, R. A., Yale, L. J., & Marqua, J. J. (2002). *Tourism: The business of travel* (2nd ed.). NJ: Prentice-Hall.

Crompton, J. L. (1979). Motivations for pleasure vacation. *Annals of Tourism Research, 6*(4), 408–424.

Crossley, J. C., Jamieson, L. M., & Brayley, R. E. (2001). *Introduction to commercial recreation and tourism: An entrepreneurial approach* (4th ed.). Champaign, IL: Sagamore Publishing.

Dann, G. M. S. (1977). Anomie, ego-enhancement and tourism. *Annals of Tourism Research, 4*(4), 184–194.

Donnelly, M. P., Vaske, J. J., DeRuiter, D. S., & King, T. B. (1996). Person-occasion segmentation of state park visitors. *Journal of Park and Recreation Administration, 14*(2), 95–106.

Geddes, A. (1994). Disney parks look to Asia for needed lift. *Advertising Age, 65*(18), 1–62.

Jones, C. B., & Robinett, J. (1993). The future role of theme parks in international tourism. *World Travel and Tourism Review 1993, 3*, 144–150.

Kozak, M. (2002). Comparative analysis of tourist motivations by nationality and destinations. *Tourism Management, 23*(3), 221–232.

Lavery, P., & Stevens, T. (1990). Attendance trends and future developments at Europe's leisure attractions. *Economist Intelligence Unit Travel & Tourism Analyst, 2*, 52–75.

Littler, D. (1995). Marketing segmentation. In: M. J. Baker (Ed.), *Marketing theory & practice* (pp. 197–212). Hampshire, England: Palgrave Macmillan.

Loker, L. E., & Perdue, R. R. (1992). A benefit-based segmentation of a nonresident summer travel market. *Journal of Travel Research, 30*(1), 30–35.

Loker-Murphy, L. (1996). Backpackers in Australia: A motivation-based segmentation study. *Journal of Travel & Tourism Marketing, 5*(4), 23–45.

Maslow, A. H. (1970). *Motivation and personality.* New York: Harper & Row.

McClung, G. W. (1991). Theme park selection: Factors influencing attendance. *Tourism Management, 12*(2), 132–140.

McCool, S. F., & Reilly, M. (1993). Benefit segmentation analysis of state park visitor setting preferences and behavior. *Journal of Park and Recreation Administration, 11*(4), 1–14.

Mill, A. S. (1985). Participation motivations for outdoor recreation: A test of Maslow's theory. *Journal of Leisure Research, 17*, 184–199.

Moutinho, L. (1988). Amusement park visitor behavior – Scottish attitudes. *Tourism Management*, *9*(4), 291–300.

Pearce, P. L. (1988). *The Ulysses factor: Evaluating visitors in tourist settings.* New York and Berlin: Springer.

Pearce, P. L. (1991). *Dreamworld: A report on public reactions to Dreamworld and proposed developments at Dreamworld.* Townsville: Department of Tourist, James Cook University.

Pearce, P. L. (1993). Fundamentals of tourist motivation. In: D. G. Pearce & R. W. Butler (Eds), *Tourism research critiques and challenges* (pp. 114–134). London: Routledge.

Plog, S. G. (1974). Why destination areas rise and fall in popularity. *Cornell Hotel and Restaurant Administration Quarterly*, *15*(November), 13–16.

Shoemaker, S. (1994). Segmenting the US travel market according to benefits realized. *Journal of Travel Research*, *32*(3), 8–21.

Shoemaker, S. (2000). Segmenting the mature market: 10 years later. *Journal of Travel Research*, *39*(2), 11–26.

Stemerding, M., Oppewal, H., & Timmermans, H. (1999). A constraints-induced model of park choice. *Leisure Sciences*, *21*(2), 145–158.

Thach, S. V., & Axinn, C. (1994). Patron assessments of amusement park attributes. *Journal of Travel Research*, *32*(3), 51–60.

Thomas, M. J. (1997). Consumer market research: Does it have validity? Some postmodern thoughts. *Marketing Intelligence & Planning*, *15*(2), 54–59.

Tourism Bureau. (2002). *Report on tourism statistics.* Taipei: Ministry of Transport and Communications.

Uysal, M., & Hagan, L. (1993). Motivations of pleasure travel and tourism. In: M. Khan, M. Olsen & T. Var (Eds), *Encyclopedia of hospitality and tourism* (pp. 798–810). New York: Van Nostrand Reinhold.

Weaver, P. A., McCleary, K. W., Lepisto, L., & Damonte, L. T. (1994). The relationship of destination selection attributes to psychological, behavioral and demographic variables. *Journal of Hospitality & Leisure Marketing*, *2*(2), 93–109.

Williams, A. (2002). *Understanding the hospitality consumer.* Woburn, MA: Butterworth-Heinemann.

Witt, C. A., & Wright, P. (1992). Tourist motivation: Life after Maslow. In: P. Johnson & B. Thomas (Eds), *Choice and demand in tourism* (pp. 33–56). London: Mansell.

Wong, K., & Cheung, P. (1999). Strategic theming in theme park marketing. *Journal of Vacation Marketing*, *5*(4), 319–332.

IMPACTS OF NO-ESCAPE NATURAL DISASTER ON TOURISM: A CASE STUDY IN TAIWAN

Tzung-Cheng Huan, Chin-Fa Tsai and Lori B. Shelby

ABSTRACT

This article highlights a new research theme on how a no-escape natural disaster (NEND), such as Taiwan's earthquake of September 21, 1999 (dubbed as 921), impacts tourists' trip decision. Nearly four years after the 921 event, a survey investigated the changes of tourists' decision-making to the area mostly affected by the disaster. Expected negative effects on travel decisions were found. Surprisingly, a tourism boom in the affected destinations was documented. The possible reasons for recovery are discussed. Furthermore, comparing the consequences of another NEND event – December 2004 tsunami, the study suggests practical research agendas in rejuvenating NEND-impacted tourism destinations. Lastly, it is recommended that future research might center on the safety issues of travel destinations.

INTRODUCTION

The aftermath of a mighty natural disaster from which the tourists may not escape often prompts tourism professionals' attention to seek for effective

Advances in Hospitality and Leisure, Volume 2, 91–106
Copyright © 2006 by Elsevier Ltd.
All rights of reproduction in any form reserved
ISSN: 1745-3542/doi:10.1016/S1745-3542(05)02005-9

crisis management plans. It is true that some disasters, such as hurricanes could be predictive in advance. Some can only be detected shortly before the event transcends such as tsunamis. However, even with an early warning system, before a tsunami wave approaches to a seashore destination, little time may exist to escape from its attack. Lastly, earthquakes represent a unique case of non-predictable natural disaster.

From a destination management point of view, the above natural disasters could be grouped into escapable and inescapable events in terms of the quickness of warning received. Hurricane belongs to escapable while tsunami and earthquake are inescapable. In theory, no-escape natural disasters (NEND) are more serious for destination crisis management than escapable events. To prevent the risk of death or injury from earthquakes, the World Tourism Organization (1998) reveals that the damage can be minimized by appropriate citing of buildings and infrastructure and by systematic efforts to eliminate unsafe infrastructure. Also, hazard maps and maps of faults along with earthquake resistant construction ensure the safety of infrastructure in earthquake prone areas (National Tsunami Hazard Mitigation Program, 2001).

However, sporadic efforts have been made in the destinations, which are likely to encounter inescapable disasters. For example, a few coastal cities in Japan have built walls to blunt the force of tsunamis and buildings have been constructed to withstand destruction by the waves (Miyazaki, 2005). Holiday makers do not want to see concrete walls in the oceanfront; however, building walls now could be a serious option in ocean resorts.

Tsunamis have continued to strike and wreck the life of human beings (Table 1) while success of preventing it has been limited in many travel destinations (Geller, Jackson, Kagan, & Mulargia, 1996; Vergano, 2001; United States Geological Survey, 1997). Because the occurrence of tsunamis is generally linked to earthquakes or under sea landslides (United States National Oceanic and Atmospheric Administration, UNESCO/Intergovernmental Oceanographic Commission, International Tsunami Information Center, Laboratoire De Geophysique, & France, 2002), their occurrence is no more predictable than earthquakes. However, since waves travel out from an origin prior to striking, e.g., a coastal resort, warning that a tsunami may strike is possible. The current "early warning" technology implemented in the Pacific basin involves wave detectors; so if a significant wave can be detected a warning of tsunami can be issued (United States National Oceanic & Atmospheric Administration et al., 2002).

Although some preventive measures are taken in destinations to lessen the damage of NEND events, little research has emphasized the psychology of

Table 1. Recent and Relatively Large Tsunami.[a]

Date UTC (YY/MM/DD)	Source Location	Deaths	Magnitude of Related Earthquake
2004/12/26	Indonesia	150,000	9.0
1994/06/02	India	238	7.2
1946/08/08	Dominican Republic	75	7.9
1946/08/04	Dominican Republic	1,790	8.1
1941/06/26	India	5,000	8.1
1929/11/18	Newfoundland, Canada	51	7.2
1928/11/18	Newfoundland, Canada	26	7.2
1918/10/11	Puerto Rico, USA	42	7.5
1909/09/22	Louisiana, USA	300	
1907/01/04	Indonesia	400	7.6
1906/01/31	Colombia	500	8.9
1883/08/27	Indonesia	36,500	
1861/03/09	Indonesia	1,700	7.0
1861/02/16	Indonesia	905	8.5
1842/05/07	Haiti	300	7.7
1797/02/10	Indonesia	300	8.0
1692/06/07	Jamaica	2,000	7.7
1774	Newfoundland, Canada	300	

[a]*Sources:* National Geophysical Data Center http://www.ngdc.noaa.gov/seg/hazard/tsu.shtml

tourists. This research is to supply the deficiencies by probing the change of destination choice sets in relation to a future visit to the most affected area caused by a NEND event in Taiwan that is related to the earthquake of September 21, 1999 (dubbed as 921).

Furthermore, this research is divided into two parts with a case study approach. The first part presents empirical information disentangling the mist behind the behavioral changes in relation to destination choice affected by a NEND event. The second part is to further discuss tourism development in an affected area after the NEND event and draw suggestions to future research on the impacts of NEND.

Background of the 921 Earthquake in Taiwan

The 921 was a 7.3 Richter scale earthquake that had its epicenter in Nantou County (Fig. 1). It broke a large concrete dam leaving one part about 10 m below another. Not far from the dam a waterfall of around 7 m appeared in a flat riverbed (see photos and map in Huan, Beaman, & Shelby, 2004). It ripped apart bridges, and collapsed houses and apartment buildings. In

The National Highway Map of Taiwan

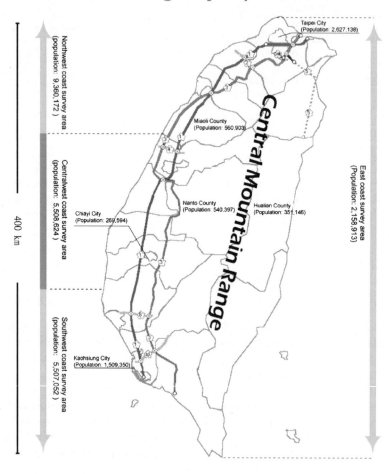

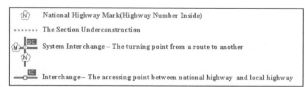

Fig. 1. The National Highway Map of Taiwan.

Taipei, which is at one end of Taiwan (over 150 km away from the epicenter), a hotel was destroyed. In fact, many homes all over west central Taiwan have a metal roof over an original roof to keep water from running into cracks created by the 921, which caused extensive damages with about 2,400 lives lost (Huang & Min, 2002; Tourism Bureau Taiwan, 2000). 38,935 buildings were completely destroyed and about 45,000 buildings suffered significant damage (The 921 Earthquake Post-Disaster Recover Commission, 2003). Nevertheless, the broken dam has been repaired with the portion broken off preserved as an historic site (Huan, in press).

The immediate and enduring psychological impacts of earthquakes are a matter of record (Goenjian, Steinberg, Najarian, Fairbanks, & Pynoos, 2000; Lewin, Carr, & Webster, 1998). Records for the 921 do not show what injuries were received by foreign tourists who experienced it or were received by domestic tourists who happened to be in the affected area. The Taiwan Ministry of Education's perception of threat was real enough to issue directives against school field trips to the Nantou area (Ministry of Education, 1999). For Nantou residents, dealing with psychological problems stemming from the 921 is continuing (Cheng, Tan, Chen, Tung, & Wang, 2003). However, interviews with psychiatric medical professionals in 2004 showed that they consider most people who suffered from serious psychological problems from it as having "recovered" (Huan, in press).

Tourism Impact Research in Relation to the 921

In an initial survey conducted shortly after the 921, the researchers examined perceptions in terms of destination image. In reporting this research, Huan et al. (2004) stated that the thought about the usefulness of image research made it clear that *for destination rehabilitation it was of limited value.* Given that a destination was rehabiliated and information about that was disseminated, any image problems had to do with the attributes of the rehabilitated destination, particularly with perceptions regarding the safety of going there given the potential for another NEND strike.

Huang and Min (2002), forecasting the recovery from the 921, concluded that after only a few years tourism has almost recovered. However, they do not discuses the level of tourism that would have occurred without it. Did the destination drop out of the consideration sets by the tourists who endured the earthquake? If so, who is replacing them and why? Unless a forecast that could addresses tourists' reaction to the events in relation to their choice sets, it appears that further research might be considered concerning the issues of tourists' decision-making.

Huan et al. (2004) presented a theory about the impact of NEND on trip decision-making. The 921 earthquake prompted the formulation of the theory. The formulation was guided by consumer behavior literature on choice sets that Crompton and Ankomah (1993) and Woodside and Lysonski (1989) among others have applied to tourism. This is tested consumer theory that describes memory as organizing potential travel destinations into choice sets that when a trip of a given type is considered a set of destinations are included, e.g., destinations that receive active consideration (the active-evoked set) and a set that does not come up for consideration (rejected/inept set). There is a proof that such organization is recognized (Woodside & Sherrell, 1977). However, no evidence shows that due to a NEND event the affected tourists removed their destination choice from their active consideration set (active-evoked set) to the rejected/inept set. The theory, proposed by Huan et al. (2004), proclaimed that recognizing the threat of a NEND at a destination causes tourists to change the choice set of the destination. However, no evidence is provided supporting such a thesis. Hem, Iversen, and Nysveen (2002) highlighted choice preferences associated with the level of risk in a study on tourists' decision-making in regard to the destination suffering from NEND. Also, the risk of being caught in a terrorism attack (King & Berno, 2002; Sonmez, Apostolopoulos, & Tarlow, 1999), earthquake, or tsunami could play a vital role in tourists' decision-making that differs from the risk portrayed in photographs in Hem et al. (2002).

METHODS

Collecting data on how the 921 affected Taiwanese residents' trip decision to the heavily affected area – Nantou County posed some challenges. Since 90% of the residents of Taiwanese who travel by private vehicles can now get to the Nantou area in a few hours, the study population is very large. An ideal survey, involving random sampling of Taiwanese holiday makers, often utilizes mailing questionnaires and telephone interview that are indeed costly. Further due to the topic of study, it also adds some difficulties in obtaining reliable information. The dilemma lies in the fact that Taiwanese are inclined to provide genius response about their emotional stress caused by disasters only to their families or close friends. Therefore, various methodological options were considered in this study. It was recognized that snowball method could be an effective way of collecting the data. The study used college students as a median to obtain the reliable information. In the spring of 2003, an initial questionnaire was developed and vetted with colleagues and students (this is about three and half years after the 921). Questions asked in the survey are quite obvious from survey results given in Tables 2 and 3. Students interviewed their relatives in appropriate categories who made recreational trips that took them an hour or more from home to a region away from their home (e.g., to a leisure farm or National Park). Each student was to obtain data from at least six relatives. Two interviews were to be with each "generation" (usually theirs, their parents, and their grand parents) allowing for coverage of the age range of traveling adults. The questionnaire was a guide for open-ended questioning with notes taken as was necessary to facilitate accurate coding of responses.

Table 2. Summary Information from the Survey.

Groups and Categories in Groups	Frequency (in Group)	Percent (of Group Total)
Visited Nantou before and after the 921		
No visit to Nantou before or after the 921	21	12
No visit to Nantou before the 921 but visited Nantou after the 921	27	15
Visited Nantou before and after the 921	91	50
Visited Nantou before 921 but not after the 921	42	23
Total	181	100
Visited Nantou before and after the 921		
Frequency increased after 921	5	6
Same frequency after 921	39	44
Frequency reduced after 921	44	50
Total (note 88 of 91 before-after reporting)	88	100
Visited Nantou before and after but reduced frequency after		
Reduced use because of the possibility of earthquake	20	45
Reduced use because of condition or service change	17	39
Other	7	16
Total (note 43 of 44 frequency reduced after 921 reporting)	44	100
Did not visit Nantou before and after the 921		
Concern with earthquake	4	20
Other	16	80
Total (note 20 of 21 not visiting Nantou responded)	20	100
Visited Nantou before the 921 but not after		
Total (note that only 30 out of 42 responded giving responses related to evoked set – see Table 3)	n.a.	n.a.

Table 3. Survey Results Concerning the Evoked Set of Respondents Who Visited Nantou Before 921 but have Not Visited after.

Scenarios Relating to Evoked Set Shift	Evoked Set	Frequency	Percent
I am waiting for things to be back to the way I have expected	Inaction	3	10.0
I think about going but do not really consider it an option	Inert	5	16.7
I started going elsewhere and no longer consider Nantou	"Out"	3	10.0
I think about going back but feel more comfortable going elsewhere	Inaction	6	20.0
I will probably eventually visit Nantou again (it is actively considered but repeatedly rejected)	Action (but low priority)	6	20.0
Because of concern with an earthquake I doubt I will go to Nantou	Inert	3	10.0
Other	n.a.	4	13.3
Total		30	100.0

Owing to Taiwan's geography (Fig. 1), the 90% of Taiwan's population toward the west can access Nantou quite quickly. Therefore, a reasonable goal for the survey was good representation from the north, west-central, and south Taiwan. It is believed that more than 99% of domestic visits from outside the Nantou area come from these three areas.

Lastly, students were not asked to collect information from a random sample of "a set of all their relatives" because that methodology did not offer clear advantages and had the potential to create problems. For example, such a selection could result in a scenario in which they have to interview relatives that they do not know well or with whom they have a poor relationship. The information obtained under those circumstances may not be reliable. In sum, the data collection objectives were (a) getting a reasonable number of interviews from the three areas mentioned above and (b) getting data from a wide range of people so as to observe any frequently occurring ways that the 921 affected tourist decision-making sets.

FINDINGS AND DISCUSSIONS

The interviews resulted in 181 usable questionnaires. Most students met the goal set for them of 6 usable interviews with relatives in appropriate segments. Only 21 people contacted chose not to respond (response rate = 88%). Of the survey respondents, 54 respondents were from the northern-west part of Taiwan (largely Taipei and northern cities), 66 were from the central-west part of Taiwan (largely cities relatively near to Nantou), and 61 were from the southern-west part of the island (largely Kaoshiung and larger southern cities). Clearly, based on population (Fig. 1), more interviews from the northern-west part of Taiwan would be expected in a random sample of Taiwanese population. However, given that the college students who employed the survey come from south-central Taiwan, the numbers of responses by area are not surprising. The final sample well presents the tourists from the three major tourist-generating regions in Taiwan.

Table 2 shows that 21 of 181 respondents did not visit Nantou before the 921 and had no intention to visit it. Twice as many respondents ($n = 42$) reported going to Nantou before the 921 but not after. Another group has only visited Nantou since the 921. This group is about the same size as the group reporting never visiting. Those who visited Nantou before and after the 921 made up 50% of respondents ($n = 91$). However, 50% of this group indicated reducing their frequency of visiting after the 921 (88 of the 91 respondents in this group reported on frequency of visits after the 921). Reduced frequency is seen by 45% of this group to be associated with the possibility of another large earthquake. Only 6% increased their frequency of visiting.

The respondents, who visited Nantou prior to the 921 but not after, have provided vital information in assessing the alteration of choice sets. Table 3 introduced the possible reaction of 30 respondents who identified themselves with an evoked set change. The evoked set membership, except for one identified as action-evoked with low priority, relates to something needing to happen to move Nantou back into the action-evoked set, where it was prior to the 921. In line with the propositions by Huan et al. (2004), the results show that the 921 event could affect the choice sets of tourists.

What has Happened at Nantou?

To this point several factors affecting the growth of tourism have not been clear regarding tourism business in Nantou. One is that destruction of tourism infrastructure in Nantou resulted in new infrastructure that meets high safety standards and, in most cases, is much more appealing to tourists than that which was destroyed. A second is how the completion of Highway

3 through Nantou (Fig. 1) would be expected to influence tourism flow volumes. Prior to the 921 Highway 3 and connectors between it and Highway 1 were in the process of being completed.

Fig. 1 shows that prior to the 921 Nantou County was viewed as a poor, agricultural area to which access was by slow and often crowded narrow roads. Although, there were some desirable destinations; however, it took effort to reach those spots from Taipei or Kaoshiung (Taiwan's largest cities). Highway 3 is a 4-lane expressway that was constructed to take pressure off Highway 1, which carries most of the north-south heavy vehicle traffic and much of the long-distance private vehicle traffic. Had the 921 not occurred, Highway 3 would have still been completed through Nantou making it easily, quickly, and conveniently reached? In addition, if it were not for 921, visitors would not find much of the first-class infrastructure they now find at Nantou.

Fig. 2 shows person trips to Nantou for last 10 years (estimated by the Nantou County government). From 1994 to 1998 change was relatively slow. In 1999 and 2000 the numbers dropped significantly because of the 921. In 2001 the number came back to normal level while by 2003 the numbers rose to twice the pre 921 level. Growth occurred with completion of Highway 3.

To further comprehend the change of visitation to Nantou and how it relates to the 921, the following two issues seem important for future tourism development in the destination. The first relates to the factors affecting repeat tourists' decision-making to Nantou that help practitioners envisage

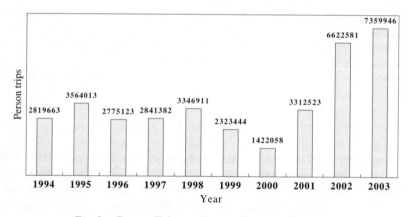

Fig. 2. Person Trips to Nantou for Last 10 Years.

the potential visitation to the area and predict the possible time that the mass tourists are likely to return. The second deals with the reasons behind the influx of infrequent, first-time visitors since the business recovery in Nantou are tied to the flow of new tourists. Given massive investment in new infrastructures and concerted efforts on rehabilitation by the government, it is likely that there would have been rapid recovery without the completion of Highway 3.

NEND Research and its Relevance to Rejuvenation of Nantou

The survey shows that a substantial number of visitors to Nantou prior to the 921 will not return to the region again. Further, the study finds a small portion of individuals who have never been to the area before are frightened to travel to the destination because of the potential threat from earthquakes. As for those who went to Nantou before 921 and continued to visit, almost half have reduced their frequency of visit and many of those reported the reduction was due to the danger of earthquake reoccurrences. Can one assume that for any NEND impacted destination, lowered trip/visit frequencies will drift back to pre earthquake levels? Huang and Min (2002) suggested that there is merely a "bang" with a drop and then the upward trend should take off again. However, what contributes to the growth is still unknown? Therefore, the tenets of Huang and Min might desires a cross validation. If the survey had showed that few people had shifted their intention to visit Nantou, it would be reasonable to reduce financial supports to recover tourism business in Nantou. However, the survey illustrated clear shifts in respect to tourists' destination choice. The future strategies may follow how the behavioral shifts should be interpreted in relation to what to do about 921.

Research Direction for Tourism Destinations Impacted by the NEND

Think about a tourism destination that was economically viable and badly damaged by a NEND, with tourists being injured and killed. This could be Nantou in the fall of 1999 or it could be one of the many destinations devastated by tsunami waves in December 2004. In either case, reconstruction is necessary if there is to be a viable destination. However, research is needed to determine appropriate steps of reconstruction or to rationalize not rejuvenating it. As discussed by Huan et al. (2004), what image people have of the destination soon after the disaster struck, is of little value in making decisions about rejuvenation. In fact, given that safety is an issue, research on the viability of rejuvenation must involve the potential to have a safe destination given how it is going to be used. As suggested earlier, building a wall to prevent damage from tsunamis is not an acceptable option for a beach area before the incident of tsunamis in south Asia. Considering what is to happen at a destination must be part of assessing if it can be attractive to visitors and acceptably safe in their eyes.

Research needs are defined when one accepts that sound analysis is required of optional development of a destination so it appeals to visitors, is economically viable, and is seen as acceptably safe. For Nantou, it is fortuitous that development along this line is already occurring and it seems to be highly appropriate. Furthermore, it is fortunate that Taiwan is one of the leaders in earthquake resistant construction and brought that capability to the rejuvenation of the Nantou area.

An aspect of consideration of options is how most visitors relate to a devastated destination. It is possible for such a destination to serve the local market. The importance of this is that all people in the market with any interest in using the destination will be aware of, and to some degree impacted, by the disaster. In this special case, viability of the destination, if reconstructed, will depend on whether the locals choose to continue using it in numbers adequate to support it. Collection of information on likely support for adequately safe options, given the costs of these options, is what is needed for rational decision-making. Appropriate research for such NENDs is not pursued further.

In contrast to a local use area being impacted by a NEND, consider what happens when a non-local-use destination like Nantou or one of the international resort destinations struck by the December 2004 tsunami is devastated. Only a few visitors would have directly experienced the NEND. Some other visitors may be closely linked because of personal relations with people injured or killed. Nevertheless, the catastrophe may be displayed in the media. However, most potential visitors can presumably look at the risk of being caught in a future NEND quite dispassionately. This is seen as behind survey results presented and behind the boom in tourism to Nantou. In spite of media coverage, some 921 damage over a wide area of Taiwan, and the Ministry of Education banning school trips, it seems clear that a very large segment of the Taiwanese population has been open to the message that the destination has been rehabilitated and it is safe to visit. In reaching out to this group, one is not trying to get someone who has placed the destination in their inept set to change its placement.

One is targeting a much easier market. For example, only a small proportion of Europeans that vacation in areas struck by the December 2004 tsunami suffered any direct consequence. Given the development of an early warning system and given that other desirable safety measures as implemented (e.g., as in Hawaii) and facilities are new, it is reasonable that most of these visitors will need very little encouragement to return. Realistically, there is no need to try to determine how large the group is that has moved the destination into their inept set. Huan et al. (2004) actually caution against pursuing choice set research soon after a NEND. The argument is that obtaining responses that are stable enough over time to be useful will not be possible until well after a NEND. Certainly, answers about whether a destination will be visited cannot be stable until it is clear what rejuvenation is being done and if one will feel safe using the destination. When choice set research may be worth doing in terms of its use in attracting visitors is commented on subsequently.

The implication of what was presented in the last paragraph is that when a non-local-use destination is struck by a NEND, research should focus on having rejuvenation resulting in a safe destination that is well positioned to be viable. Other than dealing with safety in a special way, research that is important is that, which should occur in planning for a new development. There is no mention of positioning and Nantou's competition because there really was none. However, as already noted, destinations in Kenya are looking to draw visitors for destinations struck by the December 2004 tsunami waves. If major capital construction is required to make a destination viable, prior to detail planning for construction is the appropriate time to consider repositioning and what is required for that.

One might think that forecasting use for a devastated destination would be a helpful research for rejuvenation. Several things seem clear from the literature, including the forecasting for Nantou. Given that tourism forecasting methods to deal with catastrophic events are under development (Coshall, 2000), the only value of forecasting is predicting use of the destination if the event did not occur. Having a predicted future as a baseline for comparison could be useful. Trying to predict data for after a NEND struck is going beyond current capabilities to produce valid results. Trying to predict a new trend with a few years' data after the NEND does not seem to be appropriate because there is not adequate information to determine a pattern and no proven pattern for which to estimate parameters (Hwang, Chen, & Lee, 1998; Wang, 2004).

An area in which academic research on the influence of NEND on choice set placement of destination impacts is augmenting growth. Increased

domestic visitation to Nantou by domestic tourists largely depend on transportation developments, and development of new high quality infrastructure that minimizes how a large earthquake will impact tourists and new
users. In a similar manner, it has been suggested that in the short run, for
new NEND-impacted destinations, research should focus on safety and
communicating to a wide potential market about a safe destination that
offers them something they want at a good price. When potential visitors
that have placed a destination in their inept set, e.g., a destination impacted
by the December 2004 tsunami wave, have been reached, research to examine the benefits from appealing to people with a NEND related bias
against going to the destination is appropriate. In other words, when the
potential for attracting visitors that do not take special marketing has been
exploited, research on reaching segments for which perceptions of NEND
threat influence traveling to the destination could pay dividends by facilitating tapping into a new base of users.

CONCLUSION

One arrives at what may appear to be inconsistent conclusions on examining
the impact of NEND on trip decision-making and by studying what actually
happened at the destination most affected by the 921. Actually, it was no
surprise that the survey research component of this research confirmed that
the 921 caused a number of people who had been visitors to Nantou to drop
that destination from their future consideration and caused other decision-
making shifts that impact travel to Nantou. However, in developing this
research 921 being consistent with a tourism boom at Nantou was initially a
surprise. That surprise led to understanding that drawing conclusions about
research needed in relation to rejuvenation from NEND in general depend-
ed on recognizing why rejuvenation from the 921 has progressed as it has. In
that regard, it has been recognized that making a destination impacted by
NEND safe and getting out realistic information about that is critical.

As noted, redevelopment of a destination's infrastructure to be safe and to
be appealing to a large target market is also important to success. In this
regard, research is needed on making the destination safe (e.g., by warning
systems, safe haven areas, and good construction), on seeing that the safety
message is being disseminated effectively, and on selecting and targeting the
right markets and having a destination that suits the markets targeted. This
is not to say that academic research on decision-making or developing effective forecasting models should not occur but rather that contributions to

knowledge from such research cannot be expected to be of much relevance in dealing with a crisis. In the longer term, they may allow recognition and sizing of latent markets, e.g., people requiring special attention to move a destination back into their active-evoked set.

REFERENCES

Cheng, J. J., Tan, H., Chen, C. Y., Tung, P. L., & Wang, S. Y. (2003). *Estimation of psychological impact after the 921 earthquake in Nantou area.* Retrieved September 26, 2004, from Tsao-Tun Psychiatry Center, Department of Health, Executive Yuan, Taiwan Web site: http://www.ntmhc.doh-ttpc.org/study.htm

Coshall, J. (2000). Spectral analysis of international tourism flows. *Annals of Tourism Research, 27*(3), 577–589.

Crompton, J. L., & Ankomah, P. (1993). Choice set propositions in destination decisions. *Annals of Tourism Research, 20,* 461–476.

Geller, R. J., Jackson, D. D., Kagan, Y. Y., & Mulargia, F. (1996). *Enhanced: Earthquakes cannot be predicted.* Retrieved February 7, 2005, from http://scec.ess.ucla.edu/~ykagan/perspective.html

Goenjian, A., Steinberg, A., Najarian, L., Fairbanks, L., & Pynoos, R. (2000). Prospective study of posttraumatic stress, anxiety, and depressive reactions after earthquake and political violence. *American Journal of Psychiatry, 157*(6), 911–916.

Hem, L. E., Iversen, N. M., & Nysveen, H. (2002). Effects of ad photos portraying risky vacation situations on intention to visit a tourist destination: Moderating effects of age, gender, and nationality. *Journal of Travel and Tourism Marketing, 13*(4), 1–26.

Huan, T. C. (in press). Taiwan's 921 earthquake, crisis management and research on no-escape natural disaster. In: E. Laws, & B. Prideaux (Eds), *Crisis management in tourism.* Oxfordshire, UK: CABI Publishing.

Huan, T. C., Beaman, J. G., & Shelby, L. B. (2004). No-escape natural disaster: Impact on potential tourists. *Annals of Tourism Research, 31*(2), 255–273.

Huang, J., & Min, J. (2002). Earthquake devastation and recovery in tourism: The Taiwan case. *Tourism Management, 23*(2), 145–154.

Hwang, J. R., Chen, S. M., & Lee, C. H. (1998). Handling forecasting problems using fuzzy time series. *Fuzzy Sets and Systems, 100,* 217–228.

King, B., & Berno, T. (2002). Tourism and civil disturbances: An evaluation of recovery strategies in Fiji 1987–2000. *Journal of Hospitality and Tourism Management, 9*(1), 46–60.

Lewin, T., Carr, V., & Webster, R. (1998). Recovery from post-earthquake psychological morbidity: Who suffers and who recovers? *Australian and New Zealand Journal of Psychiatry, 32*(1), 15–20.

Miyazaki, J. (2005, January 5). *How Japan handles tsunami threat.* BBC News. Retrieved February 7, 2005, from http://newsvote.bbc.co.uk

Ministry of Education (1999). *Temporarily do not go to earthquake disaster area in central Taiwan for educational sightseeing activities.* (Document No. Tai-Kao-III 88129577). Taipei, Taiwan: Ministry of Education.

National Tsunami Hazard Mitigation Program (2001). *Designing for tsunamis: Seven principles for planning and designing for tsunami hazards.* Retrieved from http://www.prh.noaa.gov/itic/library/pubs/preparedness/preparedness.html

Sonmez, S., Apostolopoulos, Y., & Tarlow, P. (1999). Tourism in crisis: Managing the effects of terrorism. *Journal of Travel Research, 38*(1), 13–18.

Tourism Bureau Taiwan (2000). *Annual report on tourism 1999, Republic of China*. Tourism Bureau, Taiwan, R.O.C. Taipei, Taiwan.

United States Geological Survey (1997). *Predicting earthquakes*. Retrieved February 7, 2005, from http://pubs.usgs.gov/gip/earthq1/predict.html

United States National Oceanic and Atmospheric Administration, UNESCO/Intergovernmental Oceanographic Commission, International Tsunami Information Center, and Laboratoire De Geophysique, France (2002). *Tsunami the great waves*. Retrieved February 7, 2005, http://www.prh.noaa.gov/itic/library/pubs/great_waves/tsunami_great_waves.html

Vergano, D. (2001). Scientists have little hope of predicting earthquakes. *USA Today* (March 3). Retrieved September 27, 2004, from http://www.usatoday.com/news/science/geology/2001-03-04-quake–predict.htm

Wang, C. H. (2004). Predicting tourism demand using fuzzy time series and hybrid grey theory. *Tourism Management, 25*(3), 367–374.

Woodside, A., & Lysonski, S. (1989). A general model of traveler destination choice. *Journal of Travel Research, 27*(4), 8–14.

Woodside, A., & Sherrell, D. (1977). Traveler evoked, inept, and inert sets of vacation destinations. *Journal of Travel Research, 16*(1), 14–18.

World Tourism Organization. (1998). *Handbook on natural disaster reduction in tourist areas*. Madrid, Spain: World Tourism Organization.

PREDICTIVE MODEL FOR REPEAT VISITORS TO SINGAPORE

Hui Tak-Kee and David Wan

ABSTRACT

It is generally accepted that repeat visitation represents an attractive, cost-effective market segment for most destinations. Given such importance, an analytical model is proposed and tested. Our model prescribes a direct, causal relationship between pull motivations, travel satisfaction, intention of repeat visit, and repeat-visit behavior. Two hundred and two survey questionnaires are collected using a systematic sampling technique. Factor Analysis is employed to reduce 14 motivational attributes to five factors. The results of the logistic regression analysis reveal that the factor 'local food and beverages' and tourists' overall satisfaction level are insignificant predictors of repeat visitation. However, the rest of the variables such as climate, attractions, and facilities are significant. Implications of the results for both researchers and practitioners are discussed.

INTRODUCTION

Over the second half of the 20th century, tourism has emerged as one of the largest and most rapidly growing sectors in the world economy. In the increasingly saturated marketplace, the success of marketing destinations has to be guided by a thorough analysis of tourist motivation and its

Advances in Hospitality and Leisure, Volume 2, 107–121
Copyright © 2006 by Elsevier Ltd.
All rights of reproduction in any form reserved
ISSN: 1745-3542/doi:10.1016/S1745-3542(05)02006-0

interplay with tourist satisfaction and loyalty. The increasing significance of tourism on a country's national economy has, therefore, aggravated an increase of exploratory research set out to provide an analytic insight into customer motivation and satisfaction.

It costs five or six times as much as in terms of money, time, and effort to attract a new customer as it does to retain an old customer (Oppermann, 1997, 1998). Thus, it is generally accepted that repeat visitation represents an attractive, cost-effective market segment for most destinations. Capturing new customers from competitors is costly because a greater degree of service improvement is needed to convince customers to switch from competitors. Besides, repeat tourists are more likely than first-timers to choose the same destination in their future holiday decision (Gyte & Phelps, 1989; Juaneda, 1996). Hence, building repeat visitation is an effective means by which a tourism destination can improve its marketing position.

A review of the literature on motivation suggests that people travel because they are 'pulled' by the external forces of the destination attributes. This motivation is implicitly linked to behavior, which could impact on their repeated visit to a place. Although 'push' factors are also explicated comprehensively in these articles, they are generated by the dynamics of demand, which is closely related to the tourists' internal desire. Thus, there are constrictions as to how tourist operators could take into account these factors in their development of destination marketing strategies.

In addition, providing high-quality service and enhancing customer satisfaction are widely recognized as important factors leading to the success of tourism industries (Stevens, Knutson, & Patton, 1995; Legoherel, 1998). Quality services and tourist satisfaction develop long-term relationships with tourists and in turn bring about destination loyalty. Visitor satisfaction has a direct impact on repeat visits, positive word-of-mouth, and revenue for a country's tourism sector. Since the costs of regenerating repeat business are substantially lower than those of attracting new clientele, it is a necessity to gain more valuable insights into understanding the bases on which satisfied tourists affiliate with repeat visitation to the country. This would aid in the better planning and formulation of specific marketing strategies.

Though repeat visit has the potential to become the backbone of tourism industry, few studies have been published examining the phenomenon of and motivation for repeat visitation (Lau & McKercher, 2004). This study aims to fill this gap and demonstrate the association between 'pull' factors i.e. tourist satisfaction and their intention of making repeat visits to Singapore in the future. In order words, it sets out to investigate a number of attributes within the Singapore context that might have an impact on tourists' perception and experience during their travel durations in Singapore. In tandem with the destination attributes identified, it will examine the strengths and weaknesses of these attributes by assessing travelers' overall satisfactions. This would derive important motivational factors resulting in tourists' likelihood of returning to Singapore in their future travel decisions.

This paper also aims to formulate a conceptual framework to study repeat visits. Based on the framework proposed, a forecasting model is constructed to help forecast the tourists' intention of making a repeat visit. The forecast would also facilitate the planning and redesigning (if any) of marketing schemes in the aid of expanding the tourism industry.

The paper is structured as follows. Firstly, it takes a look at the present situation of tourism in Singapore. Secondly, the literature on repeat tourism is reviewed. It discusses the methodology and data collection procedure in the third section. The results are presented and analyzed in the fourth section. Finally, it discusses the limitations and implications of study.

The island nation of the Republic of Singapore lies one degree north of the Equator in Southern Asia. Because of its efficient and determined government, it has become a flourishing country that excels in trade and tourism. Though physically small, Singapore is an economic giant. It has been Southeast Asia's most modern city for many decades. The city blends Malay, Chinese, Arab, Indian, and English cultures and religions. Its unique ethnic tapestry affords visitors a wide array of sightseeing and gastronomical opportunities. In addition, the country offers luxury hotels, delectable cuisine, and great shopping.

Singapore has always presented itself as a key tourist destination. Its equatorial climate welcomes both leisure and business travelers all the year round. The island republic's excellent infrastructure enables visitors to enjoy its many sites and attractions in a safe, clean, and green environment. The much-lauded Changi Airport provides air links to major cities around the world, thus making Singapore accessible to almost everyone. As such, it has always been a favorite destination for travelers, especially those from the neighboring countries.

Since the September 11 tragedy, the local tourism industry was confronted by a series of global events that saw the small island nation facing a declining global economy, turbulence in the political arena as well as international health crisis. Global troubles finally took its toll on international tourism in 2003 and the country has undoubtedly bore the brunt of the worldwide decline.

By the end of June 2003, Singapore's tourism sector has seen a strong recovery. Despite the tough economic climate aggravated by SARS, war, and terrorism, Singapore's tourism sector exceeded its target of six million visitor arrivals for 2003. Leveraging on the momentum of recovery, it is thus imperative for Singapore to fine-tune its effort in meeting and surpassing tourists' expectations to inject more destination vibrancy and enhance the country's appeal to the world market.

Key measures implemented to ride on the recovery include the introduction of the Specialized Tourist Guide scheme, the liberalization of Singapore's nightlife and entertainment scene, and the formation of the Service Quality Division to improve the service standards of tourism-related sectors and to ensure effective delivery of destination information to all visitors. Service quality is used as an experience differentiator and competitive advantage for Singapore. The local tourism board is seeking ways to institute new service standards in key tourism sectors so as to improve visitors' satisfaction and bring about greater tourism receipts for the economy.

LITERATURE REVIEW

The Repeat Visitation Phenomena

There are basically two types of tourists: first-time and repeat visitors. Although Oppermann (1997) stressed the importance of balancing the needs of first-time and repeat visitors, others cited the greater impact of repeat visitors on the well being of destination areas. For example, Gitelson and Crompton (1984) argued that it is integral that many destination areas rely on repeat visitors. This group of visitors also signifies a stabilizing influence on most destinations through their familiarity with the destination and the stable income source they provide (Oppermann, 2000). Furthermore, it costs five to six times as much in terms of time, money, and effort to attract new visitors than to convince existing tourists to return to a destination (Oppermann, 1998). Thus, concerted effort to encourage repeat visitation will not only increase revenues but also at the same time, reduce costs (Gyte & Phelps, 1989). Finally, repeat visitors can serve as informal information channels to link networks of prospective travelers to a destination through word-of-mouth communication (Reid & Reid, 1993).

While the effects of repeated visitations to a particular destination are well studied, the motivations and factors encouraging or causing repeat visitations have received comparatively less attention. In their study, Gitelson and Crompton (1984) identified five factors that might influence the repeat-visitation behavior. They are risk reduction with familiar destination, socialization with the 'like' people, fulfillment of an emotional attachment, the search for new experiences, and exposure of friends to the destination.

In another study on the motivations of first-time and repeat visitors to the Lower Rio Grande Valley in Texas, Fakeye and Crompton (1991) concluded that there were differences in the motivations for first-time and repeat visitors. First-time visitors placed greater importance on the destination's environment (i.e. temperature, exploration, and security) and the satisfaction of their curiosity about the destination. On the contrary, repeat visitors placed emphasis on the degree of social contact available at the destination.

Taking a holiday can be viewed as a high-involvement purchase, where the perceived risk is unusually high. The actual consumption of the experience is often in a foreign environment and a tourist's enjoyment of the holiday is dependent on uncontrollable factors like the mood of other members of the travel party or the weather. The unique nature of tourism product (high involvement, high-perceived risk) implies that consumers are more likely to choose a product they have 'tested' before (Dick & Basu, 1994).

Satisfaction and Repeat Visitation

Consumer satisfaction can be defined as a post-consumption evaluative judgment. Satisfaction with travel experiences based on the internal (such as psychological influences) and external forces (such as destination attributes) are likely to contribute to destination loyalty (Dann, 1977; Crompton, 1979). According to the expectation-disconfirmation model developed by Oliver (1980), consumers would develop expectations about a product before purchasing and subsequently, they would compare the actual performance with their expectations. A positive disconfirmation occurs if the actual performance is better than their expectations, that is, the consumer is highly satisfied and is more willing to purchase the product again. However, if the actual performance is below his/her expectations, negative disconfirmation will result in dissatisfaction and the customer will most likely look for other alternatives for the next purchase.

Research by Chon (1989) also contended that tourist satisfaction is based on the goodness of fit between visitor expectations about the destination and the perceived evaluation outcome of the experience at the destination area, which is simply the result of a comparison between their previous images of the destination and what they actually see, feel, and achieve at the destination. Therefore, satisfaction can be considered as a valuable concept in understanding the attractiveness of destinations (Danaher & Arweiler, 1996).

Customer loyalty is influenced by customers' satisfaction (Bitner, 1990), and in turn, satisfaction is affected by their motivation (Ross & Iso-Ahola, 1991). Similarly, tourists who have enjoyed better than expected experiences are more likely to return in future (Ross, 1993; Juaneda, 1996). Kozak and Rimmington (2000) concluded that the level of overall satisfaction with holiday experiences had the greatest impact on the intention to revisit the same destination.

Thus, the accurate identification of factors that might impact visitors' level of satisfaction would be integral to successful destination marketing because it influences customers' choice of destination, their consumption of products and services, and the decision to return (Kozak & Rimmington, 2000). However, it is also established that the more the visits to the same destination, the less the intention to visit it again.

Determinants of Visitor Satisfaction

When visiting a destination, tourists interact with many different components of the destination product, which is a package of diverse attributes that includes not only the historical sites and spectacular scenery, but also services and facilities catering to the everyday needs of tourists. Previous research have also indicated that some controllable and uncontrollable destination factors, such as the natural environment, scenery, culture, climate, and other general features (for example, the cleanliness of beach and sea, and the availability of entertainment facilities) might be among the prime determinants of tourist satisfaction. Others emphasize that holiday satisfaction does not primarily arise from beautiful scenery but also from the behavior one encounter, the information one gets, and the efficiency with which one's needs are served.

Tourists' communication with local people and service providers may also foster empathy and a feeling of safety, and thus positively affect tourist enjoyment of the host environment and skew their future destination–selection decisions. Not surprisingly, the efficiency of airport services plays a part in fostering tourist satisfaction, as the airport service encounter is generally the initial and last experience the tourists would have with the destination. The quality of these interactions and experiences form the basis for overall holiday satisfaction or dissatisfaction and the selection of future travel destinations.

Tourists' Motivations and Actual Behavior

Motivations can be defined as a set of needs and attitudes that prompts a person to act in a specific goal-directed way, and it is important that we identify these motivations to better understand actual tourist behavior (Uysal & Hagan, 1993). Measuring tourist motivations would help researchers to identify different types of tourists more easily, which in turn would give considerable insight into their travel behavior (Fodness, 1994). Research by McIntosh, Goeldner, and Ritchie (1994) revealed four basic categories of tourist motivations: physical, cultural, interpersonal, and prestige. Tourists seeking out recreation and sporting activities fall under the physical motivation category. Culturally motivated tourists travel for activities that would satisfy their curiosity about other environments, cultures, and societies. The desire to travel to meet new people or to spend time with friends and relatives concurs with the category of interpersonal motivation. Lastly, tourists motivated to travel for prestige and status reasons will seek locations and experiences that satisfy these needs.

A different outlook of tourist motivation research classifies the motivation concept into two forces, which maintains that people travel because they are pushed and/or pulled by various factors. These push–pull forces illustrate how tourists are attracted by internal motivation variables into making travel decisions and how they are pulled by external destination attributes (Uysal & Hagan, 1993). Thus, it can be concluded that push motivations are more related to personal, emotional aspects while pull motivations are connected to situational or cognitive aspects.

The Proposed Model

Although this study has elaborated on both the push and pull motivational forces, it includes only the pull motivational forces in the investigation. From the point of view of the destination marketers, the external aspects of pull motivational factors would warrant more attention so as to better cater to the needs of targeted segments of tourists. In addition, with the focus of our study on the context of Singapore, it would be more relevant to concentrate on those external (situational) and physical factors that motivate individuals to visit the country.

In essence, the model presented in Fig. 1 illustrates how pull tourist motivations might impact on satisfaction factors that in turn affect repeat visitation and behavior. The relationships of pull motivations, satisfaction, and intention of repeat visitation will be empirically examined in the next section. In general, a high level of tourist satisfaction should result in a greater intention to visit the destination again, and this will set the imperative for the forecasting of repeated-visitation behavior.

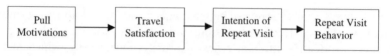

Fig. 1.   The Proposed Model on Repeat Visitation.

METHODOLOGY

Data Collection

The research sample employed in this study consists of international travelers departing from the Singapore Changi Airport. Data were collected over a two-day period at the departure hall. The researchers have used a systematic sampling approach, where questionnaires were delivered to every 5th tourists that walked past the researchers. Their willingness to participate in the survey was sought, and interested respondents were then asked to complete a self-response questionnaire.

Since this study focuses on the tourists' motivation and satisfaction, prospective respondents have to satisfy the screening question, one that serves to verify that they were indeed pleasure travelers and not visiting Singapore for business or to attend a convention.

In all, a total of 210 questionnaires were distributed for this study. Out of the collected responses, 202 questionnaires were found usable, while the rest was discarded due to the incompletion of the survey forms.

The Instrument

The questionnaire is divided into two sections. The first section requires the respondents to fill in their demographical information while section two consists of three questions. Firstly, respondents were asked to rate the importance of 14 attributes related to Singapore as a travel destination on a five-point Likert scale, with 1 being Least Satisfactory to 5 being Most Satisfactory. The second question seeks to measure tourists' overall level of satisfaction with regards to their holiday experience in the country. Finally, they were asked to state their intention of visiting Singapore again within the next three years. The dichotomous nature of this question serves as the dependent variable in our prediction model.

The survey instrument was pretested on 15 tourists in the city area to ascertain the appropriateness and clarity of the questions. As a result, minor modifications were made on some of the questions.

Data Analysis

First, demographic data of all respondents were analyzed to give a general picture of the sample characteristics. There were altogether 14 attributes. To have a better understanding of the attributes, factor analysis was first conducted on the attributes in the survey to reduce them to a more manageable size. Principal component analysis was used to extract the related factors before the varimax rotation was applied. Five factors were extracted. The factor scores were also derived to facilitate the next analysis.

Binary logistic regression analysis was used to predict the respondents' intention to make a repeat visit to Singapore. Fundamentally, it was a form of regression that is used when the dependent variable was dichotomous (e.g. with or without the intention to revisit Singapore) and the independent variables were of any type (e.g. the various factors we have previously identified). Logistic regression was then performed using the factor scores of the five identified factors, and also the overall satisfaction score as covariates to predict the tourists' intention of making a repeat visit to Singapore within the next three years. Their intention to make a repeated visit was set as the dependent variable against the independent variables ('pull' motivational factors and overall satisfaction). Apart from assuming the role of a predictor model, it could also be used to rank the relative importance of the independent variables (covariates). This would be achieved by adopting the sequential regression strategy. The ranking of the variables would aid our analysis further. The dataset was divided into two sets. The first set consisting of 180 data was used to build the model and the second set of 22 data was then used as holdout sample to test the predictive ability of the model.

RESULTS

A demographic profile of the respondents is provided in Table 1. The percentages of males and females were evenly distributed. Seven out of ten respondents were aged below 41 years old. The bulk of the travelers were from Asia, followed by those from North America (18.3 percent), Australasia (16.8 percent), and Europe (15.8 percent).

The main purpose of performing factor analysis is to reduce the 14 motivational variables and to classify the variables into independent 'pull' factors. As seen in Table 2, five factors were identified and the total variance is 75.41 percent. Factor 1, labeled 'Climate and Environment', consisted of

Table 1.   Demographic Profile of the Respondents ($N = 202$).

Characteristics	N	%	Mode
Gender			Female
Male	96	47.5	
Female	106	52.5	
Age			21–40
20 years and below	64	31.7	
21–40 years	79	39.1	
41 years and above	59	29.2	
Region of Residence			Asia
Asia	84	41.6	
Europe	32	15.8	
North America	37	18.3	
Australasia	34	16.8	
Others	15	7.4	
Annual Income			S$20,000 and below
S$20,000 and below	106	52.5	
S$20,001–30,000	73	36.1	
S$30,001 and above	23	11.4	

four variables that reflect the degree of satisfaction with local weather conditions, cleanliness of surroundings, personal security, and size of destination. Factor 2, 'Tourist Attractions and Facilities', includes four variables that relate to the variety and quality of Singapore's tourism infrastructure. Two other variables concerning tourists' satisfaction on the degree of development of Singapore, and the efficiency of its transportation infrastructure were loaded into Factor 3. Factor 4, 'Cultural Enrichment and Interaction', indicates motives to experience and learn about different cultures associated with each destination. It also measures the satisfaction of their interaction with local citizens. Lastly, Factor 5, 'Local Food and Beverage', contains two variables that reflect tourists' satisfaction with local cuisine and dining facilities.

Table 3 reveals that four out of the five identified factors turn out to be significant in the logistic regression model. Factor 5 'Local Food and Beverage' and overall satisfaction are insignificant. Intuitively, tourists' overall satisfaction should lead to repeat visit. The predictive ability based on the in-sample, in this case is 79.4 percent and it is 59.1 percent for the holdout sample. Hence, the prediction model has performed reasonably well.

Table 2. Five Categories of Motivational Characteristics.

Measures and Factors	Factor Loading	Mean
Factor 1: Climate and environment		
(26.482% of variance)		
Suitability and tolerability of weather	0.869	2.525
Degree of cleanliness of the surroundings	0.859	2.827
Manageability of the size of Singapore	0.812	2.936
Degree of security and personal safety	0.696	3.079
Factor 2: Tourist attractions and facilities		
(16.889% of variance)		
Quality of beaches and island environment	0.828	3.604
Variety and educational quality of cultural and historic sites	0.765	3.510
Variety and service quality of entertainment and nightlife attractions	0.672	3.302
Variety and service quality of shopping facilities	0.542	3.644
Factor 3: Modernity and infrastructure		
(13.188% of variance)		
Modernity of city and its environment	0.887	3.460
Efficiency and modernity of infrastructure and facilities	0.847	3.574
Factor 4: Cultural enrichment and interaction		
(10.352% of variance)		
Experience with different races and cultures	0.839	3.713
Friendliness and attitudes of local citizens	0.783	3.931
Factor 5: Local food and beverages		
(8.5% of variance)		
Variety and liking of local cuisine	0.844	3.886
Variety and service quality of good restaurants	0.681	3.579

Table 3. Estimates of the Logit Regression.

Variables	Estimate B	Wald's Statistics	p value	Exp(B)
Constant	−4.041	3.328	0.068	0.018
Factor 1	−1.072	12.213	0.000	0.342
Factor 2	−0.603	5.502	0.019	0.547
Factor 3	−0.450	3.951	0.047	0.637
Factor 4	−0.703	9.431	0.002	0.495
Factor 5	−0.386	2.239	0.135	0.680
Satisfaction	0.702	1.271	0.260	2.017

DISCUSSION

Based on the mean values in Table 2, one can easily observe that Factor 4 'Cultural Enrichment and Interaction' and Factor 5 'Local Food and Beverage' command high levels of satisfaction from visitors, and thus possess greater influence over the motivations for tourists to revisit Singapore. It is also noted that the high mean values of Factors 2 and 4 are consistent with studies conducted by Lau and McKercher (2004), and Fakeye and Crompton (1991). Lau and McKercher (2004) showed that service attractions was one of the main motivations for repeat visits to a destination, while Fakeye and Crompton (1991) established that social contact was a significant motivation for visitors to repeat their visits. In this study, Factor 4 was found to have a greater influence. Singapore's multiracial culture has resulted in an assortment of local cuisine that is unique to the destination.

The logit regression analysis yielded a Nagelkerke R^2 value of 0.265, which shows that 26.5% of the variance of the dependent variable can be explained by the covariates. As the dependent variable is dichotomous and there are more respondents who intend to revisit than those who do not, thus making the interpretation of the prediction model's R^2 problematic. From the literature review in the earlier section, it has been established that different tourists have different motivations for visiting a destination, be it for physical, cultural, interpersonal, prestige (McIntosh, Goeldner, & Ritchie, 1994), social contact or curiosity (Fakeye & Crompton, 1991). Analysis of the survey results also reveals that there are differences in the motivations to visit Singapore. Some tourists are attracted by Singapore's tourist attractions and shopping facilities, while others are eager to experience different local cultures. Thus, it would be difficult for the logit regression analysis to ascertain the main attributing covariates.

Examination of the survey responses for overall level of satisfaction shows that there are a number of respondents who do not intend to revisit although they are highly satisfied with their holiday in Singapore. Further examination of this particular group of respondents also shows that the majority of these respondents are tourists from the European regions. These respondents are polled on the reasons for not intending to revisit the country using the open-ended questions. The most frequently cited reason is that of the large geographical distance between their country of residence and the location of their destination. Other less frequently cited reasons include the expensive price for the trip to Singapore and the high cost of hotel accommodations. This finding concurs with the study conducted by Lau and McKercher (2004) where it was identified that short-haul markets provided a greater share of repeat visitors.

Scrutiny of survey responses for Factor 5 and its correlation with visitors' intention to revisit suggests that a significant number of tourists do not view local food and beverages as having a significant influence on their overall satisfaction of the holiday. Therefore, this factor is unlikely to be a strong motivator for their future visits to Singapore. In addition, the majority of this group of respondents is from the Asian region. All these may explain why the overall level of satisfaction variable and Factor 5 'Local Food and Beverages' variable are insignificant in the logistic regression analysis.

CONCLUSION AND IMPLICATIONS

The prediction model that this study has constructed provides tenable evidence that a number of factors are influential on the tourists' intention of repeat visit to Singapore. The hypothetical model is built on the foundation that the pull motivations lead to travel satisfaction (or dissatisfaction), which in turn galvanizes the intention of repeat visits.

The results reveal a slightly different outcome in terms of the relationship between pull motivations and the level of travel satisfactions. Hypothetically, as aforementioned, a higher level of travel satisfaction would result in a greater intention of repeat visitations. However, our analysis shows that the level of satisfaction is not the sole causal factor on the intention for repeat visitation. It is crucial to incorporate other considerations that might have an influence over the behavior of repeat visits. Researchers have to look into the impact of travel distance, price, and currency exchange rates on the decision of making repeat visitations.

Still, forecasting plays a major role in tourism planning. The promotion of tourism projects involving substantial sums of money requires an estimate of future demand. The prediction model based on the framework that we have proposed is certainly exploratory in nature and undeniably, further research needs to be carried out for the model to hold up.

The major findings of this study have significant managerial implications for tourist operators in Singapore. First of all, the analyses demonstrate that tourists are attracted by five different pull motivational factors, out of which four are found to be highly significant. Thus, it is suggested that destination marketers consider the practical implications of these motivational variables because they could be fundamental factors in increasing tourist satisfaction and attracting both potential and repeat travelers.

Also, different tourists visit different destinations for different motives, be it for commercial attractions, cultural enrichment, social interaction, and so forth. The reasons are multitudinous and varied, which explains why our prediction model cannot capture all the different dimensions associated with these diverse motives. To build loyalty and retain tourists, policymakers must consider both the pull motivations, which include destination attributes and the tourists actual travel experiences.

There are several limitations, which should be addressed in this study. Firstly, it has only studied the role of satisfaction of travelers on their intention to make a repeat visit. Future research can be conducted on people who have never been to Singapore. Their intention could then be measured against those of repeat visitors to examine any significant difference. Assumptions have been made in several literatures that the two groups share similar motivations, but there is still no basis for such a supposition (Lau & McKercher, 2004). An examination of the possible differences in motives would be appropriate as travel behavior is influenced by a host of factors. Secondly, although specific attributes such as satisfaction level are treated as determinants of repeat-visit intention, the amount of variables that we have identified is certainly not an exhaustive list. There exist other factors that could be included to make our study more complete.

As the tourist market for destination changes from first-timer to repeat visitors, tourist attractions in such matured destination will inevitably face declining popularity, and even financial woes. Attraction operators would find it hard to sustain if the destination sees a change in their visitor mix toward more repeat visitors. Attractions need to respond to these changes if they are to maintain, and preferably increase, the numbers of visitors they draw. Inevitably, operators must also constantly change their offerings and rely on newer 'products' to remain attractive to repeat visitors.

REFERENCES

Bitner, M. J. (1990). Evaluating service customer: The effect of physical surroundings and employees responses. *Journal of Marketing, 54,* 69–82.
Chon, K. (1989). Understanding recreational travelers' motivation, attitude and satisfaction. *The Tourist Review, 44,* 3–7.
Crompton, J. L. (1979). Motivation for pleasure vacation. *Annals of Tourism Research, 6*(4), 408–424.
Danaher, P. J., & Arweiler, N. (1996). Customer satisfaction in the tourist industry: A case study of visitors to New Zealand. *Journal of Travel Research, 34,* 89–93.
Dann, G. (1977). Anomie, ego-enhancement and tourism. *Annals of Tourism Research, 4*(4), 184–194.
Dick, A. S., & Basu, K. (1994). Customer loyalty: Toward an integrated conceptual framework. *Journal of the Academy of Marketing Science, 22,* 99–113.

Fakeye, P. C., & Crompton, J. L. (1991). Image differences between prospective, first-time, and repeat visitors to the lower Rio Grande Valley. *Journal of Travel Research, 30,* 10–16.

Fodness, D. (1994). Measuring tourist motivation. *Annals of Tourism Research, 21,* 555–581.

Gitelson, R. J., & Crompton, J. L. (1984). Insights into the repeat vacation phenomenon. *Annals of Tourism Research, 11,* 199–217.

Gyte, D. M., & Phelps, A. (1989). Patterns of destination repeat business: British tourism in Mallorca, Spain. *Journal of Travel Research, 28,* 24–28.

Juaneda, C. (1996). Estimating the probability of return visits using a survey of tourist expenditure in the Balearic Islands. *Tourism Economics, 2,* 339–352.

Kozak, M., & Rimmington, M. (2000). Tourist satisfaction with Mallorca, Spain, as an off-season holiday destination. *Journal of Travel Research, 38,* 260–269.

Lau, A. L., & McKercher, B. (2004). Exploration versus acquisition: A comparison of first-time and repeat visitors. *Journal of Travel Research, 42,* 279–285.

Legoherel, P. (1998). Quality of tourist services: The influence of each participating component on the consumer's overall satisfaction regarding tourist services during a holiday. *Proceedings of the Third International Conference on Tourism and Hotel industry in Indo-China and Southeast Asia: Development, Marketing, and Sustainability, Thailand* (pp. 47–54).

McIntosh, R., Goeldner, C., & Ritchie, B. (1994). *Tourism: Principles practices, philosophies* (7th ed.). New York: Wiley.

Oliver, R. L. (1980). A cognitive model of the antecedence and consequences of satisfaction decisions. *Journal of Marketing Research, 17,* 46–49.

Oppermann, M. (1997). First-time and repeat visitors to New Zealand. *Tourism Management, 18,* 177–181.

Oppermann, M. (1998). Destination threshold potential and the law of repeat visitation. *Journal of Travel Research, 37,* 131–149.

Oppermann, M. (2000). Tourism destination loyalty. *Journal of Travel Research, 39,* 78–84.

Reid, L. J., & Reid, S. D. (1993). Communicating tourism supplier services: Building repeat visitor relationships. *Journal of Travel & Tourism Marketing, 2,* 3–20.

Ross, E. L. D., & Iso-Ahola, S. E. (1991). Sightseeing tourists' motivation and satisfaction. *Annals of Tourism Research, 18*(2), 226–237.

Ross, G. F. (1993). Destination evaluation and vacation preferences. *Annals of Tourism Research, 20*(3), 477–489.

Stevens, P., Knutson, B., & Patton, M. (1995). Dineserv: A tool for measuring service quality in restaurants. *Cornell Hotel and Restaurant Administration Quarterly, 36,* 56–60.

Uysal, M., & Hagan, R. (1993). Motivation of pleasure travel and tourism. In: M. Khan, M. Olsen & T. Van (Eds), *Encyclopedia of Hospitality & Tourism* (pp. 798–810). New York: Van Nostrand Reinhold.

SWEDISH HOTEL SERVICE QUALITY AND LOYALTY DIMENSIONS

Peter Schofield and Nicole Katics

ABSTRACT

Relationship marketing is widely accepted as the most successful way to build customer loyalty and competitive advantage in a mature, competitive market. The study investigates customer loyalty programmes within the context of service quality in Swedish hotels using an online questionnaire survey. Five service quality factors were identified: technical, functional, environmental, technological convenience and technological product dimensions, which supports the Northern European service quality model with the addition of technological dimensions. Five loyalty programme factors were also established and factor scores were mainly undifferentiated on the basis of socio-demographic and behavioural variables. The implications of the results are discussed and recommendations for further research are made.

INTRODUCTION

Four factors have influenced the increasing focus on customer loyalty in the hospitality sector over the last decade: the notion of a customer having a

Advances in Hospitality and Leisure, Volume 2, 123–157
Copyright © 2006 by Elsevier Ltd.
All rights of reproduction in any form reserved
ISSN: 1745-3542/doi:10.1016/S1745-3542(05)02007-2

lifetime value, the sophistication of database systems, the rationale that loyalty equals an increase in profits and the increasingly competitive nature of service markets (Patterson & Ward, 2000). Loyalty programmes, as part of value creation, are a widely used strategy with the general aim of increasing the number of returning customers and increasing the amount of information about customers (Palmer, McMahon-Beattie, & Beggs, 2000). However, given their popularity, they are surprisingly ineffective (Dowling & Uncles, 1997) and represent only one way of increasing customer retention. The concept of loyalty should therefore be contextualised within a broader framework of service quality and customer satisfaction even though they do not guarantee customer loyalty (Johnson & Gustafsson, 2000). Shoemaker and Lewis (1999) argue that customer loyalty is built by focussing on three concepts: the overall service process, the use of effective database management and value creation either through added value or value recovery.

The hotel industry is no exception to this general hospitality scenario. The success of hotels is to a great extent dependent on how well customer needs and wants have been taken into account when designing and delivering the service, and the importance of overall service quality in delivering customer satisfaction is widely acknowledged. However, much of the research to date has focussed on business clients to the neglect of the leisure market for hotels (Bowen & Shoemaker, 1998). This segment is difficult to research with respect to language and cultural barriers, its highly mobile nature, high expectations and unfamiliar surroundings from the customer perspective (Orams & Page, 2000). The main objective of this study was to determine the factors of significance in hotel customer loyalty within the context of overall service quality with particular reference to information technology. Whilst the usefulness of loyalty programmes is well documented in the literature (McCleary & Weaver, 1992; O'Brien & Jones, 1995; Evans, Patterson, & O'Malley, 1997; Dowling & Uncles, 1997; O'Malley, 1998; Bowen & Shoemaker, 1998; Shoemaker & Lewis, 1999; Palmer et al., 2000), the effectiveness of elements in loyalty programmes has received much less attention. The study therefore focusses on the service quality and loyalty attributes and dimensions from the perspective of leisure customers and therefore provides an important empirical contribution to this neglected area of hotel loyalty research. The study also makes a methodological contribution to the literature because of its use of an Internet questionnaire survey. This was employed both to provide a convenient way for the hotel clients to respond to the survey and to test this method in order to identify its strengths and weaknesses in this context. The study was carried out in Sweden, a country, which has sharply increased its development and use of information technology over the last decade. As a result, it has one of the most highly computer literate populations in the world, and on that basis, they were expected to be favourably disposed to participate in an online questionnaire survey.

Relationship Marketing

Since Berry's (1983) pioneering article on relationship marketing, there has been a paradigm shift towards more personalised marketing and getting close to the customer, driven by increasing competition, a fragmented market-place, high levels of product quality resulting in the need to establish competitive advantage in other ways, more demanding customers and rapidly changing consumer behaviour (Buttle, 1996a). There is no consistent definition of relationship marketing in the literature. According to Berry (1983, p. 25), "relationship marketing is attracting, maintaining and (in multi-service organisations) enhancing customer relationships". By comparison, Lewis and Chambers (2000, p. 49) point to the necessity of: "...creating customer value and a long-term relationship", whilst Dibb, Simkin, Pride, and Ferrell (2001, p. 152) define it as "...all of the activities an organisation uses to build, maintain and develop customer relations". One of the most comprehensive definitions was provided by Grönroos (1996, p. 7) who states that "relationship marketing is to identify and establish, maintain and enhance relationships with customers and other stakeholders, at a profit, so that the objectives of all parties involved are met...this is done by a mutual exchange of fulfilments of promises". Variations on the theme are also evident in the literature, for example, one-to-one marketing (Kahan, 1998; Pitta, 1998), database marketing (Cook, 1994; Carr, 1994; Bell De-Tienne & Thompson, 1996; Schoenbacher, Gordon, Foley, & Spellman, 1997), loyalty marketing (Gould, 1998; Duffy, 1998; Shoemaker & Lewis, 1999) and interactive marketing (File, Judd, & Prince, 1995; Stokes, 2000).

The common goal is to build long-term relationships, although the concept of 'exchange relationship' within product marketing is not directly applicable to a service context because an exchange, for example, knowledge, technology, personnel or time is not straightforward in comparison to the exchange of products. Thus, the relationship itself, rather than singular exchanges within the relationship, is the fundamental concept (Grönroos, 1996). Hospitality organisations are now thinking in terms of share of customer (rather than share of market), economies of scope (in addition to economies of scale) and customer loyalty (instead of brand loyalty) (Lindgreen & Crawford, 1999). In comparison with brand loyalty – a commitment towards a product or service, customer loyalty is a commitment towards a company and its employees (Zeithaml & Bitner, 2000; Lynch, 2000). Grönroos (2000) argues that although market share may still provide important information, in order to use an organisation's resources more effectively and efficiently, the determination of the customer share of a company is a better decision-making instrument. Jiang (2000) argues that a company with greater customer share orientation tends to be based on a smaller optimal market segment size for customisation in contrast to organisations that focus only on market share. As a result, a firm can meet customers' demands better, since the targeted group is more homogeneous.

A healthy relationship is beneficial for each party, based on a balanced giving and taking. It should therefore, be in the interests of both customer and company not only to enter such a relationship, but also to sustain it. Nevertheless, Bagozzi (1995) argues that being involved in a relationship means for some people an end in itself, possibly because of the necessary effort that has to be taken. The reasons why people enter relationships have not been studied to any great extent. Grönroos (2000) suggests that the primary reason for customers is to reduce choice. Zeithaml and Bitner (2000) agree that people try to find ways to balance and simplify decision making in order to enhance their quality of life. After a reliable partner has been found, other propositions become less attractive (Sheth & Parvatiyar, 1995). Gwinner, Gremler, and Bitner (1998) undertook a study to discern the benefits a customer seeks when entering a relationship. They concluded that there were three types of benefits: 'confidence benefits', 'social benefits' and 'special treatment benefits'. Moreover, the sought benefits go beyond the core service, hence the relationship itself adds to the total value perceived by the customers (Grönroos, 2000).

Service Quality, Satisfaction and Loyalty

If relationship marketing is all about winning more customers, keeping more customers and losing less customers, the strategic aim of an organisation must become the augmentation of customer loyalty (Lewis & Chambers, 2000). The hospitality industry is characterised as highly competitive, due to globalisation, with slow growth rates and oversupplied and matured markets (Tepeci, 1999). For a customer this means increased choice, greater value for money and increased levels of service. Hence, the most common strategies hotel managers use to gain competitive advantage are either low-cost leadership through price discounting or the development of customer loyalty by providing unique benefits to customers (Kandampully & Suhartanto, 2000). Loyalty must be achieved through customer satisfaction, based on the perceived performance of the service product; hence service quality and customer satisfaction are two prerequisites of loyalty (Cronin & Taylor, 1992; Bowen & Shoemaker, 1998; Mittal & Lassar, 1998; Shoemaker & Lewis, 1999; Grönroos, 2000; McIlroy & Barnett, 2000; Zeithaml & Bitner, 2000). Although these two aspects are crucial for developing loyalty, no linear relationship exists between them (Johnson & Gustafsson, 2000).

The literature has widely acknowledged that satisfaction is not a guarantee for loyalty, although it is a prerequisite for customer retention (Anderson & Sullivan, 1993; Reichheld & Aspinwall, 1994; Mittal & Lassar, 1998; Bowen & Shoemaker, 1998; Zeithaml & Bitner, 2000; Bowen & Chen, 2001). Heskett, Sasser, and Schlesinger's (1997) research using their service–profit model found only a weak relationship between customer satisfaction and loyalty, although Fornell's (1992) study of 27 different businesses in Sweden found that highly satisfied customers were much more loyal than satisfied customers. Bowen and Shoemaker (1998) argue that the reasons for the failure of satisfaction to convert into loyalty are not related to either satisfaction or loyalty. Hotel guests may well be satisfied but not become loyal because they never return. Other guests may seek variety each time they visit the area or remain price-sensitive and shop for the best deal, although they were satisfied with the hotel. Moreover, some guests may not develop loyalty simply because they were never encouraged to do so; the hotel may never have asked or did not collect the data necessary to develop a relationship (Shoemaker & Lewis, 1999).

In recognition of the shortcomings of using satisfaction as a measurement of customer loyalty, behavioural measures such as frequency of use and monetary value are increasingly being used (O'Malley, 1998). However, "the very term loyalty implies commitment rather than just repetitive behaviour, which suggests that there is a need for a cognitive as well as a behavioural view" (Assael, 1992, p. 89). Moreover, while there is no guarantee that a satisfied guest will come back, it can be assured that a dissatisfied customer will not return (Dubé, Renaghan, & Miller, 1994). Consequently, loyalty should be contextualised within the overall quality of the service product. Thus, process (all activities involved in the service encounter from the perspective of both the consumer and the service provider), value creation (value-added and value-recovery strategies to enhance customer perceptions, especially associated with present and future service transactions) and database management/communication (effective use of guest 'knowledge' including preferences to facilitate segmentation, profiling and service customisation) are all key functions that must be addressed simultaneously (Shoemaker & Lewis, 1999).

The Economics of Loyalty

It is widely accepted that the acquisition cost of a new customer is five to six times more on top of normal service operations than keeping a satisfied customer. Moreover, long-standing customers can contribute to revenue growth by bringing more business to the same service provider as the relationship grows either through smoother and less time-intensive service encounters or through positive word-of-mouth communication without any additional costs for the company (Shoemaker & Lewis, 1999; McIlroy & Barnett, 2000; Grönroos, 2000; Bowen & Chen, 2001; Weber, 2001). Bowen and Shoemaker (1998) found that loyal customers tell, on average, 12 people about the hotel to which they feel loyal. Reichheld and Sasser's (1990) study of service quality and loyalty in nine service industries showed that improved service quality resulted in increased customer retention and higher profits. They found that a 5% increase in customer retention resulted in a 25–125% increase in profit and that the average profit per customer grew constantly over the first five years, due to the fact that the cost associated with taking care of a loyal customer declined, while the money loyal customers spent increased. Bowen and Shoemaker (1998) and Bowen and Chen (2001) have also found similar results. Reichheld and Sasser (1990) state that a premium price is often paid by old customers, because a trial discount is usually only available for new customers. For a loyal customer, the value often lies in the fact that he or she knows the firm and therefore lowers the risk of being dissatisfied. However, Grönroos (2000) points out that within a long-lasting relationship the bargaining power can easily transfer to the customer, which keeps prices down and results in a negative profit-erosion. Loyalty programmes may lead to this situation, because the 'better' the customer becomes for a company, the more 'value for money' and 'premium service' he or she receives. However, customer loyalty is particularly important to the hotel industry, because the market is mature, includes strong competition and product differentiation is small within the same segment (Bowen & Shoemaker, 1998). A common way of quantifying customer loyalty is to assess the 'lifetime value' of a customer (Shoemaker & Lewis, 1999). This is calculated through the "net present value of the net profits that can be expected over the years" (Grönroos, 2000, p. 150). Grönroos (2000) argues that if a company fails to assess a customer's lifetime value, the firm also fails to take an advantage from the relationship. However, he also points out that managers should always remember that if a customer who may not be profitable at that time, may become profitable in the future as a result of increased disposable income or changing needs.

Service Quality and Customer Loyalty

Mittal and Lassar (1998) argue that loyalty may be better explained by quality ratings than by satisfaction, because quality ratings show the state of the service provider's resources, whereas satisfaction ratings tell about the state of the consumer (Johnson, Tsirps, & Lancioni, 1995). The SERV-QUAL model (Parasuraman, Zeithaml, & Berry, 1985) and its adaptations have been used widely to measure service quality in a range of different sectors. However, the model has received much criticism for being too generic (Carman, 1990; Babakus & Boller, 1992; Buttle, 1996b;), because it has not been possible to reproduce the model's five dimensions despite repeated applications in a wide range of service industries. As a result, criticism of both the dimensionality of the scale (Babakus & Boller, 1992; Mittal & Lassar, 1996) and the associated methodology has increased in recent years (Cronin & Taylor, 1992; Buttle, 1996b). Attempts to tailor the model to particular sectors, for example, LODGSERV (Knutson et al., 1991), its hotel sector adaptation, have also met with criticism. Ekinci, Riley, and Fife-Schaw (1998) failed to replicate the five SERVQUAL dimensions using applications of the model in the hotel sector. Their findings supported Grönroos' (1990) two-dimensional model of service quality in terms of its 'technical' (result-related or 'what') and 'functional' (process-related or 'how') qualities. Rust and Oliver (1994) argued for a third dimension related to the environment 'where' the service encounter takes place. Clearly, the complexity of perceived service quality suggests that a study of hotel loyalty should be examined in the broader context of the service delivery system and its quality dimensions as seen from the consumer's perspective. Indeed, Mittal and Lassar (1998) found that loyalty was influenced by different quality dimensions than those influencing satisfaction.

Customer Loyalty Programmes

There are many reasons why organisations instigate loyalty programmes ranging from adding value to customer perceptions of a product, rewarding patronage, higher profit and extended product usage to cross selling and defence of a market position (Gilbert, 1996; McIlroy & Barnett, 2000). The use of these programmes as a tool to gain more information about a customer, thereby facilitating opportunities for customisation and manipulating consumer behaviour is also widely recognised (Palmer et al., 2000), although too many schemes overemphasise data collection resulting in data overload (O'Malley, 1998). Furthermore, Dowling and Uncles (1997) argue that the information gathered is insufficient for strategic decision making and only provides one source of market information. Additionally, Hochman (1992) argues that it takes at least two to three years to generate a return. The "decision to launch a programme is often motivated as much by fears of competitive parity as anything else, which companies rarely state publicly" (Dowling & Uncles, 1997, p. 73), although many organisations are unclear about their intentions with respect to loyalty schemes and many were introduced too quickly without assessing the needs and economics of cause and effect. As a result, "many reward programmes are widely misunderstood and often misapplied" (O'Brien & Jones, 1995, p. 75). In practice, hotels tend to use loyalty programmes as additional marketing tools and seldom as the only activity. As a result, marketing expenditure has increased (O'Malley, 1998). Moreover, once established, they are difficult to discontinue because they often spread rapidly, become the norm and then lose most of their benefits (Palmer et al., 2000)

Dowling and Uncles (1997) suggest that loyalty programmes are more effective for high-involvement than low-involvement products and services because in the case of the former, a consumer may form a relationship with the supplier. Arguably, this is the case with hotels, because customers have high interaction with employees and spend a fair amount of time on the suppliers' premises. The authors make a number of recommendations for the design of a loyalty programme. First, they suggest that it should enhance the value of the core product/service rather than using 'short-term froth' such as free gifts, which risk the devaluation of the brand. Second, they argue that managers have to evaluate the full cost of the programme; this is a difficult task because, whist visible costs such as database creation or programme launch are easy to identify, it is difficult to capture effectiveness in a formula. Third, they recommend that the reward scheme should maximise the buyers' motivation to make the next purchase. In other words, the more a member buys, the more reward should be given. Fourth, they argue that the specific market situation needs to be considered.

Customers vary in terms of their profitability for a company; the most obvious approach to customer loyalty would therefore seem to be the allocation of resources to the most rewarding customer segment. Following the '80/20 rule', marketing resources should be concentrated around the 20% of customers who produce 80% of the sales profit. However, problems arise within relationship marketing, because the most financially rewarding 20% are not necessarily the most loyal customers (Dowling & Uncles, 1997). Research by Toh, Rivers, and Withiam (1991) showed that 60% of those who were members of a hotel loyalty programme, enrolled in more than one scheme. Other research also showed evidence of 'polygamous loyalty' in that more than 80% of European business airline travellers had, on average, 3.1 memberships each (McCleary & Weaver, 1992; Dowling & Uncles, 1997). This suggests that customers tend to be more loyal to the programme rather than the service provider.

Not surprisingly, whilst loyalty programmes have been heralded as successful tools for marketing (O'Malley, 1998) and customer retention (Clayton-Smith, 1996; Shoemaker & Lewis, 1999; Palmer et al., 2000), their overall success has been questioned (Toh et al., 1991; McCleary & Weaver, 1992; O'Brien & Jones, 1995; Dowling & Uncles, 1997). However, even where companies have realised that their loyalty schemes are ineffective, they are reluctant to abandon them. McCleary and Weaver's (1992, p. 45) study of the effectiveness of hotel loyalty programmes concluded that "unless the industry as a whole drops frequent guest programmes ... individual chains are forced to maintain their programmes". A similar conclusion was reached by Toh et al. (1991, p. 52), who state that "many hoteliers would be happy to see these programmes end", but only a few chains were willing to stop their programmes. This reflects Dowling and Uncles' (1997) arguments that competition is the main reason why loyalty programmes were launched. The primary question for managers is therefore, not one of 'use or not use', but rather 'how to use' these programmes most effectively and efficiently.

O'Brien and Jones (1995) have outlined five criteria which customers use in determining the value of a loyalty programme: 'cash value', 'choice of redemption options', 'aspirational value', 'relevance' and 'convenience'. Cash value means any kind of financial reward, which results in better value for money. Redemption choice looks at the variety of rewards, which often exist due to the cross-linkage between related companies. Aspirational value considers a psychological rather than an economic aspect and tries to change customers' behaviour. Relevance refers to the speed at which any kind of reward can be achieved, and convenience looks at how easy it is for a customer to use such a programme. Dowling and Uncles (1997) argue that customers may be sensitive to the quality of these strategies; therefore care should be taken when selecting the appropriate features. By comparison, Shoemaker

and Lewis (1999) have identified six features of loyalty programmes, which
add value: financial (e.g. free night), functional (e.g. website available), temporal (e.g. priority check-in/check-out), experiential (e.g. upgrade services),
emotional (e.g. customer recognition) and/or social (e.g. interpersonal link
with service provider). A survey by Dubé and Shoemaker (2000) found that
many of these value sources were featured by company loyalty programmes.

The Role of Technology in Service Quality and Loyalty

Technology development is a key issue within the hospitality industry because it affects the service delivery system. Ten years ago, the perception of
good service in a hotel included bathroom amenities, turndown service and
the size of the mint on the pillow, whereas nowadays service is defined in
terms of time and ease of doing business, with technology as an integral part
of this hospitality experience (Lewis & Chambers, 2000). Hotel services are
particularly well suited to sale on the Internet (Yelkur & DaCosta, 2001).
Besides strategic information, in the form of electronic brochures, product
and service information, hotel history, press releases or financial reports, the
most often used features are the online directory and property information
(Gilbert, Powell-Perry, & Widijoso, 1999).

The Web is an important strategic tool for hotels; as a distribution channel, it allows customers to book hotel rooms online, using an online reservation form or by e-mail, whereas, consumers usually have to wait for a
reply. Real-time booking, a more advanced form of online reservation, is the
primary reason for the explosive growth of business-to-customer transactions in the travel industry and although technology enables hotels to offer
this service, only the minority use this opportunity to add value to their
product (Gilbert et al., 1999). Yelkur and DaCosta (2001) argue that hotel
services are particularly suited for differential pricing because of the ease of
segmenting customers and therefore suggest the use of dynamic pricing
techniques. However, the increasing number of distribution channels – global
distribution systems (GDS, central reservation systems (CRS), digital tele-
vision and wireless application protocol (WAP) – and the increasing inter-
connectivity of these distribution channels makes the maintenance of room
prices a difficult task for hotels, with the result that hoteliers argue they have
lost control of their room rates, while customers are confused and dissatisfied
by the fact that different channels quote different rates.

The Internet as a potential tool for maintaining and building customer
relationships has been widely recognised (Brown, 1997; Werthner & Klein,

1999; Gilbert et al., 1999; O'Connor, 1999), although customers may need to be trained and motivated to use it (Grönroos, 2000). New technology presents new opportunities for firms to develop the services they offer (Bitner, Brown, & Meuter, 2000). Increased information about the customer due to better technology, allows organisations to provide better customer-oriented service interactions with increased quality (Grönroos, 2000). Furthermore, technology often supports the service delivery process, with the positive effect that the service is either provided faster or the employee has more time to actually serve the customer (Brown, 1997), leading to a perceived increase in service. However, if the service encounter becomes too technology-based, emotional attachment may erode and the relationship becomes more superficial (Barnes, Dunne, & Glynn, 2000). Therefore, if the contact is only through technology, a customer is less likely to feel loyal and more prone to switch. This would be the case for self-service options, where Hackett (1992) draws attention to the problems such as the missing human element in case of service failure or the overemphasis on cost savings. Moreover, new technologies may not necessarily be accepted and appreciated by all customers and therefore any new technology needs to be introduced carefully (Grönroos, 2000).

New technologies have strongly influenced the service process (Grönroos, 2000) and have had a significant impact on the service encounter by changing the way service firms and customers interact (Barnes et al., 2000; Dabholkar, 2000). Consequently, organisations, which do not respond to changes in technology can suffer market loss and business failure (Lynch, 2000). Despite the impact of new technology, published research on hotel service quality has tended to neglect this issue in the overall assessment of service quality. This study therefore examined the importance of technology from the consumer perspective.

METHODOLOGY

A mixed-method approach was employed for the study. Thirty-nine semi-structured interviews (Sarantakos, 1998; Ibert, Baumard, Donada, & Xuereb, 2001) with hotel guests were carried out in Stockholm in July and August 2001. This qualitative data, together with variables obtained from a comparative analysis of 12 hotel and nine airline loyalty programmes, underpinned the design of the importance and performance constructs in a self-completion questionnaire survey, which was carried out in December 2001. An online procedure was used for the survey. The questionnaire was loaded onto the University of Salford website and the URL was included in a letter, distributed via e-mail, which invited subjects to access the questionnaire. Respondents were asked to rate hotel service quality and loyalty programme (process and value creation) attributes on 7-point Likert-type scales, from 'very unimportant' (1) to 'very important' (7). To increase the validity of the response set, all options associated with each attribute were clearly numbered and labelled (indicating equal distance between the values), a balanced scale was presented, an 'I do not know' option was included and the questions were kept on a comparable level of generality (Foddy, 1993; Sarantakos, 1998). As the questionnaire was designed to be self-completed, emphasis was also placed on its general 'attractiveness' in an attempt to maximise the response rate (Dillman, 1983; Ryan, 1995; Frazer & Lawley, 2000).

A pilot study, which is particularly important from the perspective of self-complete questionnaires (Riley et al., 2000; Orams & Page, 2000; Royer & Zarlowski, 2001) together with a protocol analysis was conducted in June 2001 with minor amendments being made to the wording of two scale attributes. The questionnaires were constructed in English, because the Swedish population's knowledge of English is the highest in Europe with 81% (INRA, 2001). The letter, distributed by e-mail, was also written in English; it was assumed that subjects would not access the link if they could not understand the letter. Two Swedish native speakers (one male and one female) and one Swedish linguist also evaluated the questionnaires to check for ambiguities. At this stage, the questionnaire was loaded onto the website and pre-tested to identify any coding errors. On completion and submission of the questionnaire by subjects, the data were incorporated into matrix format using Microsoft Excel. This data was then imported into SPSS version 11.0 for analysis.

One area of concern was to reconcile the distribution and sampling methods to increase the validity of the survey and the response rate. Limited opportunities to access Swedish subject natives meant that a 'snowball-sampling' method (Robson, 1993) was employed for the survey, i.e. the survey started with a few subjects, who were asked to forward the e-mail they received to other people and so on. Initially, 51 subjects were contacted directly by the researchers. They differed widely in gender, age, place of residence and occupation. Subsequently, over a period of 37 days, from 2nd December 2001 to 7th January 2002, 189 questionnaires were returned – a response rate of 38.1%. From this number 167 were useable.

The age profile of the sample was as follows: 31 (18.6%)<30 years, 74 (44.3%) 30–40 years; 18 (10.8%) 41–50 years; 30 (18.0%) 51–60 years; 13

(7.8%) 61–70 years; 1 (0.5%) >70 years. Just over half (57.2%) of the sample were male and just under one-third (29.9%) had children under 16 years of age. Approximately two-thirds (62.9%) were in the A/B socio-economic group, 34.9% in C1/C2 and 2.6% were in the D/E group. The majority (74.6%) spent three times or more in a hotel as a leisure (non-business) customer in the year prior to the survey, 31.9% stayed more than five times, 23.5% stayed three times and 10.8% four times. Moreover, in the year prior to the survey, the large majority of respondents (81.4%) spent more than one week in total in hotels, 30.2% stayed more than 15 days, 19.1% stayed between 10 and 12 days and 17.3% (between seven and nine days). Just under half of the sample (45.7%) used individual hotels, compared with 17.7% who used hotel chains and approximately one-fifth (20.1%) used both private and chain hotels; 16.5% did not state clearly whether the hotels they stayed in were privately owned or belonged to a chain. Subjects rated their hotels as follows: 5 star (7.8%), 3–4 star (88.7%) and 1–2 star (3.5%).

The snowball-sampling technique has been used hitherto primarily in qualitative research and/or with subjects with unusual characteristics who are likely to know one another (Robson, 1993). However, the Internet offers new possibilities for such a method. The main disadvantage of this sampling method is the possibility of bias within the sample, as its members may be linked with each other, which then makes it difficult to ascertain how representative of the population as a whole the subjects are (Oppenheim, 1992). Therefore, whilst this technique represents a practical method of collecting data from an otherwise inaccessible population, it also limits the generalisations that can be made from the results.

Key advantages of the online survey were firstly, that subjects' responses were anonymous, and therefore potentially more honest, and secondly, that the data could be transferred from the questionnaire to SPSS, albeit via Excel, i.e. the manual data input stage was eliminated; the overall administration of the survey was therefore more efficient and cost effective as a result. Disadvantages should also be noted. The low-response rate could be the result of the inefficient sampling method or the ease with which e-mails, particularly those from an unfamiliar source with a risk of virus infection, can be deleted. Dealing with non-responses was also time-consuming. After seven days, all subjects in the initial sample received a 'reminder' e-mail. From that point, no further action was taken. The size of the sample was not increased because of the potential for a higher non-response rate, increased bias and reduced validity (Oppenheim, 1992; Royer & Zarlowski, 2001).

RESULTS AND DISCUSSION

The Perceived Importance of Service Quality Attributes

The subjects mean ratings of the hotel attributes in terms of their general importance are given in Table 1. The top five rated attributes: clean bedrooms, safety/security, value for money, problem solving, accurate billing and efficient reservations are not unexpected and could be considered to be part of the core product offered by hotels and part of the expected product from the consumer perspective. Clean bedrooms are a direct indicator of quality regarding the service output, whilst the safety issue has received increasing attention in recent years; not only are the assets people carrying around becoming more expensive (laptops, digital and video cameras), but also personal safety has become an issue for leisure travellers, especially after September 11th. The importance of value for money is related to the characteristics of the leisure segment being sampled. It also reflects both the increasing competition and application of information technology, particularly the influence of the Internet, within the hospitality sector, which increases the bargaining power of consumers (Grant, 1998; Schofield & Fallon, 2000). The position of the item, good quality food/beverage is notable; it might be expected that subjects would have rated this item as being more important.

In the context of customer loyalty programmes, it is interesting to note that by comparison with the high ranking core product items, the existence of a 'bonus/loyalty program' is ranked 26th out of 29. Moreover, items that would normally be considered to promote loyalty such as employees who are willing to handle your special requests, employees who are sensitive to individual needs and wants, employees who make you feel special/valued and, real-time (instant response) booking via the Internet were ranked 16th or lower. This highlights the value of examining loyalty schemes within the overall context of service quality.

It is also interesting that the attributes relating to technology were rated among the least important attributes, i.e. 'online reservation facilities' (4.80), 'real-time booking via the Internet' (4.74), 'informative website' (4.57) or 'self-check-in/check-out facilities in the hotel' (3.99). Several reasons may account for this. In general, most new concepts in the hospitality sector are adopted from the airline industry, but whereas CRS were successfully introduced within the lodging industry (O'Connor, 1999), Yield Management has not lived up to initial expectations due to the greater variation in the product offered to the consumer (Lewis & Chambers, 2000). This may be

Table 1. Customer Importance Ratings on Service Quality Attributes.

Rank	Variables	Mean	Std. Deviation	Std. Error Mean
1	Clean bedrooms	6.68	0.97	0.08
2	You feel that you and your belongings are safe in the hotel	6.58	1.07	0.08
3	Value for money	6.37	1.12	0.09
4	Any problems are corrected quickly	6.34	1.02	0.08
5	Clear and accurate billing	6.11	1.14	0.09
6	Efficient reservation procedure	6.03	1.13	0.09
7	Prompt service	5.92	1.19	0.09
8	Employees who are knowledgeable and capable	5.91	1.02	0.08
9	Dependable and consistent service	5.91	1.13	0.09
10	Employees who make you feel comfortable	5.84	1.13	0.09
11	Performing services right the first time	5.80	1.14	0.09
12	Easy access by public or private transport	5.76	1.43	0.11
13	Employees who are clean, neat and appropriately dressed	5.70	1.21	0.09
14	Technology/appliances that work properly	5.59	1.28	0.01
15	Good quality food/beverage	5.27	1.42	0.11
16	Employees who are willing to handle your special requests	5.23	1.28	0.01
17	Employees who are sensitive to individual needs and wants	5.22	1.17	0.09
18	Technology/appliances that are up-to-date	5.17	1.36	0.11
19	Employees who make you feel special/valued	4.97	1.26	0.10
20	Attractive public areas	4.96	1.20	0.09
21	Online reservation facilities	4.80	1.47	0.12
22	Real-time (instant response) booking via the Internet	4.74	1.60	0.12
23	Décor in keeping with the hotel's image and price	4.69	1.13	0.09
24	Availability of leisure facilities	4.63	1.34	0.10
25	Informative website	4.57	1.51	0.12
26	The existence of a 'bonus/loyalty program'	4.13	1.55	0.12
27	Customers are recognised by hotel employees	4.07	1.69	0.13
28	Use of personal information to customise service (Guest history files)	4.07	1.40	0.11
29	Self-check-in/check-out facilities in the hotel	3.99	1.43	0.11
30	Current promotion activities communicated via the Internet	3.84	1.56	0.12
31	Hotel communicates with you via e-mail/ phone between visits	3.04	1.60	0.12

($n = 167$)

the case with the application of technology in the areas noted above. The difference in the mean ratings for 'online reservation facilities' (4.80) and 'self-check-in/check-out facilities in the hotel' (3.99) may result from the fact that the former are widely accepted in hotels, whereas self-check-in/check-outs are comparatively new to the customer. Pressures from other industry sectors may have exaggerated the importance of technology from a supply perspective without considering what customers really want.

The results of independent samples t-tests and one-way between-groups analyses of variance (ANOVA) are not presented here, but showed that customer service quality attribute importance ratings were differentiated on the basis of gender, age and nationality, but no statistically significant differences were found on the basis of socio-economic class, families with children under the age of 16, frequency of visits to hotels as a leisure customer in the previous year, number of nights spent in the hotels, the star rating of the hotels or the frequency of visits to individual hotels and hotel chains.

Factor Analysis of the Service Quality Attributes

The internal consistency of the service quality construct was assessed using reliability analysis. Three items were removed prior to factor analysis due to their low (<0.30) corrected item-total correlations (Field, 2000): easy access by public or private transport (0.23), self-check-in/check-out facilites in the hotel (0.25) and the existence of a bonus/loyalty programme (0.26). The overall α for the 28 item scale was 0.92.

The customer hotel service quality importance ratings on the 28 attributes were then factor analysed using maximum likelihood extraction and varimax orthogonal rotation because firstly, the factors were considered to be unrelated in theoretical terms (Field, 2000) and secondly, this method of extraction facilitates the identity of 'meaningful underlying dimensions" (West, 1991, p. 140). The minimum coefficient for factor items to be included in the final scale was 0.40, as recommended by Stevens (1992). The Kaiser–Meyer–Olkin (KMO) measure of sampling adequacy (0.92) was 'meritorious' (Kaiser, 1974) and the Bartlett's Test of Sphericity reached statistical significance (X^2 (378) = 3768.94 $p<0.001$), supporting the factorability of the correlation matrix.

The analysis produced a five-factor solution (with eigenvalues >1.0) that accounted for 66.50% of the overall variance before rotation (Table 2). Factor 1 (0.93 α) is a general factor and accounts for 40.12% of the

Table 2.   Factor Analysis of Subjects' Ratings on Hotel Service Quality Attributes.

Service Quality Attributes	Factor 1	Factor 2	Factor 3	Factor 4	Factor 5	Communality
Factor 1: *Technical service quality*						
Clean bedrooms	0.906					0.765
Value for money	0.818					0.643
Any problems are corrected quickly	0.906					0.700
You feel that you and your belongings are safe in the hotel	0.797					0.658
Clear and accurate billing	0.733					0.621
Dependable and consistent service	0.713					0.671
Efficient reservation procedure	0.693					0.624
Performing services right the first time	0.625					0.551
Employees who are knowledgeable and capable	0.590					0.565
Prompt service	0.586					0.652
Employees who make you feel comfortable	0.577					0.708
Employees who are clean, neat and appropriately dressed	0.531					0.559
Good quality food/ beverage	0.439					0.543
Factor 2: *Technological convenience*						
On-line reservation facilities		0.880				0.773
Real-time (instant response) booking via the Internet		0.870				0.773
Informative website		0.609				0.661
Current promotion activities communicated via the Internet		0.578				0.683
Factor 3: *Functional service quality*						
Customers are recognised by hotel employees			0.836			0.639
Employees who make you feel special/valued			0.667			0.700
Employees who are sensitive to individual needs and wants			0.639			0.717

Table 2. (Continued)

Service Quality Attributes	Factor 1	Factor 2	Factor 3	Factor 4	Factor 5	Communality
Employees who are willing to handle your special requests			0.619			0.679
Use of personal information to customize service (Guest history files)			0.597			0.603
Hotel communicates with you via e-mail/phone between visits			0.408			0.511
Factor 4: *Technological product attributes*						
Technology/appliances are up-to-date				0.815		0.828
Technology/appliances that function				0.792		0.806
Factor 5: *Service environment*						
Availability of leisure facilities					0.768	0.676
Attractive public areas					0.683	0.673
Décor in keeping with its image and price					0.446	0.638
Eigenvalue	11.234	3.054	1.868	1.416	1.048	
Variance (%)	40.123	10.908	6.673	5.057	3.742	
Cumulative variance (%)	40.123	51.032	57.704	62.762	66.504	
Cronbach's α	0.93	0.83	0.83	0.88	0.72	
Number of items (Total = 16)	13	4	6	2	3	

Note: Only loadings above 0.4 are displayed.

variance. It loads on 13 attributes including nine of the 10 highest rated customer importance ratings on the service quality attributes, which relate to the technical aspects of service quality. It was therefore named, 'technical service quality'. This outcome supports Grönroos' (1984) argument that the technical quality is the dominating quality, because the benefits a customer seeks are "embedded in the technical solution". Factor 2 (0.83 α) accounts for 10.91% of the variance in the data and loads on on-line reservation facilities, real-time (instant response) booking via the Internet, informative website and current promotion activities communicated via the Internet. These attributes relate to 'technological convenience'. Factor 3 (0.83 α) accounts for 6.67% of the variance and loads on employees who make you feel special/valued, employees who are sensitive to individual needs and wants, employees who are willing to handle your special requests, use of personal information to customise service (Guest History Files), and hotel communicates with you via e-mail/phone between visits. It has therefore been labelled, 'functional service quality'. The small amount of variance explained notwithstanding, this factor indicates that 'personalised service' is important to the subjects and therefore supports the findings of Surprenant and Solomon (1987), Brown and Swartz (1989) and Grönroos (1997). Factor 4 (0.88 α) accounts for 5.06% of the variance and loads on two attributes: technology/appliances are up-to-date and technology/appliances that function; this seems to suggest, 'technological product attributes'. Factor 5 (0.72 α) accounts for only 3.74% of the variance. It loads on the availability of leisure facilities, attractive public areas, and décor in keeping with its image and price and therefore represents the 'service environment' or 'servicescape', which includes the physical setting where the service is provided (Zeithaml & Bitner, 2000). Research by Wakefield and Blodgett (1996) found the servicescape to be important both in keeping customers in a facility as long as possible and in influencing repeat visits.

The results would seem to broadly support the findings of Ekinci et al. (1998), which in turn, support Grönroos' (1990) model of service quality rather than the the SERVQUAL (Parasuraman et al., 1985) or LODGSERV (Knutson et al., 1991) models. Additionally, given that factor 5 supports an environmental dimension in addition to the 'technical' and 'functional' service quality dimensions, the outcome supports the findings of Rust and Oliver (1994), who also identified an environmental component. Despite the relatively low importance ratings on the technical attributes, factors 2 and 4 have highlighted the importance of technology in the hotel marketing mix and service product provision in terms of technological convenience and product dimensions. These two technological aspects are distinct from the environmental dimension and reflect the increasing importance of technology – the driving force for organisational change (Lynch, 2000). Technology has become an integral part of the hospitality service delivery system highlighting the need to rearrange traditional concepts relating to space and time (Hagel & Armstrong, 1997). Lovelock (2000) points out that technology not only changes the nature of the operation, but also the personal contact between customers and employees and even more significantly requires a rethinking of market parameters and segmentation variables. The establishment of factor 2 in particular highlights the importance of technology and the fact that because the Internet is an interactive medium, customers are more than just passive recipients in the process (Hoffman, Novak, & Chatterjee, 1995).

The clear importance of technology notwithstanding, the technical service quality factor explained 40.12% of the variance in the data and the large majority of attributes loading on this dimension highlight the key role of employees in providing the various aspects of service quality – employees are part of the hospitality product (Lewis & Chambers, 2000). High labour turnover including part-time jobs, distressed working situations, low employee satisfaction or commitment caused by inexperienced, underqualified, underpaid and overstretched employees have an impact on the service encounter. This situation can arise if management fails to clarify both relevant objectives and how employees should achieve them through the provision of an effective and efficient output to achieve an appropriate outcome for the customer. Consequently, managers should not disregard the importance of job design, employee selection and development, as they are important attributes of internal service quality (Heskett, Jones, Loveman, Sasser, & Schlesinger, 1994) and directly influence the service performance. Chenet, Tynan, and Money (2000) argue that addressing these issues results in employees' trust and commitment, which they see as the foundation and the key part of internal service quality. The overall goal would be professionalism, which includes aspects such as the knowledge and expertise to fulfil the tasks and the effective use of scarce resources, resulting in a level of service required by the customer (Paraskevas, 2001).

Differentiation in Service Quality Importance Ratings on the Factors by Customer Characteristics

A one-way between groups multivariate analysis of variance (MANOVA) was used, after preliminary assumption testing, to determine the existence of differences between customer segments on the factor scores. Due to the differences in sample sizes between sub-groups, Box's test of the homogeneity of variance–covariance matrices was employed.

For the variable gender, a non-significant Box's test statistic ($p = 0.13$) showed that the assumption of homogeneity was met. Levene's test of equality of error variances ($p > 0.07$) also showed non-significant statistics for all dependent variables. The MANOVA results showed no statistically significant difference between the factor scores on the basis of resident gender. This was also the case for customer age, socio-economic class, families with children under the age of 16, frequency of visits to hotels as a leisure customer in the previous year, number of nights spent in the hotels, the star rating of the hotels and the frequency of visits to individual hotels and hotel chains (Table 3).

Table 3.   MANOVA Results for Service Quality Importance Factors by
                 Customer Characteristics.

	Box's Test	Levene's Test	F	P	Pillai's Trace	Partial η^2
Gender	0.13	p>0.07	1.95	0.09	0.06	0.06
Age	0.06	p>0.20	1.35	0.12	0.20	0.04
Socio-economic class	0.05	p>0.30	0.97	0.54	0.28	0.06
Families with children under the age of 16	0.03	p>0.20	0.66	0.66	0.02	0.02
Nationality*	0.06	p>0.05	3.40	0.001	0.19	0.10
Frequency of visits to hotels in the previous year	0.01	p>0.10	1.11	0.31	0.20	0.04
Number of nights spent in the hotels	0.01	p>0.10	0.94	0.55	0.15	0.03
The star rating of the hotels	0.02	p>0.20	1.24	0.18	0.26	0.05
Fequency of visits to individual hotels and hotel chains	0.01	p>0.10	1.5	0.11	0.13	0.04

*Significant difference

For customer nationality (see Table 3), preliminary assumption testing using Box's ($p = 0.06$) and Levene's ($p > 0.05$) tests showed no significant violations and there was a statistically significant difference between the factor scores ($F = 3.40$; $p < 0.001$; Pillai's Trace = 0.19; partial $\eta^2 = 0.10$). When the results for the factors were considered separately, the only difference to reach statistical significance using a Bonferroni adjusted α level of 0.01 to reduce the chance of a type 1 error (Tabachnick & Fidell, 1996) was on factor 1 (technical service quality): $F(2) = 15.57$; $p < 0.001$; partial $\eta^2 = 0.16$. The statistic results from the substantial and significant difference in the mean scores between the English and Swedish customers and between the English and 'other' customers. The English customers' mean importance scores on all attributes that load on factor 1 were between 2 and 3 scale points below those of the other nationalities. However, the validity of the result is reduced by the small size of the English customers segment ($n = 24$). The fact that the differentiation has emerged on the technical aspects of service and not on other dimensions may reflect the relative ease with which customers can evaluate service attributes which load on this factor in comparison with, for example, those in the functional service quality dimension.

The Perceived Importance of Loyalty Programme Attributes

The subjects' ratings on the loyalty programme attributes are given in Table 4. 'Flexible times for check-in/check-out' (5.78) is the most important attribute. This supports the work of Bowen and Chen (2001), who found that customer loyalty was 'boosted' if customers could check-in when they arrived, even if it was before check-in time. Unfortunately, this feature not

Table 4.   Customer Ratings on Loyalty Programme Attributes.

Rank	Variables	Mean	Std. Deviation	Std. Error Mean
1	Flexible times for check-in/check-out	5.78	1.36	0.11
2	Price discount	5.31	1.41	0.11
3	Free breakfast	5.25	1.70	0.13
4	Double room at single room rate	4.98	1.61	0.12
5	Free use of health club facilities	4.85	1.90	0.15
6	Priority check-out or invoice sent later	4.82	1.58	0.12
7	Fresh fruit and mineral water in your room	4.79	1.65	0.13
8	The room of your choice	4.69	1.77	0.14
9	Room upgrading	4.64	1.66	0.13
10	Free night	4.57	1.77	0.14
11	If the hotel is about to be fully booked, the hotel will contact you and give you the opportunity to make your regular reservation	4.54	1.72	0.13
12	Free night for partner	4.51	1.77	0.14
13	Free daily newspaper of your choice	4.44	1.73	0.13
14	Free rental car (for stays of more than five nights)	4.27	1.82	0.14
15	Free movie channel/free "pay-per-view"	3.86	1.74	0.13
16	Free laundry service (one article every other day)	3.83	1.93	0.15
17	General discount on hotel restaurant	3.81	1.67	0.14
18	Free local phone/fax	3.77	1.88	0.15
19	Special direct number for reservations	3.73	1.68	0.13
20	One free meal for two in hotel restaurant	3.70	1.83	0.14
21	General discount on laundry service in the hotel	3.67	1.85	0.14
22	Welcome gift	3.14	1.73	0.13
23	Travel/shopping voucher (5% of the money you spent in the hotel)	3.07	1.61	0.12
24	Welcome drink	2.99	1.62	0.13
25	Customised minibar	2.72	1.65	0.13
26	Free babysitter for up to 3 h a day	2.63	1.83	0.15

($n = 167$)

only depends on the interaction of the hotel and the customer itself but on other customers. Managers always try to maximise occupancy, so problems arise if guests would like to check-out late, because new customers may have to wait to check-in, given that rooms need to be cleaned. This issue becomes more critical in the case of short breaks because quality time is limited and customers try to maximise their experience. Potentially, a service experience could suffer greatly, e.g. guests who plan to ski would prefer to arrive early to spend the day on the slopes and depart late for the same reason. Losing a half day and/or switching to alternative arrangements for changing clothes or showering can leave a bad impression and potentially creates a 'halo-effect', resulting in a dissatisfied customer, even if the stay in the hotel equalled or exceeded expectations. Whilst this attribute is ranked first in this scale, it is interesting to note that 12 items (39%) in the general service quality scale received a higher rating.

Price discount (5.31), free breakfast (5.25), double room at single room rate (4.98), free use of health club facilities (4.85) and priority check-out or invoice sent later (4.82) are also considered to be very important to customers. The third rank position of free breakfast adds another dimension to the findings of Danaher and Mattsson (1994), who identified that breakfast had the most important impact on overall satisfaction of hotel guests. It is therefore perhaps not unexpected that a 'free' breakfast is rated so highly. What is more unexpected is the rank order of certain other items. For example, room up-grading (4.64), free night (4.57) and free night for partner (4.51) are rated as being less important than fresh fruit and mineral water in your room (4.79).

The results of independent samples *t*-tests and one-way between-groups ANOVA are not presented here, but showed that, as was the case with the service quality ratings, loyalty programme attribute importance ratings were differentiated on the basis of gender, age and nationality, but not on the basis of socio-economic class, families with children under the age of 16, frequency of visits to hotels as a leisure customer in the previous year, number of nights spent in the hotels, the star rating of the hotels or the frequency of visits to individual hotels and hotel chains.

Factor Analysis of the Loyalty Programme Attributes

The internal consistency of the loyalty construct was assessed using relia-bility analysis (Asubonteng, McLeary, & Swan, 1996). The reliability ana-lysis showed that three items had corrected item-total correlations below 0.30: if the hotel is about to be fully booked, the hotel will contact you and give you the opportunity to make your regular reservation (0.25), fresh fruit and mineral water in your room (0.27) and free breakfast (0.28). These items were removed; this produced an overall α coefficient for the scale of 0.91.

The ratings on the remaining 23 attributes were then factor analysed. The decision rules for the analysis remained unchanged from the previous analysis; maximum likelihood extraction and varimax orthogonal rotation were used and the minimum coefficient for factor items to be included in the final scale was 0.40 (after Stevens, 1992). The KMO measure of sampling adequacy (0.86) was 'meritorious' (Kaiser, 1974) and the Bartlett's Test of Sphericity reached statistical significance (X^2 (276) $= 2261.39$ $p<0.001$), supporting the factorability of the correlation matrix.

The analysis produced a five-factor solution (with eigenvalues > 1.0) that accounted for 60.74% of the overall variance before rotation (Table 5). Factor 1 (0.78 α) is a general factor and accounts for 13.46% of the variance. It loads on free daily newspaper of your choice, flexible times for check-in/check-out, priority check-out or invoice sent later, the room of your choice, free local phone/fax, room upgrading, free use of health club facilities, double room at single room rate, special direct number for reservations and free movie channel/free "pay-per-view". This includes six of the nine highest rated loyalty scheme attributes, which suggests that it generally represents 'high priority primary benefits'. Factor 2 (0.82 α) accounts for 10.59% of the variance in the data and loads on one free meal for two in hotel restaurant, general discount on hotel restaurant, travel/shopping voucher (5% of the money you spent in the hotel), free rental car (for stays of more than five nights) and free baby-sitter for up to three hours a day. It has therefore been labelled 'free or discounted secondary benefits'. Factor 3 (0.80 α) accounts for 10.26% of the variance and loads on free night, free night for partner and price discount. It has therefore been labelled, 'value for money'. Factor 4 loads on some of the least important attributes (what Dowling & Uncles, 1997 refer to as 'short-term froth'): welcome drink, welcome gift and customised minibar. (0.77 α); it has therefore been labelled, 'low priority extras'; it accounts for 9.49% of the variance. Factor 5 (0.85 α) accounts for only 7.52% of the variance. It loads on general discount on laundry service in the hotel and free laundry service (one article every other day). It has therefore been labelled 'free or discounted laundry service'.

Differentiation in Loyalty Programme Importance Ratings on the Factors by Customer Characteristics

The MANOVA results showed no statistically significant difference between the factor scores on the basis of resident gender, age, frequency of visits to

Table 5. Factor Analysis of Subjects' Ratings on Loyalty Programme Attributes.

Loyalty Programme Attributes	Factor 1	Factor 2	Factor 3	Factor 4	Factor 5	Communality
Factor 1: *High priority primary benefits*						
Free daily newspaper of your choice	0.644					0.501
Flexible times for check-in/check-out	0.604					0.451
Priority check-out or invoice sent later	0.598					0.413
The room of your choice	0.589					0.431
Free local phone/fax	0.519					0.483
Room upgrading	0.442					0.410
Free use of health club facilities	0.439					0.450
Double room at single room rate	0.438					0.431
Special direct number for reservations	0.422					0.342
Free movie channel/free "pay-per-view"	0.410					0.327
Factor 2: *Free or discounted secondary benefits*						
One free meal for two in hotel restaurant		0.696				0.685
General discount on hotel restaurant		0.655				0.617
Travel/shopping voucher – 5% of the money spent		0.609				0.513
Free rental car (for stays of more than five nights)		0.508				0.501
Free babysitter for up to 3 h a day		0.448				0.342
Factor 3: *Value for money*						
Free night			0.853			0.782
Free night for partner			0.853			0.823
Price discount			0.487			0.411
Factor 4: *Low priority extras*						
Welcome drink				0.748		0.673
Welcome gift				0.655		0.623
Customised mini bar				0.527		0.370

Table 5. (*Continued*)

Loyalty Programme Attributes	Factor 1	Factor 2	Factor 3	Factor 4	Factor 5	Communality
Factor 5: *Free or discounted laundry service*						
General discount on laundry service in the hotel					0.921	0.566
Free laundry service (one article every other day)					0.602	0.850
Eigenvalue	8.089	2.367	1.733	1.338	1.050	
Variance (%)	33.706	9.861	7.221	5.577	4.375	
Cumulative variance (%)	33.706	43.566	50.787	56.364	60.739	
Cronbach's α	0.78	0.82	0.80	0.77	0.85	
Number of items (Total = 16)	10	5	3	3	2	

Note: Only loadings above 0.4 are displayed

Table 6.   MANOVA Results for Loyalty Programme Importance Factors by Customer Characteristics.

	Box's Test	Levene's Test	F	P	Pillai's Trace	Partial η^2
Gender	0.23	$p > 0.10$	0.62	0.65	0.02	0.02
Age	0.07	$p > 0.01$	1.15	0.28	0.17	0.01
Socio-economic class*	0.20	$p > 0.19$	1.71	0.003	0.48	0.10
Families with children under the age of 16*	0.34	$p > 0.02$	3.09	0.01	0.09	0.09
Nationality	0.05	$p > 0.05$	1.61	0.10	0.10	0.05
Frequency of visits to hotels in the previous year	0.27	$p > 0.15$	1.18	0.23	0.21	0.04
Number of nights spent in the hotels	0.22	$p > 0.10$	1.02	0.43	0.16	0.03
The star rating of the hotels	0.06	$p > 0.03$	1.28	0.15	0.27	0.05
Fequency of visits to individual hotels and hotel chains	0.32	$p > 0.16$	0.68	0.80	0.06	0.02

*Significant differences

hotels as a leisure customer in the previous year, number of nights spent in the hotels, the star rating of the hotels and the frequency of visits to individual hotels and hotel chains (Table 6). However, customer ratings were differentiated on the basis of socio-economic class and families with children under the age of 16 (preliminary assumption testing using Box's and Levene's tests showed no significant violations). For socio-economic class, when the results for the factors were considered separately, the only difference to reach statistical significance using a Bonferroni-adjusted α level of 0.01 (Tabachnick & Fidell, 1996) was on factor 4 (low priority extras): $F(9) = 2.74$; $p = 0.006$; partial $\eta^2 = 0.15$. It is interesting to note that the socio-economic class group D/E rated the three attributes that load on factor 4 significantly higher in importance than the other groups. For families with children under the age of 16, when the results for the factors were considered separately, the only difference to reach statistical significance was on factor 1 (high priority primary benefits): $F(1) = 5.97$; $p = 0.01$; partial $\eta^2 = 0.001$. Whilst the effect size is small (Cohen, 1988), it is interesting that the customers with no children under the age of 16 produced significantly higher ratings on all 10 of the attributes which load on factor 1.

CONCLUSION

Relationship marketing, with the aim of increased customer loyalty, is a key issue in hospitality marketing. The purpose of this study was to investigate the key issues in customer loyalty, within the context of overall service quality, in the hitherto neglected leisure consumer market segment for Swedish hotels using an online questionnaire survey. The context was critical because both loyalty programmes and their outcome for the consumer are embedded within the overall quality of the service product output; the two concepts are interrelated and cannot be evaluated independently.

The technical, functional and environmental dimensions of service quality have emerged as being important factors in Swedish hotel service products, from the consumer perspective. This outcome generally supports the North European School's service quality model rather than the North American model and specifically supports the findings of Rust and Oliver (1994) and Ekinci et al. (1998). Technology has also emerged as a distinctive dimension. Whilst other service quality attributes, particularly those relating to the core service, were perceived as being more important, it is nevertheless an important underlying dimension. Customer recognition of the importance of technology, particularly the Internet, supports research by Hoffman et al.

(1995), Hagel and Armstrong (1997), and Lynch (2000), which highlighted its importance in the hospitality industry. The results have underlined the significance of the Internet as a medium for accessing, organising and communicating information and promoting customer loyalty by facilitating continuity, either by making it easier to make a reservation, more convenient to check-in/check-out, easier to find a particular service product, or demonstrate how the particular product can be provided.

The importance of technology was not unexpected given the significance of personalised service for the loyal hotel customer. Shoemaker and Lewis (1999) have argued that customer loyalty is some function of an organisation's ability to meet an individual customer's demands better than competitors and develop a relationship that cannot easily be reproduced by competitors. This ability is dependent, to a certain extent, on effective database management to satisfy individual needs, build the foundation for one-to-one marketing and make the transition from market share to customer share.

The particular importance of the technical service quality factor and the key direct role of employees in the large majority of attributes loading on this dimension (although they critically influence the outcome in all of the service dimensions identified), underlines the inseparability of both staff from the product and production from consumption. This reflects the work of Reichheld (1996), who found that service outlets with the highest customer retention also had the best employee retention. Heskett et al.'s (1994) research also established causal links in achieving success in service businesses, which illustrates the mutual dependency that exists among service output and employees' performance and the importance of customer retention for long-term business success (Rust & Zahorik, 1993). Zeithaml and Bitner (2000, p. 295) argue that management must firstly, "hire the right people", secondly, "provide needed support systems", thirdly, "develop people to deliver service quality" and finally, "retain the best people" in order to provide a customer-oriented service that is reliable and dependable, leading to customer satisfaction.

The integration of the service delivery system and new technology is becoming an increasingly important factor in the customer loyalty equation because technology can effectively improve the service product, including its technical service quality. The emergence of the technology and technical sevice quality dimensions here indicates the necessity of a 'high tech high touch' (Naisbitt, 1982) approach because the more customers are faced with high tech, the more they want high touch; the fewer contacts with staff that customers have, the more important the quality of each contact becomes" (Albrecht & Zemke, 1985, p. 8).

The relatively low level of importance given, by customers, to the existence of a 'bonus/loyalty program' among other general service quality attributes and the fact that 12 (39%) of the attributes in the general service quality scale were rated higher than the first ranked attribute on the loyalty programme scale are interesting results. They suggest that the overall quality of service experienced by the customer, particularly on the items perceived to be most important by the consumers, is likely to have a significant impact on customer satisfaction and loyalty, although satisfaction does not automatically result in loyalty (Reichheld & Aspinwall, 1994; Heskett, Sasser, & Schlesinger, 1997; Mittal & Lassar, 1998; Bowen & Shoemaker, 1998; Bowen & Chen, 2001). Approximately one-third of the variance in the loyalty programme ratings was accounted for by the high priority primary benefits factor, which includes six of the nine highest rated loyalty scheme attributes. Moreover, subjects' ratings were not differentiated on the basis of socio-demographic or behavioural variables. This suggests that emphasis could be placed on these aspects of service to promote customer loyalty, although the overall service product context must be considered, particularly given that subjects' ratings on the general service quality factors were also undifferentiated for the most part indicating a degree of shared dimensionality among the leisure consumers.

The advantages of identifying the consumer priorities with respect to loyalty programme sought benefits notwithstanding, overall the findings suggest that the implementation of an effective relationship marketing strategy requires a focus on overall service quality. Within this framework, given that the provision of service that relates to the extrinsic needs is substantially more important to customers than that which relates to intrinsic needs, resource management should emphasise the need to raise and/or maintain the standards of the core service product with the loyalty programme features adding value in terms of the key benefits identified. Given both that loyalty programmes should be considered as long-term strategies and that once introduced, they can become part of the overall service product, it would seem that the findings lend some support to the previous research that questions their success (inter alia Toh et al., 1991; O'Brien & Jones, 1995; Dowling & Uncles, 1997). The results also support the position that customer loyalty is built by focussing on three concepts: the overall service process, the use of effective database management and value creation either through added value or value recovery (Shoemaker & Lewis, 1999).

The outcome for the consumer from the hotels' service product output was not measured in this study. Future research in this area could include a measure of customer satisfaction to compare the effect of loyalty attributes, service quality attributes and a combined scale on overall satisfaction. An overall measure of customer loyalty could also be obtained to compare the predictive ability of the scales and to assess the relative influence of different quality dimensions on satisfaction and loyalty. Clearly, technology will develop rapidly and its influence on both the individual elements of the hotel service product mix, their interrelationship and more importantly, the outcome for the consumer, in terms of satisfaction and loyalty, requires ongoing investigation. The on-line survey and the snowball sample used in the research were exploratory. Moreover, given the small sample used in the study and the fact that this segment is difficult to research because of its mobility and high expectations, further work is needed to explore the key issues associated with the use of this data collection tool and sampling technique and to examine further their methodological strengths and weaknesses.

REFERENCES

Albrecht, K., & Zemke, R. (1985). *Service America! Doing business in the new economy*. Homewood: Dow Jones-Irwin.

Anderson, E. W., & Sullivan, M. W. (1993). The antecedents and consequences of customer satisfaction for firms. *Marketing Science, 12*(Spring), 125–143.

Assael, R. (1992). *Consumer behaviour and marketing action* (4th ed.). Boston: PWS-Kent.

Asubonteng, P., McLeary, K. J., & Swan, J. E. (1996). SERVQUAL revisited: A critical review of service quality. *Journal of Services Marketing, 10*(6), 62–81.

Babakus, E., & Boller, G. W. (1992). An empirical assessment of the SERVQUAL scale. *Journal of Business Research, 24*, 253–268.

Bagozzi, R. P. (1995). Reflections on relationship marketing in consumer markets. *Journal of the Academy of Marketing Science, 23*(1), 272–277.

Barnes, J. G., Dunne, P. A., & Glynn, W. J. (2000). Self-service and technology: Unanticipated and unintended effects on customer relationships. In: T. A. Swartz & D. Iacobucci (Eds), *Handbook of service marketing and management* (pp. 89–102). Thousand Oaks: Sage Publications Inc..

Bell DeTienne, K., & Thompson, J. A. (1996). Database marketing and organizational learning theory: Toward a research agenda. *Journal of Consumer Marketing, 13*(5), 12–34.

Berry, L. L. (1983). Relationship marketing. In: L. L. Berry, G. L. Shostack & G. D. Upah (Eds), *Emerging perspectives of service marketing* (pp. 25–28). Chicago: American Marketing Association.

Bitner, M. J., Brown, S. W., & Meuter, M. L. (2000). Technology infusion in service encounters. *Journal of the Academy of Marketing Science, 28*(1), 138–149.

Bowen, J. T., & Chen, S. (2001). The relationship between customer loyalty and customer satisfaction. *International Journal of Contemporary Hospitality Management, 13*(5), 213–217.

Bowen, J. T., & Shoemaker, S. (1998). Loyalty: A strategic commitment. *Cornell Hotel and Restaurant Administration Quarterly, 39*(1), 12–25.

Brown, S. A. (1997). *Breakthrough customer service: Best practices of leaders in customer support*. Toronto: Wiley.

Brown, S., & Swartz, T. (1989). A gap analysis of professional service quality. *Journal of Marketing, 53*(2), 92–98.

Buttle, F. (1996a). Relationship marketing. In: F. Buttle (Ed.), *Relationship marketing: Theory and practice* (pp. 1–16). London: Paul Chapman Publishing Limited.

Buttle, F. (1996b). SERVQUAL: Review, critique, research agenda. *European Journal of Marketing, 30*(1), 8–32.

Carman, J. M. (1990). Consumer perceptions of service quality: An assessment of the SERVQUAL dimensions. *Journal of Retailing, 66*(Spring), 33–55.

Carr, M. (1994). Database marketing: Talking direct to our listening customers. *Market Intelligence and Planning, 5*(6), 12–14.

Chenet, P., Tynan, C., & Money, A. (2000). The service performance gap: Testing the re-developed causal model. *European Journal of Marketing, 34*(3/4), 472–495.

Clayton-Smith, D. (1996). Do It All's loyalty programme – and its impact on customer retention. *Managing Service Quality, 5*(6), 33–37.

Cook, S. (1994). Database marketing: Strategy or tactical tool? *Marketing Intelligence Planning, 12*(6), 4–7.

Cronin J. J. Jr., & Taylor, S. A. (1992). Measuring service quality: A re-examination and extension. *Journal of Marketing, 56*(July), 55–68.

Dabholkar, P. A. (2000). Technology in service delivery. In: T. A. Swartz & D. Iacobucci (Eds), *Handbook of service marketing and management* (pp. 103–110). Thousand Oaks: Sage Publications.

Danaher, P. J., & Mattsson, J. (1994). Customer satisfaction during the service delivery process. *European Journal of Marketing, 28*(5), 5–16.

Dibb, S., Simkin, L., Pride, W. M., & Ferrell, O. C. (2001). *Marketing concepts and strategies* (4th ed.). Boston: Houghton Mifflin.

Dillman, D. A. (1983). Mail and other self administered questionnaires. In: P. Rossi, J. D. Wright & A. B. Anderson (Eds), *Handbook of survey research* (pp. 195–230). New York: Academic Press.

Dowling, G. R., & Uncles, M. (1997). Do customer loyalty programs really work? *Sloan Management Review, 38*(4), 71–82.

Dubé, L., Renaghan, L. M., & Miller, J. M. (1994). Measuring customer satisfaction for strategic management. *Cornell Hotel and Restaurant Administration Quarterly, 35*(1), 39–47.

Dubé, L., & Shoemaker, S. (2000). Brand switching and loyalty for services. In: T. A. Swartz & D. Iacobucci (Eds), *Handbook of service marketing and management* (pp. 381–400). Thousand Oaks: Sage Publications.

Duffy, D. L. (1998). Customer loyalty strategies. *Journal of Consumer Marketing, 15*(5), 435–448.

Ekinci, Y., Riley, M., & Fife-Schaw, C. (1998). Which school of thought? The dimensions of resort hotel quality. *International Journal of Contemporary Hospitality Management, 10*(2), 63–67.

Evans, M. J., Patterson, M., & O'Malley, L. (1997). Consumer reactions to database-based supermarket loyalty programmes. *The Journal of Database Marketing, 4*(4), 307–320.

File, K. M., Judd, B. B., & Prince, R. A. (1995). The effect of interactive marketing on commercial customer satisfaction in international financial marketing. *Journal of Business and Industrial Marketing, 10*(2), 69–75.

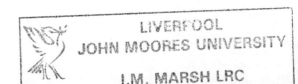

Foddy, W. (1993). *Constructing questions for interviews and questionnaires: Theory and practice in social research.* Cambridge: Cambridge University Press.

Fornell, C. (1992). A national customer satisfaction barometer: The Swedish experiences. *Journal of Marketing, 56*(January), 6–21.

Frazer, L., & Lawley, M. (2000). *Questionnaire design and administration.* Queensland: Wiley.

Gilbert, D. C. (1996). Airlines. In: F. Buttle (Ed.), *Relationship marketing: Theory and practice* (pp. 131–144). London: Paul Chapman.

Gilbert, D. C., Powell-Perry, J., & Widijoso, S. (1999). Approaches by hotels to the use of the Internet as a relationship marketing tool. *Journal of Marketing Practice: Applied Marketing Science, 5*(1), 21–38.

Gould, B. (1998). Notes of caution for relationship marketing. *The Antidote, 3*(5), 25–26.

Grant, R. M. (1998). *Contemporary strategy analysis* (3rd ed.). Oxford: Blackwell.

Grönroos, C. (1984). A service quality model and its marketing implications. *European Journal of Marketing, 18*(4), 36–44.

Grönroos, C. (1990). Relationship approach to the marketing function in service contexts: The marketing and organizational behaviour context. *Journal of Business Review, 20*(1), 3–12.

Grönroos, C. (1996). Relationship marketing: Strategic and tactical implications. *Management Decision, 34*(3), 5–14.

Grönroos, C. (1997). Keynote paper: From marketing mix to relationship marketing towards a paradigm shift in marketing. *Management Decision, 35*(4), 322–339.

Grönroos, C. (2000). *Service management and marketing: A customer relationship management approach* (2nd ed.). Chichester: Wiley.

Gwinner, K. P., Gremler, D. D., & Bitner, M. J. (1998). Relational benefits in service industries: The customer's perspective. *Journal of the Academy of Marketing Science, 26*(2), 101–114.

Hackett, G. P. (1992). Investment in technology: The service sector sinkhole? *Sloan Management Review, 34*(Winter), 97–103.

Hagel, J., & Armstrong, A. G. (1997). *Net gain.* Boston: Harvard Business School Press.

Heskett, J. L., Jones, T. O., Loveman, G. W., Sasser,, W. E., Jr., & Schlesinger, L. A. (1994). Putting the service-profit chain to work. *Harvard Business Review, 72*(2), 164–174.

Heskett, J. L., Sasser, W. E. Jr., & Schlesinger, L. A. (1997). *The service profit chain.* New York: The Free Press.

Hochman, K. (1992). Customer loyalty programmes. In: E. L. Nash (Ed.), *The direct marketing handbook* (pp. 781–799). New York: Irwin McGraw-Hill.

Hoffman, D., Novak, T., & Chatterjee, D. (1995). Commercial scenarios for the web: Opportunities and challenges. *Journal of Computer Mediated Communication, 1*(3), 23–30.

Ibert, J., Baumard, P., Donada, C., & Xuereb, J. (2001). Data collection and managing the data source. In: R. Thiétart (Ed.), *Doing management research: A comprehensive guide* (pp. 172–195). London: Sage Publication.

INRA (International Research Association) (2001). Europeans and language. *INRA (Europe) European coordination office S.A. for the education and culture directorate-general* (pp. 1–60). Brussels: The Education and Culture Directorate-General Unit.

Jiang, P. (2000). Segment-based mass customization: An exploration of a new conceptual marketing framework. *Internet Research: Electronic Networking Applications and Policy, 10*(3), 215–226.

Johnson, M. D., & Gustafsson, A. (2000). *Improving customer satisfaction, loyalty and profit: An integrated measurement and management system.* San Francisco: Jossey-Bass.

Johnson, R. L., Tsirps, M., & Lancioni, R. A. (1995). Measuring service quality: A systems approach. *Journal of Services Marketing*, (5), 6–19.

Kahan, R. (1998). Using database marketing techniques to enhance your one-to-one marketing initiatives. *Journal of Consumer Marketing*, 15(5), 491–493.

Kaiser, H. F. (1974). An index of factorial simplicity. *Psychometrika*, 39, 31–36.

Kandampully, J., & Suhartanto, D. (2000). Customer loyalty in the hotel industry: The role of customer satisfaction and image. *International Journal of Contemporary Hospitality Management*, 12(6), 346–351.

Knutson, B., Stevens, P., Wullaert, C., Patton, M., & Yokoyama, F. (1991). LODGSERV: A service quality index for the lodging industry. *Hospitality Research Journal*, 24, 277–284.

Lewis, R. C., & Chambers, R. E. (2000). *Marketing leadership in hospitality: Foundations and practices* (3rd ed.). New York: Wiley.

Lindgreen, A., & Crawford, I. (1999). Implementing, monitoring and measuring a programme of relationship marketing. *Marketing Intelligence and Planning*, 17(5), 231–239.

Lovelock, C. H. (2000). Functional integration in services: Understanding the links between marketing, operations and human resources. In: T. A. Schwartz & D. Iacobucci (Eds), *Handbook of services marketing and management* (pp. 421–437). London: Sage.

Lynch, R. (2000). *Corporate strategy* (2nd ed.). London: Prentice-Hall International.

McCleary, K. W., & Weaver, P. A. (1992). Do business travelers who belong to frequent guest programs differ from those who don't belong? *Hospitality Research Journal*, 15(3), 51–64.

McIlroy, A., & Barnett, S. (2000). Building customer relationships: Do discount cards work? *Managing Service Quality*, 10(6), 347–355.

Mittal, B., & Lassar, W. M. (1996). The role of personalization in service encounters. *Journal of Retailing*, 72(1), 95–109.

Mittal, B., & Lassar, W. M. (1998). Why do customers switch? The dynamics of satisfaction versus loyalty. *Journal of Services Marketing*, 12(3), 177–194.

Naisbitt, J. (1982). *Megatrends: Ten new directions transforming our lives.* New York: Random House.

O'Brien, L., & Jones, C. (1995). Do rewards really create loyalty? *Harvard Business Review*, 73(Jan–June), 75–82.

O'Connor, P. (1999). *Electronic information distribution in tourism and hospitality.* Wallingford: Cab International.

O'Malley, L. (1998). Can loyalty schemes really build loyalty? *Marketing Intelligence & Planning*, 16(1), 47–55.

Oppenheim, A. N. (1992). *Questionnaire design, interviewing and attitude measurement.* London: Continuum.

Orams, M. B., & Page, S. J. (2000). Designing self-reply questionnaires to survey tourists: Issues and guidelines for researchers. *Anatolia: An International Journal of Tourism and Hospitality Research*, 11(2), 125–139.

Palmer, A., McMahon-Beattie, U., & Beggs, R. (2000). A structural analysis of hotel sector loyalty programmes. *International Journal of Contemporary Hospitality Management*, 12(1), 54–60.

Paraskevas, A. (2001). Internal service encounters in hotels: An empirical study. *International Journal of Contemporary Hospitality Management*, 13(6), 285–292.

Parasuraman, A., Zeithaml, V. A., & Berry, L. L. (1985). A conceptual model of service quality and its implications for future research. *Journal of Marketing*, 49(Fall), 41–50.

Patterson, P. G., & Ward, T. (2000). Relationship marketing and management. In: T. A. Swartz & D. Iacobucci (Eds), *Handbook of service marketing and management* (pp. 317–342). Thousand Oaks: Sage Publications.

Pitta, D. A. (1998). Marketing one-to-one and its dependency on knowledge discovery in database. *Journal of Consumer Marketing, 15*(5), 468–480.

Reichheld, F. F. (1996). *The loyalty effect: The hidden force behind growth, profits and lasting value.* Boston: Harvard Business School Press.

Reichheld, F. F., & Aspinwall, K. (1994). Building high-loyalty business systems. *Journal of Retail Banking, 16*(2), 21–29.

Reichheld, F. F., & Sasser, W. E. Jr. (1990). Zero defections quality comes to service. *Harvard Business Review, 68*(September–October), 105–111.

Robson, C. (1993). *Real world research: A resource for social scientists and practitioner-researchers.* Oxford: Blackwell.

Royer, I., & Zarlowski, P. (2001). Sampling. In: R. Thiétart (Ed.), *Doing management research: A comprehensive guide* (pp. 141–171). London: Sage.

Rust, R. T., & Oliver, R. L. (1994). Service quality: Insights and managerial implications from the frontier. In: R. T. Rust & R. L. Oliver (Eds), *Service quality: New directions in theory and practice* (pp. 24–57). Thousand Oaks: Sage.

Rust, R. T., & Zahorik, A. J. (1993). Customer satisfaction, customer retention and market share. *Journal of Retailing, 69*(Summer), 193–215.

Ryan, C. (1995). *Researching tourist satisfaction: Issues, concepts, problems.* London: Routledge.

Sarantakos, S. (1998). *Social research.* London: Macmillan Press.

Schoenbacher, D. D., Gordon, G. L., Foley, D., & Spellman, L. (1997). Understanding consumer database marketing. *Journal of Consumer Marketing, 14*(1), 5–19.

Schofield, P., & Fallon, P. (2000). Measuring the importance of critical factors in restaurant service quality performance evaluation: A triadic perspective. *Proceedings of the Consumer Satisfaction Research in Tourism and Hospitality Conference*, Oxford Brookes University, 25 November 2000 (pp. 159–182).

Sheth, J. N., & Parvatiyar, A. (1995). Relationship marketing in consumer markets: Antecedents and consequences. *Journal of the Academy of Marketing Science, 23*(4), 255–271.

Shoemaker, S., & Lewis, R. C. (1999). Customer loyalty: The future of hospitality marketing. *Hospitality Management, 18*, 345–370.

Stevens, J. P. (1992). *Applied multivariate statistics for the social sciences* (2nd ed.). Hillsdale, NJ: Erlbaum.

Stokes, D. (2000). Entrepreneurial marketing: A conceptualisation from qualitative research. *Qualitative Market Research: An International Journal, 3*(1), 47–54.

Surprenant, C., & Solomon, M. (1987). Predictability and personalization in the service encounter. *Journal of Marketing, 51*(3), 86–96.

Tabachnick, B. G., & Fidell, L. S. (1996). *Using multivariate statistics* (3rd ed.). New York: Harper & Row.

Tepeci, M. (1999). Increasing brand loyalty in the hospitality industry. *International Journal of Contemporary Hospitality Management, 11*(5), 223–229.

Toh, R. S., Rivers, M. J., & Withiam, G. (1991). Frequent-guest programs: Do they fly? *The Cornell Hotel and Restaurant Administration Quarterly, 36*, 46–52.

Wakefield, K. L., & Blodgett, J. G. (1996). The effect of the servicescape on customers' behavioral intentions. *The Journal of Services Marketing, 10*(6), 45–51.

Weber, K. (2001). Association meeting planners' loyalty to hotel chains. *Hospitality Management, 20,* 259–275.

Werthner, H., & Klein, S. (1999). *Information technology and tourism – a challenging relationship.* Vienna: Springer-Verlag.

West, R. (1991). *Computing for psychologists – statistical analysis using SPSS and Minitab.* Chur: Harwood Academic Publishers.

Yelkur, R., & DaCosta, M. M. (2001). Differential pricing and segmentation on the Internet: The case of hotels. *Management Decision, 39*(4), 252–261.

Zeithaml, V. A., & Bitner, M. J. (2000). *Service marketing* (2nd ed.). London: Irwin McGraw-Hill.

VALUE RELEVANCE OF EQUITY, EARNINGS AND CAPITAL STRUCTURE IN THE RESTAURANT INDUSTRY

Arun Upneja and Nan Hua

ABSTRACT

This paper seeks to accomplish three objectives. First, based on prior research, this paper attempts to infer the value relevance of earnings and equity for firm valuation in the restaurant industry. The second objective is to document the joint information content of earning and equity in firm valuation. Finally, the model tested above is used to evaluate the relevance of capital structure for firm valuation in the static capital structure framework. The empirical results indicate that the incremental R^2 associated with earnings was found to be generally less than the incremental R^2 associated with equity. The adjusted R^2 of the model that included both earnings and equity ranged from 0.54 to 0.77. The results suggest that the addition of capital structure variables have no incremental explanatory power in explaining the market value of firm, in the presence of earnings and equity.

Advances in Hospitality and Leisure, Volume 2, 159–178
ISSN: 1745-3542/doi:10.1016/S1745-3542(05)02008-4

INTRODUCTION

This paper seeks to accomplish three objectives. First, based on research in the accounting and finance literature, this paper attempts to infer the value relevance of earnings and equity for firm valuation in the restaurant industry. The second objective of the paper is to document the joint information content of earning and book value of equity in firm valuation. Finally, the model tested above is used to evaluate the relevance of capital structure for firm valuation in the static capital structure framework.

Research on firm valuation using financial statements has a long history (e.g., Beaver, Kettler, & Scholes, 1970; Ball & Brown, 1969; Dechow, 1994; Hayn, 1995; Ou & Penman, 1989). The financial statement data are widely circulated and considered reliable because independent accountants audit the financial statements of publicly traded firms. Multiple classes of people use the financial statements; for example, researchers, financial analysts and other participants in the financial markets all use this data for various purposes. Different classes of users of financial statements use them for different purposes. For example, investors are concerned with the return on investment, whereas a creditor is more likely to focus on getting paid for material supplied or services rendered to the firm. Financial analysts use the financial statements for prediction and valuation. The analysts attempt to predict many outcome variables, such as future sales, profit margins and market share. From these predictions they can then use financial models to value the firm. Academic researchers also retain a keen interest in valuation research using financial statements.

If the industry has been in existence for a long time and is very mature then the cash flows (profitability) are generally predictable. If constant innovation is taking place in a particular industry, it is very difficult to project the cash flows in future. For example, the web-based industry is characterized by a very rapid growth rate. It is very difficult to predict the direction and speed at which technology is moving. Contrast web-based industries with relatively stable electric utilities. Utilities are a special case because they are regulated by the states and are required to earn no more or less than some benchmark rate, which is set by the state. In this special case, earnings are a function of firm assets. In other words, the earnings can be reliably estimated from the total assets of a utility. However, in an industry characterized by rapid change, earnings are a function of strategic steps taken by the managers of the firm. Value of firms in the utility industry is derived mainly from its asset holding and the value of web-based firms is derived purely from the potential earnings, totally unrelated to the underlying assets. Most industries fall between the two extremes of a scale that is anchored on one side by the utility industry and the web-based industry on the other. Therefore, it is reasonable to assume that firm value is a function of both the income-generating assets and future potential of the firm.

The present value of all future expected cash flows (see Brealey & Myers, 1984 for an extended discussion) is the most popular approach in the firm valuation literature. This is known as a discounted cash flow (DCF) approach. Under the DCF approach, future cash flows are discounted by some discount rate to arrive at a present value. The DCF does not specify the term "cash flows" and there are many different operationalizations of the construct. Capitalization of earnings, dividends and cash flows from operations are the three most popular ways to operationalize the future cash flows construct. Capitalization of "economic value added" by the firm is a more recent approach to firm valuation. Two major assumptions have to be made under the DCF approach: (1) all future cash flows have to be estimated and (2) an estimate is also required for the risk-adjusted discount rate. In practice, it is very difficult to make accurate forecasts about the future cash flows. Therefore, many researchers use proxies that may be more accurate than using estimates of multiyear forecasts. This paper uses one such specification of the DCF where no explicit forecasts are made about the future cash flows; instead, the net income from operations is used to surrogate for future cash flows and used in the valuation model. One assumption of many DCF models is that because the firm is a going-concern entity, the liquidation value of the firm can be ignored. Some models explicitly include a measure of the liquidation value of the firm. The book value of assets is assumed to surrogate for the liquidation value of the firm and is included in the model tested.

Finally, the model derived is used to test a part of the static capital structure theory. Under the static analysis, firms weigh the advantages /disadvantages of borrowed funds versus internally generated funds. This process of continuous evaluation leads to target ratios. Given the controversy in the literature over static analysis versus the pecking order theory as an explanation for capital structure, this paper does not take a position on whether firms are adjusting towards target ratios. However, this paper does provide some evidence on the value relevance of debt ratios for firm valuation.

LITERATURE REVIEW AND MODEL DEVELOPMENT

The valuation model developed by Ohlson (1994) starts with the following familiar equation:

$$\text{MVF}_{i,t} = \sum_{\tau=1}^{\infty} R_f^{-\tau} E_t(\tilde{d}_{t+\tau}) \tag{1}$$

where $\text{MVF}_{i,t}$ is the market value of firm i at time t; R_f, the one plus the risk-free rate of return; $\tilde{d}$, the dividends at time t; and E, an expectations operator.

In this case it is assumed that dividends are being used to operationalize the construct of "cash flows". From this model, Ohlson (1994) uses the clean surplus relation along with assumptions about the stochastic properties of accounting data to show that both book value and earnings possess incremental information content with respect to each other. The clean surplus relation states that changes in the book value of the firm are equal to the earnings of the firm, adjusted for dividends and capital contributions. Ohlson (1994) uses the clean surplus relation to express the market value of the firm as a function of book value and earnings. In other words, the future stream of dividends is replaced in the market valuation function with the current book value and the future stream of earnings. The final analysis shows that the market value of a firm is a weighted average of earnings and book value:

> Specifically, the core of the valuation function expresses value as a weighted average of (i) capitalized current earnings (adjusted for dividends), and (ii) current book value.

Ohlson (1994) also demonstrates the special cases where either earnings or book value are sufficient as "sole value indicators". For example, the utility industry is required by law to set prices in such a way as to obtain a fixed return on assets. Given the risk characteristics of the utility industry, value of the firm is simply a function of the assets of the firm.

Collins, Pincus, and Xie (1999) provide empirical support for the inclusion of net book value in the valuation model:

> More specifically, we conjecture that the simple earnings capitalization model is mis-specified due to the omission of book value of equity from the price-earnings model.

The motivation for Collins et al. (1999) stems from the anomalous negative price/earnings relation reported by Jan and Ou (1995) for loss firms. Jan and Ou (1995) find that when earnings per share are regressed on price per share, the coefficient on earnings is significantly negative for all 19 years examined in the study. For firms reporting losses, it appeared that greater the loss, greater is the stock price of the firm. However, using multiple analyses and a detailed investigation of this issue, Collins et al. show that the anomalous negative relation disappears when book value of equity is added to the relation. Overall, there is a significant positive relation between price and earnings and this relationship continues to be either significantly positive or zero in yearly regressions.

Collins et al. (1999) motivate the inclusion of book value in the price/ earnings relation on three grounds: as a scale proxy, as a complementary value indicator to earnings and as an abandonment (or adaptation value) option. The scale proxy argument is from Barth and Kallapur (1995) and is summarized below. The complementary value indicator argument is due to Ohlson (1994) and has been described above. The abandonment option argument (Barth, Beaver, & Landsman, 1997; Berger, Ofek, & Swary, 1996; Burgstahler & Dichev, 1997) is the value of the assets at liquidation. Even if the firm is liquidated, the assets have some value. The value of the assets may be less in a liquidation situation than the value in a going-concern situation. The argument is that this liquidation value can be proxied for by the book value of the firm. The concept of adaptation value is very similar and argues that the assets can be deployed in their next best use. The value of the assets in their next best use is the adaptation value.

Barth and Kallapur (1995) provide econometric support for including some measure of size as a scale proxy. Cross-sectional financial research based on accounting data often involves grouping of firms that vary in size. The variation in the magnitudes of the variables included in the study lead to biased coefficient estimates. In addition, scale differences in the cross-sectional data also lead to "heteroscedastic regression errors which can cause biased standard error estimates and estimation inefficiency". They consider three ways to deal with the heteroscedastic error variance caused by scale differences. The first method used by financial researchers is to deflate the variables by a scale proxy. Some of the common variables used are total assets, equity, sales or the total outstanding number of shares. The second method deals a scale proxy as an independent variable. The third to uses White (1980) heteroscedasticity-consistent standard error estimates.

Barth and Kallapur find that magnitude of the bias in the coefficients and the heteroscedasticity problems in the errors increases when a scale variable is used to deflate the variables. They also find that the bias in the coefficients is of less concern when the scale proxy is used as an independent variable. Finally, they also show that even if the errors are heteroscedastic, if a scale proxy is included in the regression, the White (1980) standard errors are close to the true errors. Therefore, they suggest, "When scale differences are

of concern, accounting researchers should include a scale proxy as an independent variable". In Eq. (1), book value of equity (a scale proxy) should
be included if the price/earnings relation is moderated by size.

  There are other variables that can be used as scale proxies (e.g., total assets
or total sales). However, given the theoretical arguments advanced by Ohlson
(1994) and empirical evidence presented by Collins et al., book value of
equity is included in the price/earnings relation as an independent variable
along with earnings. Eq. (2) is the theoretical model tested in this paper.

$$\mathrm{MVE}_{i,t} = \frac{\sum\limits_{1}^{n} \mathrm{CF}_{i,t}}{1 + t_{i,t}} + \left(\frac{\mathrm{BV}}{1 + t_{i,t}}\right) \tag{2}$$

where $\mathrm{MVE}_{i,t}$ is the market value of equity for firm i at time t; $\mathrm{CF}_{i,t}$, the cash
flows of firm i at time t; and BV, the book value of the firm equity.

  Eq. (2) uses a discount rate to calculate the present value of the terminal
value of the firm. However, Maydew (1993) shows that varying the discount
rates between firms does not cause any significant increase in the explanatory power of the models of firm valuation. Therefore, the discount rates
are dropped. As mentioned before, capitalization of earnings is one approach to operationalize the construct of future cash flows. Future cash
flows can be replaced with earnings. In other words, inclusion of the earnings is sufficient for capitalizing the future cash flows of the firm.

  In summary, theoretical support for replacing the future cash flows construct with earnings and the addition of book value is provided by Ohlson
(1994). Collins, Pincus, and Xie (1999) provide empirical support for including book value of equity in the presence of earnings for firm valuation.
Barth and Kallapur (1995) express econometric reasons for including a
measure of size as a scale proxy in the relation between the market value of
firm equity and earnings. The empirical model that is tested in the paper is
shown in Eq. (3).

$$\mathrm{MVE} = \mathrm{Earnings} + \mathrm{Net\ Book\ Value} \tag{3}$$

  Collins, Maydew, and Weiss (1997) have also used this model and the
methodology in their research on the changes in the value relevance of
earnings and book values. Collins et al. (1997) find that there has been no
decrease in the joint value relevance of earnings and book value over the last
40 years. They also report that the slight decrease in the value relevance of
earnings has been replaced by an increase in the value relevance of the book
value. Collins et al. also show that the increase in the value relevance of
book value (at the expense of earnings) is due to the "increasing frequency

and magnitude of one-time items, the increasing frequency of negative earnings, and changes in average firm size". (Collins et al., 1997).

Much research attention has been focussed on whether firms adjust their capital structure ratios towards some form of optimum ratios. For example, Taggart (1977) and Marsh (1982) provide evidence that firms are optimize debt ratios in some form or the other. There is plenty of evidence that suggests that the management make certain decisions about the capital structure during the process of creating a profitable firm. Some of the decisions involve trade-off between different kinds of debt. For example, the pecking order theory suggests that firms prefer external debt to equity. However, excess of external debt increases the bankruptcy risk of the firm. Therefore, the alternative explanation to the static theory is that the process of making decisions leads to a particular capital structure and the capital structure observed at any point in time is the end product of the process rather than the objective of the process. Some of the papers that argue different aspects are Myers (1984), Kester (1986) and Rajan and Zingales (1995). Given the controversy in the literature over static analysis versus the pecking order theory as an explanation for capital structure, this paper does not take a position on whether firms are adjusting towards target ratios. The attempt in this paper is to provide some evidence on the value relevance of debt ratios for firm valuation in the static structure framework.

There is very limited research on financial aspects of publicly traded restaurant firms in the hospitality literature. Marler (1993) examines off balance sheet financing issues in the restaurant industry. Kim (1997) explores the determinants of debt ratios (short-term, long-term and total debt ratios). Upneja and Dalbor (1999) examine the relationship between debt financing and marginal tax rates and help explain the trade-off between leasing and debt financing. They show that by using tax rates that simulate the prefinancing tax rates faced by the firm, the spurious negative relationship between postfinancing debt rates and magnitudes of debt financing by firms is eliminated.

DATA COLLECTION AND OPERATIONALIZATION OF VARIABLES

Data Sources

The financial data are collected from the 2005 version of the annual and the quarterly COMPUSTAT. The primary/secondary/tertiary file was combined with the full coverage tape and all firms trading in the NYSE, AMEX and NASDAQ were included. Firms in the SIC code 5812 (Eating-places) are included in the study. Due to small sample size of restaurant firms before 1991, the time period selected for this study is 1991–2004. If the data for any firm could not be found for a particular year, then that firm-year was dropped. For example, if 1995 earnings were not available for Wendy's, none of the information relating to Wendy's for 1995 was collected. If any of a firm's short-term debt ratio, long-term debt ratio or total debt ratio is greater than 10, the corresponding firm-year observations were dropped. Firms with assets above the 90 percentile and losses beyond 90 million dollars were also deleted to exclude the effect of a few very large firms and outliers.

Except for price and outstanding shares, the annual version of the COMPUSTAT contains financial data stated on a fiscal yearend basis. The price and outstanding data are stated on a calendar year-end basis. As explained below, the price and outstanding share data are collected from the quarterly COMPUSTAT and all other financial data are collected from the annual COMPUSTAT.

Model

The empirical model that is tested in this paper relates the market value of a firm's equity to the book value of equity and earnings (see Eq. (3)).

The statistical model tested in the paper is:

$$\text{MVE}_{i,t+1/4} = \text{NI}_{i,t} + \text{NBV}_{i,t} \tag{4}$$

Because earnings and net book value will not predict the market value of the firm exactly, the intercept and an error term are added to the regression equation.

$$\text{MVE}_{i,t+1/4} = \beta_0 + \beta_1 \text{NI}_{i,t} + \beta_2 \text{NBV}_{i,t} + \varepsilon \tag{5}$$

where $\text{MVE}_{i,t+1/4}$ is the market value of equity for firm i at the end of the first quarter following the end of the fiscal year t; $\text{NI}_{i,t}$, the earnings from operations (before extraordinary earnings and unusual items) for the firm i, for the fiscal year t; and $\text{NBV}_{i,t}$, the net book value of equity for firm i at the end of fiscal year t.

Dependent Variable

Multiplying the stock price with outstanding shares operationalizes the dependent variable. The stock price and the outstanding shares are measured at the end of the first quarter following the end of the fiscal year. The dependent variable is measured at the end of the first quarter because there is usually a lag between the fiscal yearend and the release of financial information by the firm. The auditors need some time to audit and certify the financial assertions made by the management in the financial statements. The time required by the auditors is a function of the complexity of the operations, other workload of the auditing firm and statutory requirements for reporting. The assumption widely used in the literature is that by the end of the first quarter of a fiscal year, financial information (pertaining to the previous year) is available to market participants. Therefore, the stock price at the end of first quarter is considered to have impounded the financial performance of the previous fiscal year. For example, if a firm has December 31 as the fiscal yearend, the release of its financial information will take place during the next 90 days. For consistency and ease of data collection purposes, it is assumed that the market has impounded the financial information by March 31. Similarly, for firms with fiscal yearend January 31, the market price on April 30 is assumed to be the date by which the market has impounded the financial information about the previous year. Therefore, multiplying the stock price with outstanding shares (measured at the end of the first quarter following the end of the fiscal year) operationalized the market value of the firm (dependent variable).

Independent Variables

Earnings are operationalized as income from operations before unusual and extraordinary items. The net book value of the firm is operationalized as the difference between the total assets and total liabilities of the firm. Both of the variables are measured at the end of the fiscal year and collected from the annual COMPUSTAT.

Additional Independent Variables

The third objective of the study was to evaluate the relevance of capital structure for firm valuation. Three variables, representing the debt level of the firm, were added to the regression equation. The three variables are short-term debt ratio, long-term debt ratio and the total debt ratio. The total debt of the firm was divided into short term and long term and the ratios were calculated by dividing the debt by total assets. For example, short-term debt ratio was calculated by dividing short-term debt by total assets. Each of the ratios was then added individually as independent variables to the regression equation that contained both earnings and the net book value of equity.

The following were the three equations tested in the study:

$$MVE_{i,t+1/4} = \beta_0 + \beta_1 NI_{i,t} + \beta_2 NBV_{i,t} + \beta_3 STDR_{i,t} + \varepsilon_{i,t} \qquad (6)$$

$$MVE_{i,t+1/4} = \beta_0 + \beta_1 NI_{i,t} + \beta_2 NBV_{i,t} + \beta_3 LTDR_{i,t} + \varepsilon_{i,t} \qquad (7)$$

$$MVE_{i,t+1/4} = \beta_0 + \beta_1 NI_{i,t} + \beta_2 NBV_{i,t} + \beta_3 TDR_{i,t} + \varepsilon_{i,t} \qquad (8)$$

where STDR is the short-term debt ratio; LTDR, the long-term debt ratio; and TDR, the total debt ratio.

A significant coefficient on the capital structure variables would demonstrate the valuation implication of capital structure above and beyond what is conveyed by earnings and net book value. Moreover, if capital structure variables have valuation implication, then a significant increase in the adjusted R^2 should be observed. If either the capital structure variables are not value-relevant for valuation or the information is already contained in the book value of equity or earnings, the corresponding coefficients will not be statistically significant at reasonable confidence level and the adjusted R^2 exhibiting a significant decrease.

RESULTS AND DISCUSSION

Table 1 presents the descriptive statistics for the sample firms. The number of firms with data on COMPUSTAT (meeting the criteria of this research) varies from 61 in 2004 to 116 in 1996. Given the tragedy happened in 2001 and accompanying economy slowdown, a significant decline is observed in the number of restaurant firms in the stock market. However, when the attention is directed to the average market value, equity and net income, a monotonic increase pattern through the years is observed with only a few setbacks. Generally, firms traded in the stock market benefit from stock market listing as they can raise equity capital, which facilitates their growth. Through the time, those that survive in the market tend to see a growth in size and an increase in earnings from operations. For example, the average market value of equity for these publicly traded restaurant firms has increased from $139.47 million to almost $492.37 million. Correspondingly, the mean book value of equity has also increased from $39.53 million to

Table 1. The Statistics of Restaurant Firms in the 2005 Edition of COMPUSTAT for the Years 1991–2004. (All Amounts are in Millions of Dollars).

Year	No. of firms	Market Value of Equity		Mean Book Value of Equity		Net Income		STDR		LTDR		TDR	
		Mean	Std. Dev.	Mean	Std. Dev.	Mean	Std. Dev.	Mean	Std. Dev.	Mean	Std. Dev.	Mean	Std. Dev.
1991	66	139.47	213.06	39.53	57.67	3.28	10.50	0.28	0.23	0.20	0.21	0.52	0.30
1992	76	169.31	265.52	46.56	62.67	4.66	10.21	0.19	0.10	0.18	0.19	0.42	0.24
1993	86	143.59	213.56	43.39	52.12	3.70	9.47	0.21	0.13	0.17	0.18	0.43	0.25
1994	96	118.76	201.91	45.68	63.77	3.09	9.27	0.23	0.28	0.19	0.17	0.46	0.33
1995	109	127.01	266.83	42.95	60.30	1.34	12.43	0.27	0.49	0.22	0.22	0.54	0.53
1996	115	121.37	229.05	54.72	78.40	2.47	13.01	0.22	0.14	0.19	0.19	0.49	0.41
1997	109	148.62	281.00	60.09	105.58	2.91	17.03	0.25	0.25	0.21	0.22	0.51	0.34
1998	103	123.86	286.38	60.93	112.20	4.97	18.98	0.32	0.61	0.26	0.23	0.63	0.69
1999	102	112.13	200.31	59.44	101.74	5.53	16.65	0.29	0.29	0.26	0.24	0.64	0.67
2000	100	122.39	255.27	53.94	103.00	1.60	21.26	0.32	0.34	0.26	0.25	0.69	0.74
2001	85	213.54	389.51	76.06	127.36	4.43	24.60	0.30	0.45	0.28	0.32	0.65	0.67
2002	79	198.38	365.04	88.78	147.57	9.74	24.42	0.30	0.57	0.23	0.23	0.60	0.59
2003	77	322.30	538.90	109.70	183.72	10.28	29.66	0.28	0.48	0.26	0.26	0.62	0.61
2004	61	492.37	733.24	130.68	248.48	17.82	34.75	0.23	0.20	0.27	0.34	0.59	0.40
All years	1264	170.04	338.31	62.83	115.44	4.90	19.14	0.27	0.37	0.23	0.23	0.55	0.52

$130.68 million. The mean earnings from operations have increased from $3.28 million to $17.82 million.

The first objective is to evaluate the value relevance of book value and net income in firm valuation. Table 2 presents the adjusted R^2s from the models that include only net book value, only net income and both of these variables together. It is clear from the tables that both earnings and the equity variables are significant predictors of market value. The adjusted R^2 of equity ranges from 0.49 to 0.73 and that of earnings ranges from 0.44 to 0.76. Equity had a higher adjusted R^2 (as compared to earnings) in 10 of the 14 years examined, one year they were about equal and earnings had a higher adjusted R^2 in three years. This is a very puzzling result because it is

Table 2.   The Adjusted R^2 from Regression of Market Value of Firm on
Equity and Earning Variables.

Year	Adj. R^2			Incremental Information[a]		
	Equity	Earnings	Equity + Earnings	Incremental R^2 of equity	Incremental R^2 of earnings	Common R^2 [b]
1991	0.73	0.61	0.75	0.14	0.02	0.59
1992	0.70	0.62	0.71	0.09	0.01	0.61
1993	0.58	0.46	0.60	0.14	0.02	0.44
1994	0.51	0.48	0.59	0.11	0.08	0.40
1995	0.70	0.50	0.74	0.24	0.04	0.46
1996	0.70	0.58	0.77	0.19	0.07	0.51
1997	0.73	0.48	0.74	0.26	0.01	0.47
1998	0.56	0.56	0.66	0.10	0.10	0.46
1999	0.50	0.63	0.67	0.04	0.17	0.46
2000	0.49	0.44	0.54	0.10	0.05	0.39
2001	0.67	0.45	0.70	0.25	0.03	0.42
2002	0.61	0.69	0.72	0.03	0.11	0.58
2003	0.67	0.65	0.71	0.06	0.04	0.61
2004	0.54	0.76	0.76	0.00	0.22	0.54
All years	0.60	0.59	0.67	0.08	0.07	0.52

[a]The incremental R^2 for equity is calculated as the difference in adjusted R^2 between the model with both net income and equity and the model with only earnings, in other words the increase in adjusted R^2 when equity is added to a model that includes earnings. Similarly, the incremental R^2 for earnings is calculated as the difference in adjusted R^2 between the model with both earnings and equity and the model with only equity. Both Wilcoxon and T tests suggest Equity, Earnings and Equity + Earnings are statistically different at 5% significance level.
[b]The common R^2 is the common explanatory power of both equity and earnings. It is calculated by subtracting the incremental R^2 of equity and the incremental R^2 of earnings from the adjusted R^2 of the model that includes both equity and earnings. For example, the common R^2 of 1991 is calculated by subtracting 0.14 and 0.02 from 0.75.

generally believed that earnings are more important for firm valuation. However as explained before, if the restaurant industry is very mature, it is possible that the earnings of restaurant firms are heavily dependent on the total assets of the firm.

Incremental information of the variables is also calculated. The incremental R^2 for equity is calculated as the difference in adjusted R^2 between the model with both net income and equity and the model with only earnings, in other words the increase in adjusted R^2 when equity is added to a model that includes the earnings variable. Similarly, the incremental R^2 for earnings is calculated as the difference in adjusted R^2 between the model with both earnings and equity and the model with only equity. The incremental R^2 procedure allows us to compare the additional information content of a variable, in the presence of another variable. It appears from the data that the book value of equity is more informative than the earnings in 11 of the 14 years tested. Both Wilcoxon and T tests suggest Equity, Earnings and Equity + Earnings are statistically different at the 5% significance level. The incremental R^2 of the book value of equity ranges from 0.00 to 0.26 with a mean of 0.12. The incremental R^2 of earnings ranges from 0.01 to 0.22 with a mean of 0.07.

The common R^2 is calculated by subtracting the incremental R^2 of earnings and book value of equity from the adjusted R^2 that includes both the terms. For example, the common R^2 of 0.59 for 1991 is calculated by subtracting 0.14 and 0.02 from 0.75. The common R^2 procedure allows in drawing inferences about the information contained in two variables that are common to both of them. The common portion of the explanatory power of equity and earnings ranges from 0.39 to 0.61.

The second objective of the paper is to evaluate the overall significance of a model that includes both net income and the net book value of equity. Table 3 presents the results of estimating Eq. (6). Overall the model is quite effective in estimating the market value of the firm as the adjusted R^2 range from 0.54 to 0.77. The equity variable is significant at the 1% level for all the years in the study except 2004. The earnings variable is significant at the 1% level in 10 of the 14 years, and significant at the 5% level for all the years examined.

The third objective of the paper is to evaluate the information content of capital structure variables for equity valuation in the presence of book value of equity and earnings. The book value of equity and operating earnings are referred as the control variables in this part of the paper. Tables 4–6 report annual regression results from Eqs. (6–8). Short-term debt ratio is significant only in 1994 (Table 4), long-term debt ratio only in 1995 and 1997

Table 3.   The Market Value of Firms on Earnings from Continuing
Operations and Book Value of Equity.

Market value $= \beta_0 + \beta_1 \text{Equity} + \beta_2 \text{Earnings} + \varepsilon$

Year	β_0	β_1	β_2	Adj. R^2	No. of Observations
1991	27.89	5.45	2.37	0.75	66
	(16.70)	(2.10)	(0.38)		
1992	16.82	6.57	2.62	0.71	76
	(21.47)	(3.27)	(0.53)		
1993	20.12	5.6	2.37	0.60	86
	(19.65)	(2.35)	(0.43)		
1994	27.65	8.38	1.43	0.59	96
	(16.65)	(2.01)	(0.29)		
1995	−5.57	5.84	2.9	0.74	109
	(17.31)	(1.42)	(0.29)		
1996	10.94	6.26	1.73	0.77	115
	(13.15)	(1.09)	(0.18)		
1997	22.02	2.54	1.98	0.74	109
	(16.40)	(1.17)	(0.19)		
1998	21.44	6.58	1.14	0.66	103
	(18.98)	(1.22)	(0.21)		
1999	40.62	7.27	0.53	0.67	102
	(13.40)	(1.01)	(0.17)		
2000	54.83	4.08	1.13	0.54	100
	(21.01)	(1.18)	(0.24)		
2001	41.67	3.76	2.04	0.70	85
	(27.64)	(1.25)	(0.24)		
2002	47.36	8.85	0.72	0.72	79
	(25.49)	(1.62)	(0.27)		
2003	91.84	7.23	1.41	0.71	77
	(39.46)	(2.19)	(0.35)		
2004	155	17.05	0.24*	0.76	61
	(52.08)	(2.30)	(0.32)		
All years	49.1	7.28	1.35	0.67	1264
	(6.30)	(0.44)	(0.07)		

Note: All significant at 5% level. Standard errors are reported in parentheses.
*Not significant at 5% level.

(Table 5) and total debt ratio only in 1994 and 1997 (Table 6). Moreover,
Table 7 reports the adjusted R^2 from regressions of market value of firm on
equity, income from operations and variables representing the capital structure of the firm. The incremental R^2 of the capital structure variables (in the
presence of control variables) is also reported. The incremental R^2 of the
short-term debt ratio ranges from −0.01 to 0.03 and the cross-sectional time

Table 4.   Test for Short-Term Debt Ratio (1991–2004).

Market value $= \beta_0 + \beta_1\text{Equity} + \beta_2\text{Earnings} + \beta_3\text{STDR} + \varepsilon$

Year	β_0	β_1	β_2	β_3	Adj. R^2
1991	26.42 (26.09)	2.38 (0.39)	5.44 (2.11)	4.52 (61.24)	0.75
1992	44.95 (41.37)	2.59 (0.53)	6.41 (3.28)	−134.34 (168.73)	0.70
1993	33.20 (34.56)	2.33 (0.44)	5.66 (2.37)	−54.48 (118.16)	0.60
1994	−22.63 (22.06)	1.71 (0.29)	8.46 (1.91)	164.09* (50.11)	0.62
1995	−10.73 (19.62)	2.93 (0.30)	5.82 (1.43)	15.43 (27.25)	0.74
1996	−19.55 (24.80)	1.81 (0.19)	6.27 (1.09)	118.29 (81.26)	0.77
1997	14.22 (23.14)	1.99 (0.19)	2.57 (1.19)	28.16 (56.34)	0.74
1998	20.27 (21.72)	1.15 (0.21)	6.58 (1.23)	3.12 (27.75)	0.66
1999	35.73 (19.14)	0.53 (0.17)	7.30 (1.02)	14.93 (41.54)	0.66
2000	57.00 (29.00)	1.13 (0.25)	4.08 (1.19)	−5.90 (53.91)	0.53
2001	27.63 (34.95)	2.07 (0.25)	3.81 (1.27)	41.54 (55.13)	0.70
2002	48.42 (29.31)	0.72 (0.27)	8.85 (1.64)	−0.96 (39.19)	0.71
2003	101.08 (47.30)	1.39 (0.36)	7.28 (2.23)	−18.73 (71.95)	0.71
2004	158.50 (80.32)	0.24 (0.33)	17.03 (2.35)	−2.00 (238.57)	0.75

Note: Short-term debt ratio, calculated by dividing short-term debt into total assets. Standard errors are reported in parentheses.
*Significant at 5% level.

series incremental R^2 is 0.00. Only in 1994, the adjusted R^2 of the model that includes the short-term debt ratio (along with control variables) is greater than the adjusted R^2 of the model that just includes the control variables. The incremental R^2 of the long-term debt ratio ranges from −0.01 to 0.01 and the cross-sectional time series incremental R^2 is 0.01. The adjusted R^2 of the model that includes the long-term debt ratio (along with control variables) is greater than the adjusted R^2 of the model that just includes the control variables only in 1995 and 1997. The incremental R^2 of the total debt

Table 5.   Test for Long-Term Debt Ratio (1991–2004).

Market value $= \beta_0 + \beta_1 \text{Equity} + \beta_2 \text{Earnings} + \beta_3 \text{LTDR} + \varepsilon$

Year	β_0	β_1	β_2	β_3	Adj. R^2
1991	46.82	2.38	4.85	−85.63	0.75
	(22.28)	(0.38)	(2.14)	(67.11)	
1992	35.61	2.55	6.48	−85.08	0.71
	(29.20)	(0.54)	(3.27)	(89.53)	
1993	33.99	2.36	5.29	−72.32	0.60
	(25.56)	(0.43)	(2.38)	(85.03)	
1994	21.22	1.42	8.54	33.84	0.58
	(22.48)	(0.29)	(2.05)	(79.05)	
1995	−41.12	2.96	6.46	146.41*	0.75
	(22.36)	(0.29)	(1.41)	(60.20)	
1996	10.04	1.74	6.27	4.60	0.76
	(17.64)	(0.18)	(1.10)	(56.66)	
1997	−18.22	2.08	2.46	161.40*	0.75
	(23.05)	(0.19)	(1.15)	(65.39)	
1998	−12.15	1.23	6.56	110.55	0.66
	(29.86)	(0.21)	(1.22)	(76.14)	
1999	32.46	0.55	7.24	26.32	0.66
	(21.17)	(0.17)	(1.02)	(52.72)	
2000	28.42	1.17	4.26	90.88	0.54
	(29.79)	(0.24)	(1.18)	(72.87)	
2001	49.80	2.02	3.78	−21.09	0.70
	(38.33)	(0.25)	(1.27)	(77.51)	
2002	72.91	0.62	9.29	−85.74	0.72
	(40.23)	(0.30)	(1.72)	(106.25)	
2003	51.57	1.45	7.40	139.18	0.71
	(59.77)	(0.36)	(2.22)	(140.40)	
2004	139.70	0.31	16.71	53.58	0.75
	(78.81)	(0.40)	(2.54)	(169.64)	

Note: Long-term debt ratio, calculated by dividing long-term debt into total assets. Standard errors are reported in parentheses.
*Significant at 5% level.

ratio ranges from −0.01 to 0.03 and the cross-sectional time series incremental R^2 is 0.01. The adjusted R^2 of the model that includes the total debt ratio (along with control variables) is greater than the adjusted R^2 of the model that just includes the control variables only in 1994 and 1997. Formal Wilcoxon and T tests suggest Equit + Earnings (EE), EE + STDR, EE + LTDR and EE + TDR are not statistically different at all reasonable significance level.

Table 6.   Test for Total Debt Ratio (1991–2004).

Market value = $\beta_0 + \beta_1$Equity + β_2Earnings + β_3TDR + ε

Year	β_0	β_1	β_2	β_3	Adj. R^2
1991	52.37 (33.16)	2.33 (0.39)	5.12 (2.13)	−42.14 (49.29)	0.75
1992	59.21 (39.94)	2.55 (0.53)	6.22 (3.27)	−90.57 (72.07)	0.71
1993	46.81 (34.81)	2.32 (0.43)	5.41 (2.36)	−55.60 (59.83)	0.60
1994	−41.91 (27.94)	1.61 (0.29)	9.18 (1.94)	129.38* (42.65)	0.62
1995	−30.05 (23.18)	2.97 (0.29)	6.03 (1.42)	39.96 (25.38)	0.74
1996	−9.29 (19.42)	1.77 (0.18)	6.42 (1.10)	37.30 (26.15)	0.77
1997	−35.31 (30.00)	2.09 (0.19)	2.62 (1.16)	99.11* (43.39)	0.75
1998	11.50 (26.42)	1.17 (0.21)	6.56 (1.23)	13.62 (25.09)	0.66
1999	37.36 (18.95)	0.53 (0.17)	7.27 (1.02)	4.38 (17.86)	0.66
2000	50.73 (28.73)	1.14 (0.25)	4.09 (1.18)	5.21 (24.78)	0.53
2001	27.62 (40.96)	2.06 (0.25)	3.80 (1.27)	19.65 (37.84)	0.70
2002	58.98 (38.07)	0.70 (0.28)	8.91 (1.64)	−15.46 (39.47)	0.71
2003	86.80 (59.19)	1.41 (0.37)	7.27 (2.23)	11.12 (58.35)	0.71
2004	109.01 (114.24)	0.35 (0.41)	16.53 (2.55)	71.97 (148.39)	0.75

Note: TDR: Total debt ratio, calculated by dividing total liability into total assets. Standard errors are reported in parentheses.
*Significant at 5% level.

CONCLUSIONS AND RECOMMENDATIONS FOR FUTURE RESEARCH

It appears from the results that both variables, book value of equity and earnings, are very important for the market valuation of firm equity. The adjusted R^2 ranged from 0.54 to 0.77. Therefore, there is no reason to exclude either book value of equity or earnings as control variables while

176   ARUN UPNEJA AND NAN HUA

Table 7.   Market Value of Firm on Equity, Income from Operations.

| Year | Adjusted R^2 [a] | | | | No. of Incremental Information [b] | | |
	Equit + Earnings (EE)	EE + STDR	EE + LTDR	EE + TDR	Incremental R^2 of STDR	Incremental R^2 of LTDR	Incremental R^2 of TDR
1991	0.75	0.75	0.75	0.75	0.00	0.00	0.00
1992	0.71	0.70	0.71	0.71	−0.01	0.00	0.00
1993	0.60	0.60	0.60	0.60	0.00	0.00	0.00
1994	0.59	0.62	0.58	0.62	0.03	−0.01	0.03
1995	0.74	0.74	0.75	0.74	0.00	0.01	0.00
1996	0.77	0.77	0.76	0.77	0.00	−0.01	0.00
1997	0.74	0.74	0.75	0.75	0.00	0.01	0.01
1998	0.66	0.66	0.66	0.66	0.00	0.00	0.00
1999	0.67	0.66	0.66	0.66	−0.01	−0.01	−0.01
2000	0.54	0.53	0.54	0.53	−0.01	0.00	−0.01
2001	0.70	0.70	0.70	0.70	0.00	0.00	0.00
2002	0.72	0.71	0.72	0.71	−0.01	0.00	−0.01
2003	0.71	0.71	0.71	0.71	0.00	0.00	0.00
2004	0.76	0.75	0.75	0.75	−0.01	−0.01	−0.01
All years	0.67	0.67	0.68	0.68	0.00	0.01	0.01

Note: EE: Regression equation with both equity and earnings from continuing operations; STDR: short term debt ratio; LTDR: long term debt ratio; TDR: total debt ratio.
[a]Both Wilcoxon and T-tests suggest Equity + Earnings (EE), EE + STDR, EE + LTDR and EE + TDR are not statistically different at all reasonable significance level.
[b]Please see Table 2 for a definition of incremental R^2.

doing research on stock valuation. For example, it is commonly believed that restaurants do well when the economy is doing well. Book values of equity and earnings have to be controlled for when evaluating the impact of economic factors on firm value. Therefore, the inclusion of "economic conditions variable" to predict the market value of restaurant firms would be one extension of this line of research. These results provide the baseline numbers for evaluating the information content of other relevant variables.

The results in this paper also provide a way to evaluate the value-relevance of other variables in predicting market value of restaurant firms. The claim is that for a variable to be value relevant, it has to provide information content beyond what is already contained in the book value of equity and earnings. Operationally, this is achieved by including potential value-relevant variables in the model to evaluate if there is a significant increase in the adjusted R^2.

One of the drawbacks of this research is that it is ex-post research, i.e., both the dependent and the independent variables are measured at year-end.

In other words, it is known already that net income and equity are both significantly related to market value of the firm. The next phase of this line of research is to find those variables that help predict the income for next year. For example, given that the health of the economy is significantly related to financial performance of the firms, what is the association between leading indicators of the economy and financial performance of the restaurant industry?

REFERENCES

Ball, R., & Brown, P. (1969). An empirical evaluation of accounting income numbers. *Journal of Accounting Research, 6*, 159–178.

Barth, M., Beaver, W., & Landsman, W. (1997). *Relative valuation roles of equity book value and net income as a function of financial health.* Unpublished manuscript, Stanford University.

Barth, M. E., & Kallapur, S. (1995). *The effects of cross-sectional scale differences on regression results in empirical accounting research.* Unpublished manuscript, Stanford University.

Beaver, W., Kettler, P., & Scholes, M. (1970). The association between market determined and accounting determined risk measures. *The Accounting Review, XLV*(4), 654–682.

Berger, P., Ofek, E., & Swary, I. (1996). Investor valuation of the abandonment option. *Journal of Financial Economics, 42*, 257–287.

Brealey, R., & Myers, S. (1984). *Principles of corporate finance* (2nd ed.). New York: McGraw-Hill.

Burgstahler, D. C., & Dichev, I. D. (1997). Earnings, adaptation and equity value. *The Accounting Review, 72*, 187–215.

Collins, D. W., Maydew, E. L., & Weiss, I. S. (1997). Changes in the value-relevance of earnings and book values over the past forty years. *Journal of Accounting & Economics, 24*, 9–67.

Collins, W., & Xie, H. (1999). Equity valuation and negative earnings: The role of book value of equity. *Accounting Review, 74*, 29–61.

Dechow, P. (1994). Accounting earnings and cash flows as measures of firm performance: The role of accounting accruals. *Journal of Accounting and Economics, 18*, 3–42.

Hayn, C. (1995). The information content of losses. *Journal of Accounting and Economics, 20*, 125–153.

Jan, C., & Ou, J. (1995). *The role of negative earnings in the evaluation of equity stocks.* Unpublished manuscript, New York University and Santa Clara University.

Kester, C. W. (1986). Capital and ownership structure: A comparison of United States and Japanese manufacturing corporations. *Financial Management, 15*, 97–113.

Kim, W. (1997). The determinants of capital structure choice in the US restaurant industry. *Tourism Economics, 3*, 329–340.

Marler, J. H. (1993). Off balance sheet lease financing in the restaurant industry. *Journal of Hospitality Financial Management, 3*(1), 15–28.

Marsh, P. (1982). The choice between equity and debt: An empirical study. *Journal of Finance, 37*, 121–144.

Maydew, E. (1993). *An empirical evaluation of earnings and book values in security valuation.* Unpublished manuscript, University of Iowa.

Myers, S. C. (1984). The capital structure puzzle. *Journal of Finance, 39*, 575–592.

Ohlson, J. (1994). *Earnings, book value, and dividends in equity valuation.* Unpublished manuscript, Columbia University.

Ou, J., & Penman, S. (1989). Financial statement analysis and the prediction of stock returns. *Journal of Accounting and Economics, 11,* 295–329.

Rajan, R. G., & Zingales, L. (1995). What do we know about capital structure? Some evidence from international data. *Journal of Finance, 50,* 1421–1460.

Taggart, R. A. (1977). A model of corporate financing decisions. *Journal of Finance, 32,* 1467–1484.

Upneja, A., & Dalbor, M. (1999). An examination of leasing policy, tax rates, and financial stability in the restaurant industry. *Journal of Hospitality & Tourism Research, 23,* 85–99.

White, H. (1980). A heteroskedasticity-consistent covariance matrix estimator and a direct test for heteroskedasticity. *Econometrica, 48,* 817–838.

THE RELATIONSHIP AMONG TRUSTWORTHINESS, TIME LAPSE, AND ONLINE RESERVATION IN THE HOSPITALITY AND TOURISM INDUSTRY

David Y. Chang, France Bélanger and Muzaffer Uysal

ABSTRACT

Internet technology has changed the way information is distributed and the way people do business in the industry. Its impacts have been well studied, but the time element seems to be ignored for the investigation of risks taken and trustworthiness held by online shoppers. The time element should be included because pre-travel plans are usually made and a time lapse does exist between "the time a reservation is made" and "the time the reservation is confirmed." This study proposes an online purchasing model to investigate the relationships among trustworthiness, time lapse, and online reservation activities. A significant correlation was found between trustworthiness and online reservations but despite such significance, time lapse neither sways the trustworthiness nor leads to low reservation retention.

Advances in Hospitality and Leisure, Volume 2, 179–198
ISSN: 1745-3542/doi:10.1016/S1745-3542(05)02009-6

INTRODUCTION

Internet technology is one of the greatest innovations to the economy simply because it changes the way information is formed and how it circulates. The hospitality and tourism industry has been receptive to the benefits offered by such an innovation (O'Connor, 1999), but it also faces a growing challenge brought by the savvy online shoppers who quickly adapt to the usage of the Internet technology for information gathering and comparison to search for a better business deal.

This type of transformation was actually foreseen back by Froschl and Werthner (1997) who studied the ongoing changes for the travel segment in relation to the way the hospitality and tourism industry implements information technology (IT). They concluded that travel business "is an information business," "is undergoing a structural change," and "is going electronic." These remarks seem to provide a good notation for the change in today's competition driven by the Internet technology since the travel business is information-oriented and the Internet is a non-boundary media being widely adopted as the common platform for information transmission. Inevitably, the nature, frequency, and concentration of travelers' booking activities are altered along with the adoption of Internet technology simply because of the intensity of information involved.

Information indeed links travel business and IT together seamlessly. As Internet technology, one kind of IT, expedites the way product or price information flows, the way people do business in the hospitality and tourism industry must be changed as well. Travelers need information to decide whether or not to purchase or re-purchase products and/or services before they actually move in a geographical distance to consume them. Today, many of them are dependent on the Internet technology to gather information for such a decision making. According to the TIA (Travel Industry Association) report, as of 2003 there were 64 million adults in the US gone online for travel information.

Using Internet technology not only is a convenient way to search information for travel planning (Suskind, Mark, Bonn, & Dev, 2003; Weber & Roehl, 1999; Kierzkowski, McQuade, Waitman, & Zeisser, 1996), but also is a major means for potential travelers to seek bargains and better deals (Tofa, 1998). A number of studies have investigated the impacts of Internet technology in the hospitality and tourism industry but none has tried to explore the risk issues taken by the online shoppers from the perspective of *trustworthiness*. As noted by many researchers, Internet shopping involves more uncertainty and risk than traditional shopping simply because of the way information transmits. When gathering and analyzing the travel information provided by an Internet vendor, a shopper's perception of *trustworthiness* in the vendor plays a critical role. It is the authors' opinion that an Internet vendor gets selected by a savvy online shopper because the vendor is *trusted* to have the capability in handling the risk-related issues pertaining to online business.

Apparently, if an Internet vendor has the capability to cope with the risks associated with the Internet technology, and can successfully demonstrate such a capability to the public that it can minimize the risks pertinent to online booking or shopping activities, it can likely increase an online shopper's confidence level in doing online business with the company. Once this confidence level is established and sustained consistently, the Internet vendor is likely to win and accumulate the online shopper's trustworthiness. The researchers believe that if an online shopper has an unbreakable trustworthiness in an Internet vendor, he or she would perceive the risk associated with online booking or shopping activities as a tiny issue when doing business with that vendor. However, the risk issue relative to online businesses in the hospitality and tourism industry should be studied together with the *time* element because travelers tend to make travel plans before the actual trips take place. Indubitably, there is "a period of time" between "the time the reservation is made" and "the time the reservation is confirmed." Whether or not this "period of time," a waiting time, changes online shoppers' trustworthiness in their Internet vendors becomes an important issue in studying technology topic for the field of hospitality and tourism management.

Primarily, this study attempts to answer two research questions: (1) Do previously studied antecedents of trustworthiness in the field of electronic commerce (e-commerce) hold in the context of the field of the hospitality and tourism? (2) Will "time lapse" alter an online shopper's trustworthiness in an Internet vendor and further influence his or her online booking activities? To answer these questions, an online purchasing model is proposed to investigate the relationships among online shoppers' trustworthiness, the time lapse that they waited, and their shopping or booking activities.

The paper starts by the review of the contemporary changes driven by the Internet technology with key related literature, followed by a discussion about the online purchasing model proposed, illustrating how its constructs are defined and obtained, and then moves to the discussions of methodology and results. The research concludes with some comments and discussions about the overall findings and the necessity of including the time element in IT-related studies. The findings are expected to be exploratory in hopes of serving for a stepping stone for future research since the issues discussed were not yet fully studied in the field of hospitality and tourism management.

LITERATURE REVIEW

As well recognized by the world, the Internet-enabled business has spurred growth and prosperity in the global economy. This effect can be realized and sustained through the growth of the online retail sales in recent years. For example, according to Forrester Research Inc., online retail sales grew 15% to $51.35 billion in 2001, 48% to $76 billion in 2002, and reached $95.76 billion in 2003, a growth of 26% from previous year. This figure is expected to continue increasing and reaches near $230 billion accounting for 10% of total US retail sales by 2008 and climbs to $316 billion by 2010. In its recent report (August 2004), the growing population of online shopping households combined with retailer innovations and site improvements will give the online business a very promising future and drive it to account for 12% of total retail sales in 2010, up from nearly 7% in 2004. Furthermore, analysts believe that between this year and 2010, online sale is expected to grow at a 14% compound annual growth rate.

The online shopping population and retail sales reported above give a quick glance at the changes driven by Internet technology. These figures also provide a perspective for the impacts caused by the Internet on hospitality and tourism business since the industry has been rated among the top three product or service categories purchased via the Internet since 1996 (Tweney, 1997). For the travel-related online sales alone, the research firm eMarketer projected in October 2003 that worldwide online travel bookings in the US will account for 30% of worldwide travel bookings by 2005. Moreover, TIA reported that as of 2003, 42.2 million travelers were "online travel bookers," who have actually made travel purchases online, and 29% of them made all of their travel purchases or reservations online, rising 6 percentage points since 2002.

In some specific studies focusing on the travel segment of the hospitality and tourism industry, the statistics are also very remarkable. According to the studies of Forrester Research, approximately 30 million US web travel households will buy travel online this year, for which they will spend $53 billion and this will reach 46.4 million households, spending nearly $111 billion. As the online booking captures more of leisure travelers' spending, it will snag 59% of the travelers' budgets this year for travel plans including vacation packages, cruises, and hotels and are poised for another greater growth (Harteveldt, Leaver, & Yuen, 2004). eMarketer's report further estimates that online travel sales in the travel segment will constitute approximately 40% of all online business-to-consumer (B2C) commerce in the US. Moreover, Forrester Research (September 2004) recently predicted that, including all segments of the hospitality and tourism industry, the Internet will produce 34% of revenues in 2009, yielding a projected $40.1 billion for the industry. These reports suggest that travel-related online shopping business in the hospitality and tourism industry is expected to continue to be the leading revenue producer among all online business segments.

Therefore, a clear message is received that online business in the hospitality and tourism industry has been and will continue to be very strong. It is no secret that Internet shopping removes many geographic barriers between customers and merchants and thus establishes new distant merchant–customer relationships that are different from those in the traditional business model. Other than acclaiming the favorable future of the online business, an Internet vendor should demonstrate its competency in dealing with online shopping or booking activities. The online shopper's trustworthiness emerges to be important as product, service, and price information provided on the Internet by other competitors can be easily delivered to the online shoppers. As a possible result, without putting trustworthiness into the equation of doing online business, an online shopper's purchasing decision might be easily changed in the last minute because of the newly attractive information received.

Froschl and Werthner's (1997) remarks mentioned earlier (i.e., information business, undergoing a structural change, and business goes electronic), directly link the impacts of IT to the nature of the business in the hospitality and tourism industry. Indeed, their arguments provided explanations for the exciting figures estimated by the research organizations discussed earlier and indicated how the hospitality and tourism business has been changing under the force driving change of IT. Their findings are just consistent with and reinforce the work of Schertler, Schmid, Tjoa, and Werthner (1994), who have been regarding hospitality and tourism as an information business since 1994. Recent literature also found that because of the dependence of the information and the Internet technology, the pricing structure of the industry "nearly transparent to the customer" (Carroll & Siguaw, 2003) and the last-minute deals are now considerably easier to find because they are offered by a number of Internet vendors (Shapiro, 2003).

Furthermore, Internet vendors, including the own websites of the service providers, not only acknowledge the changes described earlier but also promote them through their marketing policies. Online shoppers thus quickly learn how to strike a better deal through the comparison of the product and price information provided on the Internet. Better deal or lower price is believed to be a major incentive for online shoppers. Olearchik (2003) found that "price" is the factor resulting in the explosion of Internet booking. Evidently, because product and price information are made available on the Internet, their easy accessibility has made online business in the hospitality and tourism industry more competitive. Shaw (2002) had noticed that the use of the online booking, especially through the third-party websites, has made the yield management very complex for the industry.

As known, most travelers have to plan their trips first and then leave their original environment to move to a geographically distant place to experience the products and services booked in the plans. In other words, a pre-travel planning must be conducted, and sufficient and accurate product and price information can make this planning easier and future trip more pleasant. The Internet thus became the most convenient platform for this type of planning simply because it offers abundant product and price information.

Therefore, a business relationship can be established as early as an online shopper books products and services on the Internet. However, such a relationship can still possibly be changed because it is just a result of the pre-travel planning process. Not only it can be changed, it can also be cancelled. In other words, it creates a time lapse between "the reservation booked" and "further confirmation made." This time lapse is the time element discussed earlier and might be a unique factor distinguishing the e-commerce activities of the hospitality and tourism industry from others.

It is the author's opinion that Internet vendors should not assume that online shoppers are loyal and static and simplify the sophistication and complexity of their travel planning process. Imaging how fast and easy a traveler can alter his or her travel plan if other product and price information is available throughout the time waiting for the plan to be executed or confirmed.

AN ONLINE PURCHASING MODEL

Travelers cannot physically check the quality of a product or service before making a purchase, or monitor the safety and security of sending sensitive personal and financial information through the Internet to a party whose behaviors and motives may be hard to predict. Therefore, when selecting an

Internet vendor for online shopping, travelers usually are taking a certain degree of risk and would like to foresee such a risk in any possible way they can in order to assess this vendor thoroughly and avoid any potential hazards. This risk is viewed as a mixture of various variables, such as a company's characteristics, technology competencies, quality of product and/or service offered, environmental and/or industry events, etc. Overall, these variables are termed "risk factors" in the study.

The concept of risk is not new and indeed has been discussed in various scales depending on the research domains and objectives in different disciplines. It is an extremely complicated issue in strategic management as well as in financial management. Regardless, as briefly mentioned earlier, if an Internet vendor can consistently demonstrate its capability of handling the *risk factors* well to the public, it can likely increase an online shopper's confidence level about doing online business with it. As a result, the Internet vendor can win and accumulate the online shopper's trustworthiness. Once an online shopper has an unbreakable trust in an Internet vendor, he or she would feel comfortable to depend on the information provided by the vendor for travel planning and might not consider the risk factors as seriously as do other new shoppers. Over time, this would result in establishing an even stronger trustworthiness.

The question is: As the actual travel date nears, how strong can this trustworthiness be? Can it be defeated by other more attractive product and price information offered by other Internet vendors? In other words, the time lapse discussed earlier could be a possible factor causing any change to the reservation made in today's information world and should be studied. Fig. 1 illustrates a research model for this attempt and tries to address the relationships among trustworthiness, time lapse, and online shopping or booking activities.

Trustworthiness (T)

The new distant relationships constructed by Internet technology bring in a salient issue, online shopper's trustworthiness, for the online business in the hospitality and tourism industry. Although the importance of trust is widely recognized, there is widespread disagreement about its definition and characteristics. Bélanger, Hiller, and Smith (2002) had defined trustworthiness in e-commerce as "the beliefs about whether Web merchants possess qualities that make them deserving of trust " (p. 253). By adopting their definition, in this study, the *trustworthiness* is defined as *the shopper's perception of*

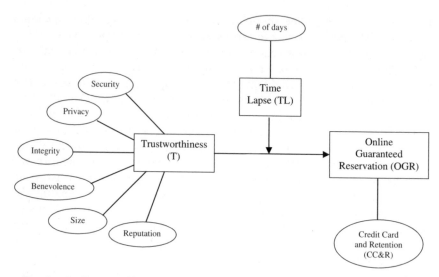

Fig. 1. An Internet Shopping Model in the Hospitality and Tourism Industry.

confidence in online purchase or booking activities and such a perception of
confidence is the belief possessed by the online shopper about the capability of
the Internet vendors conducting online business. In other words, this perception or belief is the confidence an online shopper has about *what* and *how* the
products and/or services will be sold online by an Internet vendor. Chang,
Madanoglu, and Chu (2003) conducted a perception study and found that
there are four types of online shoppers in the hospitality and tourism industry: image-orientated shoppers, practical shoppers, sentimental shoppers, and defensive shoppers. They were categorized according to the
different perceptions and beliefs online shoppers hold.

In this study, the researchers focus on the issue of trust and believe that
trustworthiness overall is a variable related to the holistic online shopping
experience. It needs to be developed and accumulated over time on the basis
of the perception of confidence that exists in the four aspects of relationships:
human-to-human, human-to-machine, human-to-organization, and organi-
zation-to-organization. Given that the interest of the study is under the scope
of B2C e-commerce, the research domain of the study fits with the categories
of human-to-machine and human-to-organization (i.e., the Internet vendor).

In the literature discussing human–computer interface and ergonomics, trust
is identified as a factor affecting human choice of the use of computerized

systems (Muir, 1997). Using Internet technology to shop online is an activity that necessarily entails primary interactions with computer systems. In some sense, an online reservation system with which an online shopper interacts is analogous to the salesperson in a traditional shop. An online shopper's perception of confidence in this computerized medium (salesperson) is likely to affect his or her trust in the online shopping activities. Lee and Moray (1992) stated that human trust in an automated or computerized system depends on three factors: (1) the perceived technical competence of the systems, (2) the perceived performance level of the system, and (3) the human operator's understanding of the underlying characteristics and processes governing the system's behavior. They defined technical competence of a system as its ability to perform the tasks it is supposed to perform, while performance level includes such parameters as speed, reliability, and availability.

The first two factors can be viewed together as the capability an Internet vendor has in performing the security and privacy control. According to Cheung and Lee (2001), the *security* control refers to the Internet vendors' ability to fulfill security requirements, such as authentication, encryption, and non-repudiation. The *privacy* control is conceived as an Internet vendor's ability in protecting an online shopper's personal information collected from its electronic transactions from unauthorized use or disclosure. Thus, the *security* and *privacy* are important elements in online shopping activities and are included in the research model as variables of the trustworthiness.

The third factor suggested by Lee and Moray (1992) was not well defined in their study due to its self-explanatory nature. It is not included in the model because of the lack of its explanation. However, the model included some other variables that have been studied by a long line of research in the field of e-commerce for the investigation of the formation of trustworthiness. One of the typical studies is the work of Mayer, Davis, & Schoorman (1995) in which three factors – ability, integrity, and benevolence – were found consistently related to trust. The ability factor is more technical-oriented and is very close to the capability of handling security and privacy control discussed earlier. Hence, it is redundant to have it included in the model. However, the other two factors – integrity and benevolence – are too important to be excluded. According to Mayer et al. (1995), *integrity* includes honesty and sincerity, and *benevolence* means favorable motives without acting opportunistically or manipulatively. These definitions are adopted for the study as they are consistent with the literature reviewed earlier.

Therefore, these four variables (i.e., *security, privacy, integrity*, and *benevolence*) are believed to have influence on an online shopper's perception

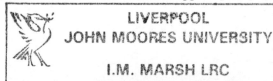

of confidence in an online shopping medium and thus can affect the process of building up the online shopper's trustworthiness in an Internet vendor. However, literature also found that other factors such as *size* and *reputation* can also impact the degree of trust in an Internet vendor (Jarvenpaa, Tractinsky, & Vitale, 2000; Chang & Weaver, 2003). The lack of previous experience or comments of other shoppers can make online shoppers weigh in size and reputation in their assessment of the risk taken in conducting online purchase with an Internet vendor. Jarvenpaa et al. (2000) found that an online shopper's trust in an Internet vendor is positively related to a company's size that the shopper perceived. Chang and Weaver (2003) also found that size and reputation are perceived as two most important factors in online shopping activities in the field of hospitality and tourism.

In the research, *size* is defined as the consumer's perception of the company's size, not necessary the actual size. The literature suggests that a company's size assist online shoppers in forming their impressions regarding the concern of trust of an organization. According to Doney and Cannon (1997), online buyers use size as a signal to know if an online seller can be trusted. They found that online shoppers tend to believe that large organizational size comes from high volume of sales, which implies that other buyers trust the organization and have conducted business successfully with it. Online shoppers also believe that large size signals that an Internet vendor must have the necessary expertise and resources to support its online reservation systems including customer and technical services; and, that the vendor is able to absorb the risk of product failure and to compensate buyers accordingly (Chow & Holden, 1997; Chang & Weaver, 2003). Therefore, size should be regarded as an important factor in the process of an online shopper building trustworthiness toward an Internet vendor.

Another factor *reputation* is defined as the extent to which online shoppers believe that an Internet vendor is honest and concerned about its customers (Doney & Cannon, 1997). The marketing literature suggests that reputation is a valuable asset that requires a long-term investment of resources, effort, and attention to customer relationships (Smith & Barclay, 1997; Chang & Weaver, 2003). A good reputation signals past forbearance from opportunism (Smith & Barclay, 1997). In the industrial buyer context, the seller's reputation has been positively related to the buyer's trust in the seller (Anderson & Weitz, 1989; Ganesan, 1994). Hence, reputation is selected as it can influence the process of the formation of trustworthiness in online shopping activities.

All these six variables, *security, privacy, integrity, benevolence, size*, and *reputation*, are considered important elements that can affect an online shopper's trustworthiness in an Internet vendor, and further influence the decision-making process to reach a final purchasing decision.

Time Lapse (TL)

The recent study conducted by Bhatnagar and Ghose (2004) indicated that online shoppers' search patterns and duration depend on the type of information they seek. While reiterating and recognizing the importance of information for online business, they did not investigate the time element in their research. However, as known from the literature, to hospitality and tourism business, most travels tend to make travel plans ahead of time and thus it creates "a period of time." As discussed earlier, this type of time element should not be ignored in studying online shopping activities. In this study, the "a period of time" is termed *time lapse*.

Time lapse is defined as "the certain period of time" exists between "*the reservation*" and "*the affirmation*" of an online booking activity. The meaning of *the reservation* is self-explanatory. It simply represents the result of the information search and booking activities. *The affirmation* is referred as the point the online shopper gives his or her credit card information to hold what was reserved or purchased earlier. However, because most Internet vendors ask for credit card information at the time the reservation was being made (most likely at the end of the reservation process), *the certain period of time* in this case would be very little (almost none). Therefore, *the affirmation* should also consider the action of cancellation for a confirmed reservation and accept other deal offered by other Internet vendor. In other words, affirmation has two meanings in this study: it either *confirms the original booking* or *replaces the original confirmed booking with other Internet vendor's offer*.

Whether or not an actual consumption of the booking occurs or a penalty of cancellation is charged is not a concern of the study. It is the authors' opinion that when an online shopper is willing to release his or her sensitive credit card information over the Internet to confirm the reservation booked earlier, there must be a degree of trustworthiness involved. Similarly, if an online shopper is willing to pay penalty and cancels the confirmed reservation and goes to other Internet vendor, the degree of trustworthiness of the shopper is questionable.

This reasoning is based on the role of information discussed earlier in the travel business. Because information, such as better price or better products, offered by other Internet vendors is ramping around in the Internet and is likely to be delivered to online shoppers, if an online shopper waits a period of time and still decides to release his or her credit card information to confirm and keep the booking in exchange for the products and service that are promised to be provided later, there must be a certain amount of trust-worthiness held by the online shopper toward the Internet vendor selected.

Although it is logically understandable, it is implausible for one to assume that as the travel time approaches, the number of possible future search for a better deal diminishes, especially given the consideration of the con-venience and abundant information available on the Internet. It is also inappropriate to assume that online shoppers are unsophisticated or have not fully adapted to the Internet technology and simplify the complexity of a traveler's pre-travel planning process. The time element, *time lapse*, certainly is an important factor for the study of risk and trustworthiness in online purchasing activities and should be included in the model.

Online Guaranteed Reservation (OGR)

In the field of hospitality and tourism, reservation is a very important ac-tivity as the carrying capacity is likely to be limited in any hotel, restaurant, airplane, or tourist destination. The reservation can be conducted and formed in various ways, but from the perspective of law it is considered a contract between the buyer and the seller. For example, a contract for a room between an innkeeper and a guest must satisfy the essential elements – contractual capacity, mutuality, legality, consideration, proper form, and genuine consent (Cournoyer, Marshall, & Morris, 1999).

This contract is a mutual agreement and the agreement can take many forms, including walk-in, confirmed reservation, guaranteed reservation, pre-paid reservation, and blank reservation. Once a reservation is made and confirmed, it is valid and binds the service provider to provide the service in the right format that was mutually agreed with. If the service provider cannot accommodate due to the overbooking or other reasons, it will be in breach of contract and liable for damages (Cournoyer et al., 1999).

One of these forms, *guaranteed reservation*, especially fits the research topic. In the traditional shopping activities, it is defined as *the guest promises to pay for the products or services reserved (e.g., a hotel room), even if the guest never takes possession of it* (Cournoyer et al., 1999). This definition harmonizes the definition of time lapse discussed earlier: as long as an online shopper gives credit card information to confirm the reservation made ear-lier, an *online guaranteed reservation* is established. In the case the time lapse is almost none as discussed, an *online guaranteed reservation* can also be established when an online shopper retains the confirmed reservation. In both cases, a certain degree of trustworthiness is seen.

Therefore, the definition of *online guaranteed reservation* (OGR) emerges: it is established when an online shopper releases the credit card information to confirm and further retain (CC&R) the reservation. Using it as the threshold, this study can investigate the possible effect of time lapse on trustworthiness simply because it puts a stop on the waiting time between *the action of booking* (i.e., the reservation) and *the action of affirmation*, which are the two points of time used to measure the time lapse.

METHODOLOGY

As discussed earlier, the study attempts to answer two research questions: (1) Do previously studied antecedents of trustworthiness in the field of e-commerce hold in the context of the hospitality and tourism industry? (2) Will "time lapse" alter an online shopper's trustworthiness in an Internet vendor and further influence his or her online booking activities? To answer these questions, a model was proposed (Fig. 1) and a questionnaire was developed on the basis of the literature study to test the model.

The questionnaire consists of three parts: The first part deals with the respondents' online shopping and booking experience and the issue of time lapse (TL); the second part contains the statements regarding the six factors (e.g., integrity, benevolence, reputation, size, security, and privacy) that contribute to the respondent's trustworthiness (T) in the Internet vendors about his or her shopping and booking activities experienced; the last part of the survey includes general demographic questions.

Because the research is exploratory and is an attempt to investigate the unknown but possible influence of the time element in online booking activities for the field of hospitality and tourism management, convenient samples were used. The questionnaires were distributed to students on campus of a state university last year three weeks before and after the one-week Thanksgiving holiday. Only those who had experiences of making pre-travel plans and reservations on the Internet in the previous year were included in the study to accord the definition of online shoppers. The response rate was 87.9%.

The sample size for the study is 473 after excluding the outliers who made reservations more than 120 days before the OGR was established. The average time to complete the survey was between 8 to 10 minutes. Several statistical techniques were used to answer the research questions set forth in order to achieve the research objectives.

RESULTS

Some key descriptive information regarding the respondents was obtained (Table 1). Among the respondents who had made pre-travel plans and reservations online in the previous year, 49% were female. Approximately 70.3% of the respondents were between 18 and 25 years of age and 22.4% between 26 and 35. A great portion of the respondents (95.7%) believed that they have a very good computer literacy (rated 4 or 5 in the Semantic Differential scale). In addition, in the Likert-type scale of 1–5, 91.6% rated themselves as 4 or 5 indicating that they felt comfortable using the Internet for travel planning on their own. Of the respondents, 87.9% believed that if they want to they are capable of using an Internet technology even if there is no one around to show them how to use it.

In order to answer the first research question "do previously studied antecedents of trustworthiness hold in the context of the hospitality and tourism

Table 1. Key Descriptive Information of the Respondents.

	Scale	$N = 473$
Gender	Male	50.2%
	Female	49.4%
Age	Under 18	1.9%
	18–25	70.3%
	26–35	22.4%
	36–50	5.4%
Self-evaluation about having good computer literacy	Very good	48.3%
	—	47.4%
	—	3.1%
	—	1.2%
	Very poor	—
I would feel comfortable using the Internet for travel planning on my own	Strongly agree (= 5)	48.2%
	Agree	43.4%
	Neither agree or disagree	6.5%
	Disagree	1.2%
	Strongly disagree (= 1)	0.7%
I would be able to use an Internet application system even if there was no one around to show me how to use it	Strongly agree (= 5)	49.4%
	Agree	38.5%
	Neither agree or disagree	10.2%
	Disagree	1.3%
	Strongly disagree (= 1)	0.6%

industry," a multiple regression analysis was conducted. The six antecedents selected from the literature are "security," "privacy," "integrity," "benevolence," "size," and "reputation." The result of the multiple regression analysis (Table 2) shows that four elements are significant besides *benevolence* and *reputation*. However, the variance explained by these significant elements are relatively small ranging from 31% (*size*) to 19% (*security*) and the regression model can explain approximate only 34% of the variance in the overall perception of trustworthiness with regard to the pre-travel planning. Although the relationships among these four variables and the trustworthiness are significant, it does not seem strong enough overall. In addition, the negative value in *size* indicates a result that contradicts findings suggested in the literature. It is possible that online shoppers might believe that most Internet vendors are capable of handling online business using the common implementation of Internet technology regardless of size.

Although it was found that the respondents who did not establish an OGR accounted for only 18% and most of them retain it for the future trips, unfortunately the effect of the time element cannot be seen from this result. As the research is interested in knowing "whether or not the time lapse alters a consumer's trustworthiness in an Internet vendor and further influences the online booking activities," the time lapse (TL) is an important factor that needs to be addressed.

Therefore, the respondents were categorized into two groups according to the length of the TL reported. A cutoff point of 21 days was selected for this categorization on the basis of the inspection of the data frequency in which a pattern regarding the respondents' actions of affirmation was clearly seen.

Table 2. Multiple Regression Analysis (Stepwise method) – the Determinants of Trustworthiness for Online Travel Reservation.

Antecedents of Trustworthiness	B	Significance[*]	R^{2}[**]
(Constant)	2.53		
Security	0.313	0.002	0.191
Integrity	0.301	0.002	0.214
Privacy	0.292	0.005	0.286
Size	−0.184	0.009	0.310

Dependent variable: trustworthiness (T)
Independent variables: the six antecedents
Overalltrustworthiness = $2.53 + (0.31 * \text{Security}) + (0.30 * \text{Integrity}) + (0.29 * \text{Privacy}) - (0.18 * \text{Size})$
Adjusted $R^{2} = 0.343$

[*]$p < 0.01$.
[**]R^{2} of each element; independent variables: the six antecedents.

In addition, the cutoff point seems to divide the respondents into two groups with approximate equal number of samples: 47% ("less than or equal 21 days") vs. 53% ("more than 21 days"). The null hypothesis for the first research question can thus be developed as *There is no difference regarding reaching an online guaranteed reservation in the respondent's latest online travel planning in terms of the time lapse* and a χ^2 test of independence was called for the test of this hypothesis.

The assumption of expected frequency was met and the non-significant value of Pearson χ^2 suggests that the analysis failed to reject the null hypothesis (Table 3). Hence, the result indicates that there is *no* difference in making an OGR between the two groups of respondents after waiting a certain period of time – either they have waited for or less or more than 21 days.

However, it is the researchers' opinion that the differences between these two groups should be further investigated in order to validate the result of the χ^2 test for a more accurate interpretation. Therefore, a follow-up *t*-test was conducted. The value of means (Table 4) reveals that the responses were not much different in the perspective of the time lapse, which confirms the result of the χ^2 test. The result also suggests that the respondents' perceptions about the elements of the trustworthiness were not much different either. Only the elements *benevolence* and *size* were found significant indicating that they might have some influences on CC&R.

This result is interesting because it confirms the result of the regression analysis earlier about the impact of *size*, but also contradicts the finding about the *benevolence* in the same regression model. However, before reaching any inconsistent remark about the findings, one should direct attention to the value of means between the two groups who establish or did not establish the OGR (Yes vs. No). It appears that the difference is relatively small (3.02 vs. 2.98; Table 4). Therefore, the result of the multiple regression analysis indicating that *benevolence* is not a significant factor for trustworthiness should be considered valid.

Table 3. χ^2 Test of Independence for Hypothesis 1.

Time Lapse (TL)	Give Credit Card Information and Retain the Reservation (CC&R)	
	Yes %	No %
TL ≤21 days	79.4*	20.6**
TL >21 days	83.2	16.8

*Pearson χ^2 is 1.045 and $p = 0.30$.
**0 cells (0.0%) have expected count less than 5.

Table 4. Group Statistics and Independent Samples Test.

CC&R		N	Mean	Levene's Test	
				F	Significance
Security	Yes	388	3.64	0.760	0.324
	No	84	3.42		
Privacy	Yes	389	3.07	0.293	0.565
	No	84	3.05		
Integrity	Yes	389	3.36	1.365	0.247
	No	84	3.29		
Benevolence	Yes	389	3.02	6.671	0.008
	No	84	2.98		
Size	Yes	389	3.36	6.213	0.016
	No	84	3.33		
Reputation	Yes	389	3.29	1.323	0.232
	No	84	3.12		
Time lapse	Yes	389	35.54	0.017	0.888
	No	84	34.36		

Furthermore, the correlation between time lapse (TL) and trustworthiness (T) was found significant at the 0.012 probability level. This raises the possibility that variance of TL might be able to be explained by the six elements of T. To further ensure this interpretation is correct, a multiple regression analysis was again utilized. The result found illustrates that only *privacy* is significant at a level of 0.05 and *size* might also be significant at a level of 0.10. However, this regression model overall is weak and the six elements can explain only 22% of the variance in TL. This suggests that although the correlation of the trustworthiness and time lapse is significant, the period of time waited can *not* be significantly explained by the six elements of the trustworthiness.

CONCLUDING COMMENTS

Because Internet technology can expedite information transmission, it has been a significant force driving change to online business for the hospitality and tourism industry. An online shopper might be able to strike a better deal easily in the last minute for the travel plans prior to the actual trips. This study introduced the time element into the investigation of the trustworthiness held by an online shopper attempting to understand its effect for the pre-travel planning. The low correlation among the variables of the model increases the difficulty to conduct statistical analysis as well as to interpret the final results. However, by utilizing various univariate and bivariate statistic techniques, the study was able to obtain some exploratory results.

First of all, a significant relationship is found between trustworthiness and online guaranteed reservation. *Secondly*, although the correlation of trustworthiness and time lapse is found significant, time lapse does not significantly sway an online shopper's trustworthiness in an Internet vendor during the process of pre-travel planning. *Thirdly*, no evidence found indicates that time lapse will lead to a replacement of the original confirmed reservation with other deals offered by other Internet vendors. *Finally*, the scenario of "last-minute decision for a better deal" believed possibly exists in today's information economy (Shapiro, 2003; Carroll & Siguaw, 2003) is not found in the study.

Interestingly, one additional finding obtained from the study is that the frequency table evidently reveals that the period of time waited by the respondents in both groups (waited more than 21 days vs. waited less than 21 days) tends to center on some certain time spots: one week (12.3%), two weeks (14.6%), three weeks (18.3%), one month (i.e., four weeks or 30 days; 24.7%), and two months (i.e., 60 days; 15.8%). Although sporadic cases appear on various waiting periods, the counting of days using "week" or "month" as the unit for the "waiting time" or "deadline" set by the respondents themselves seems clear.

Moreover, the fact that 82% of the respondents have used Internet technology to make their pre-travel plans provides a promising future for online business in the hospitality and tourism industry. In addition, the individual's high confidence level about using Internet technology for the pre-travel planning suggests that Internet vendors perhaps is on the right track in developing their Internet-based systems. However, Internet vendors should also pay more attention to the way information is distributed – because if most online shoppers are found with little challenges in using Internet technology, it is conceivable that price and product information provided on the Internet can be easily gathered and compared. This will make online business more challenging and competitive.

DISCUSSIONS

The correlations among the elements of trustworthiness, time lapse, and credit card & retention were small resulting in a great challenge to analyze the data collected. It also diminishes the necessity of adopting other multivariate statistic techniques, such as path analysis or structural equation modeling for an in-depth analysis. One of the possible explanations is that the sample was collected before and after the one-week Thanksgiving break from the students on campus. The "latest pre-travel planning online" is likely to bind with the trip home for the Thanksgiving holiday. It is possible that the respondents were *determined* to return home for the holiday regardless. In other words, "the must-have trip" results in a high retention of the online guaranteed reservation. It also masks the *possible and real* influence of time lapse pertinent to the process of pre-travel planning and thus distorts the possible effect on trustworthiness that the research is interested in discovering. A future study interested in the similar subject should take this into consideration for better selections in sample frame and timing of data collection.

However, this study did raise the concern about the speed and the way information circulates through Internet technology. It is understandable that when lots of marketing information is automatically delivered to a traveler's e-mail and computer directly, the chance for one to receive a better deal on travel package is relatively high. Although the time element introduced in the research was found no influence on an online shopper's trustworthiness, because the dramatic competition is greatly driven by the force of IT for the hospitality and tourism industry, it is still an important topic deserving another empirical study with regard to any online shopping activities. One might find the long-standing concept of "loyal customer" is challenged.

REFERENCES

Anderson, E., & Weitz, E. (1989). Determinants of continuity in conventional industrial channel dyads. *Marketing Science, 8*, 310–323.

Bélanger, F., Hiller, J., & Smith, W. J. (2002). Trustworthiness in electronic commerce: The role of privacy, security, and site attributes. *Journal of Strategic Information Systems, 11*(December), 245–270.

Bhatnagar, A., & Ghose, S. (2004). An analysis of frequency and duration of search on the Internet. *Journal of Business, 77*(2), 311–320.

Carroll, B., & Siguaw, J. (2003). The evolution of electronic distribution: Effect on hotels and intermediaries. *Cornell Hotel and Restaurant Administration Quarterly, 44*(4), 38–50.

Chang, D. Y., Madanoglu, M., & Chu, Y. (2003). Toward e-commerce in the hospitality and tourism industry: An exploratory survey of consumers' perception. *Proceedings of the 2003 EuroCHRIE Congress* (pp. 14–18). Bad Honnef, Germany.

Chang, D. Y., & Weaver, P. A. (2003). The Use of online application systems in the hospitality and tourism industry: A satisfaction analysis. *Proceedings of Eighth Annual Graduate Education and Graduate Students Research Conference, USA*, (Vol. 8, pp. 43–47). Las Vegas, Nevada, USA.

Cheung, C. M. K., & Lee, M. K. O. (2001). Trust in Internet shopping: Instrument development and validation through classical and modern approaches. *Journal of Global Information Management, 9*(3), 23–35.

Chow, S., & Holden, R. (1997). Toward an understanding of loyalty: The moderating role of trust. *Journal of Managerial Issues, 9*(3), 275–298.

Cournoyer, M. G., Marshall, A. G., & Morris, K. L. (1999). *Hotel, restaurant, and travel law: A preventive approach* (5th ed.). New York: Delmar Publishers.

Doney, P. M., & Cannon, J. P. (1997). An examination of the nature of trust in buyer–seller relationships. *Journal of Marketing, 61*(2), 35–51.

Froschl, K. A., & Werthner, H. (1997). *Informed decision making in tourism management – closing the information circuit.* New York: Springer.

Ganesan, S. (1994). Determinants of long-term orientation in buyer–seller relationships. *Journal of Marketing, 58*(2), 1–19.

Harteveldt, H. H., Leaver, S., & Yuen, E. (2004). *Online leisure travel forecast 2004–2009.* Trend Report. Forrester Research Inc., <http://www.forrester.com>

Jarvenpaa, S. L., Tractinsky, N., & Vitale, M. (2000). Consumer trust in an Internet store. *Information Technology and Management, 1*, 45–71.

Kierzkowski, A., McQuade, S., Waitman, R., & Zeisser, M. (1996). Marketing to the digital consumer. *McKinsey Quarterly, 33*, 4–21.

Lee, M. K. O., & Moray, N. (1992). Trust, control strategies, and allocation of functions in human–machine systems. *Ergonomics, 35*, 1243–1270.

Mayer, R. C., Davis, S. F., & Schoorman, F. D. (1995). An integrative model of organizational trust. *Academy of Management Review, 20*(3), 709–734.

Muir, B. M. (1997). Trust between humans and machines, and design of decision aids. *International Journal of Man–Machine Studies, 27*, 527–539.

O'Connor, P. (1999). *Electronics information distribution in tourism and hospitality.* Oxford, UK: CAB International.

Olearchik, J. (2003). Increasingly Internet. *Travel Agent, 311*(7), 76.

Schertler, W., Schmid, B., Tjoa, A. M., & Werthner, H. (1994). *Information and communication technologies in tourism.* New York: Springer.

Shapiro, M. (2003). Booking last minute: A primer. *The Washington Post,* July 20, TRAVEL, P01.

Shaw, R. (2002). Hoteliers use independent web sites to fill empty rooms. *Hotel & Motel Management, 217*(12), 1–3.

Smith, J. B., & Barclay, D. W. (1997). The effects of organizational differences and trust on the effectiveness of selling partner relationships. *Journal of Marketing, 61*, 3–21.

Suskind, A., Mark, M., Bonn, A., & Dev, C. S. (2003). To look or book: An examination of consumers' apprehensiveness toward Internet use. *Journal of Travel Research, 41*, 256–264.

Tofa, A. (1998). Why book on line? One view. *Travel Weekly, 57*(45), 4–5.

Tweney, D. (1997). Making money on the web: What is really working? *InfoWorld, 19*(36), 63–64.

Weber, K., & Roehl, W. S. (1999). Profiling people searching for and purchasing travel products on the World Wide Web. *Journal of Travel Research, 37*(3), 291–298.

YOUTH PATRONS' TRIP PREFERENCES AND PERCEPTIONS OF ACCOMMODATIONS IN SWITZERLAND

Colin Johnson, Thouraya Gherissi Labben and
Joseph S. Chen

ABSTRACT

*This research compares youth tourists' trip preferences and their percep-
tions of accommodation in Switzerland among visitors staying at three
different types of properties (e.g., hard budget, budget, and mid-sector).
Attractive price was found to be the most critical reason for the selection
of accommodation for those staying at hard budget properties. Proximity
to points of interest represents the main reason for choosing budget and
mid-sector accommodations. When examining the differences in preferences for eating outlets, the respondents from the mid-sector lodging facilities prefer full-service restaurants while the other groups of visitors
prefer to use self-service eateries. The study further finds that the youth
guests of hard budget properties express reluctance in joining evening
activities that are fee-paying. Managerial implications along with suggestions for future study are provided in the conclusion.*

Advances in Hospitality and Leisure, Volume 2, 199–211
Copyright © 2006 by Elsevier Ltd.
All rights of reproduction in any form reserved
ISSN: 1745-3542/doi:10.1016/S1745-3542(05)02010-2

INTRODUCTION

Although youth travel in Europe has existed from the beginning of the eighteenth century (Horak & Weber, 2000) with origins in the "Grand Tour" undertaken by the offspring of the aristocracy there has been little academic research on the subject. As the French say, "Les voyages forment la jeunesse." The latter statement has recently been statistically proven with youths who travel demonstrating higher grades than those who stay at home (Rozycki & Winiarski, 2005). Mass youth tourism is more recent, however, appearing in the last 30 years, mainly as a result of societal and economic developments which have brought increasing affluence, leisure, and liberalization (Carr, 1998).

At a general level, it has become apparent that youth are playing an increasingly important commercial role in society. In the US, 8–24 year-olds spend $164 billion per year, save $54 billion, and e-commerce is growing four times faster among on-line 18–24 year-olds than among adults (Harris Interactive.com, 2003). It has also become clear that youth have their own lifestyle; music and fashion being the two most obvious influences on youth culture (Sellars, 1998). To date this sector has been under-researched (Carr, 1998; Horak & Weber, 2000; Richards & Wilson, 2003). Analysis of the youth tourism sector is, therefore, hindered by both a lack of basic data and a lack of empirical studies on the subject.

While they do not represent a homogenous market segment, young tourists share certain characteristics with older age-groups and at the same time display distinct differences. Heterogeneity is apparent in terms of the customer profile, the reason for traveling, and the needs expressed. There is an obvious interest from a commercial viewpoint in determining the market potential of young tourists. Young people in industrial economies often have relatively high disposable income, and unlike older tourists do not suffer from the "time poverty syndrome" (Sellars, 1998). They are not "burdened" with the responsibilities of mortgages or children, and therefore have high mobility (Beus-Richembergh (1997) in Horak & Weber, 2000).

There are a number of associations concerned with advancing the youth tourism agenda (e.g., The Federation of International Youth Travel Organizations, International Student Travel Confederation) but data on even such basic areas as size of market, growth rate, market niches, etc. are extremely vague. Over a decade ago, a World Tourism Organization conference concluded that youth tourism was not fully recognized by the travel industry. It was estimated that the youth tourism sector represented 20% of international arrivals (World conference concludes youth tourism underestimated, 1992).

By 2000 there were 182 million tourism trips by European young tourists within their own countries as well as 53 million international trips within Europe and 7 million inter-continental trips. Young people from other continents contributed 4 million international trips to Europe. This represents an 11% increase in the number of trips over 1993 (Horak & Weber, 2000). Specific countries have also made assessments of the youth market, for example, with Canada estimating the youth tourism market at C$12 billion in 2004 and that the sector was rising rapidly, accounting for almost 23% of the total Canadian travel sector (Student Youth Travel Association, 2004). Important trends that may be identified from the market are that the average age of travelers is getting younger, with the average age of a youth traveler now 3–4 years younger than it was 20 years ago, and that people are traveling further from home, and are more risk oriented, looking for more adventurous destinations (Student Youth Travel Association, 2004). On a global level, it has been estimated that the youth travel market will increase to 25% by 2006 (Mintel International Group, 2004).

There have been several attempts to classify youth tourism, although none have gained universal acceptance. Carr (1998) provides a useful synopsis, dividing youth tourists by mode of travel (i.e. either "institutionalized," organized by a tour operator, or "independent"); others classify by activity during the vacation (e.g., "wanderers" and "participants"). It is also possible to segment according to type of accommodation, which identifies three different types of young tourists: those who stay in commercially operated accommodation, those who stay in young persons' hostels (thereby spending less on accommodation than on other things), and those who stay in the visiting friends and relatives sector (Carr, 2002). Carr (1998) proposes seven different segments, including international/domestic, short-term/long-term, and institutional/non-institutional. Also of note are a number of newer tourism labels among the categories, namely "alternative" and "experience" tourists.

Another method of determining market segments was suggested in a study by Richards and Wilson (2003). The study provided a classification that extended the understanding away from simply back-packers and provided different categories of youth tourist ("Backpacker," "traveler," and "tourist"). This was useful as it came out of definitions as perceived by the youth tourists themselves.

One of the main problems in "youth tourism," in common with many areas of tourism research, is in the definition of the concept. The age limits of youth tourism have been fixed variously, by different authors, between 15 and 35 years. This paper will use the range 15–25 years of age, as preferred by various government agencies (Australia Now, 1998).

In terms of the differences between youth tourists and regular ones, Horak and Weber (2000) and Richards and Wilson (2003) stress that there is an educational and cultural element of youth tourism. Activities also linked to sporting events and recreation is also a distinctive feature (Furtwingler (1991) in Carr, 1998.) Related studies also emphasize that youth culture generally has strong leisure, play, fun, and entertainment components (Sellars, 1998; Richards & Wilson, 2003). It is this blend of adventure, education, relaxation, and often work that makes youth travel so different, manifested in the "not a tourist" self-identity (Richards & Wilson, 2003).

It has been claimed that in many cases even companies that have specifically attempted to cater for the youth tourism market do not, in practice, meet those needs (Carr, 1998). The youth market appears to have a somewhat negative image in the eyes of the tourism industry, which believes that young tourists are not important to host countries, as there is a stereotype of a budget (backpacker) traveler, staying only for a short period, unreliable by nature, and behaving irresponsibly (Horak & Weber, 2000; Carr, 1998).

In reality, however, the reverse has been shown to be the case. Research has shown inter alia that young tourists spend average or above-average sums, make long visits (sometimes lasting even for months), are "civilized" and socially sensitive, are open to new tourism products, use information technology, and, especially important for the destination, they are constructing a "travel career" (Richards & Wilson, 2003).

Purpose of Study

This research aims to examine the differences in trip preferences and perceptions of accommodation among youth patrons staying at three different types of lodging facilities. Consequently, five research questions are investigated as follows:

1. Are there any differences in reasons of choosing accommodations among the youth patrons of hard budget, budget, and mid-sector accommodations?

2. Are there any differences in selecting eating outlets among the youth patrons of hard budget, budget, and mid-sector accommodations?

3. Are there any differences in attending evening activities among the youth patrons of hard budget, budget, and mid-sector accommodations?

4. Are there any differences in duration of stay among the youth patrons of hard budget, budget, and mid-sector accommodations?

5. Are there any differences in the perceptions of accommodation price among the youth patrons of hard budget, budget, and mid-sector accommodations?

METHODOLOGY

Owing to the lack of an apparent definition of youth tourists, this research attempts to evaluate youth tourists in a rather holistic perspective and operationally defines youth tourists as travelers in the ages of 15–25. The classification may help enrich marketing applications to a wide range of student travelers such as high school, and university learners. To determine the youth tourists' consumption patterns, a series of on-site surveys were carried out from July to mid-September of 2002 in the French-speaking region of Switzerland.

Survey questionnaires were collected from a range of different types of accommodation and festivals and 1,179 valid questionnaire responses were obtained. As regards accommodation, a representative sample of hotels, hostels, backpackers, etc. was selected. Since Switzerland is an international travel destination for youth tourists, questionnaires written in French, English, German, and Italian were used in the survey. The questionnaire covered the following themes: individual consumer behavior, accommodation, eating, cultural, and entertainment service preferences, along with personal data.

To ensure the validity of the measurement variables, the questionnaire was first screened by Swiss hospitality practitioners as well as professors, researchers, and students from the Ecole hôtelière de Lausanne. A pilot test using a draft questionnaire was conducted among multilingual youths in the city of Lausanne to further strengthen the validity and reliability of the study variables.

The study divided the population into three groups according to the types of facilities in which the respondents stayed: (1) hard budget, (2) budget, and (3) mid-sector. Hard budget accommodations include youth hostels, school dormitories, and guesthouses. Budget accommodations comprise hotels receiving rating of one to two stars. Mid-sector accommodations refer to three-star hotels.

The descriptive analyses were used to revaluate the factors influencing the selection of accommodation, eating outlet, and leisure activities among the three groups of youth tourists who stayed at the different type of lodging facility. In addition, tourists' perception of price on lodging facilities was also examined. Correspondence analyses were adopted to find out the similarities and differences in relation to the selection of accommodations and evening activities. Correspondence analysis is a multivariate technique used to depict the relative position of objects and variables in a single mapping. It scales the rows and columns in corresponding units, enabling graphical representation in the same low-dimensional space (Malhotra, 1996). It is used to obtain compact representations of respondents' perceptions and preferences, providing in effect a "photograph" of the market. Correspondence analysis has been used recently in tourism research, notably by Chen and Uysal (2002), Chen (2001), and Chen and Gursoy (2000).

RESULTS AND DISCUSSIONS

Reasons for Selection of Accommodations

As may be seen from Table 1, for hard budget properties, the guests tend to see attractive price as the most important choice attribute. However, the guests from budget and mid-sector lodging facilities believe that the proximity to centers of interest is more critical. A further examination on the differences in the reasons of selecting accommodations shows some distinct variations among the three study populations. Guests from budget accommodations are influenced by recommendation from families and friends, and the proximity to center (see Fig. 1). For those staying at mid-sector accommodations, they see referrals from travel agencies and services offered by the property as important considerations for hotel choice (see Fig. 1).

Table 1. Reasons of Choosing Accommodations among Youth Patrons Staying in a Different Type of Lodging Facility.

	Hard Budget		Budget		Mid-Sector	
	%	Rank	%	Rank	%	Rank
1. Proximity to centers of interest	30.2	2	47.5	1	46.0	1
2. Recommendation from families and friends	14.4	3	17.5	3	11.9	4
3. Referral from a travel agency	2.3	5	3.7	5	7.4	5
4. Attractive prices	44.2	1	24.3	2	15.4	3
5. Services offered	8.9	4	7.0	4	19.3	2

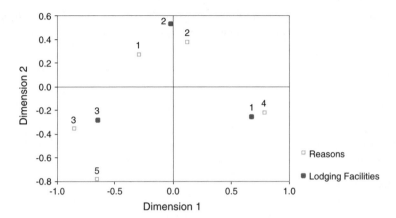

Fig. 1. Reasons of Choosing Accommodations among Youth Patrons. Note: (a) Regarding Lodging Facilities: 1 = Hard Budget; 2 = Budget; 3 = Mid-Sector. (b) Regarding Reasons: 1 = Proximity to Centers of Interest; 2 = Recommendation from Families and Friends; 3 = Referral from a Travel Agency; 4 = Attractive Prices; 5 = Services Offered.

Choice of Seating Outlets

Regarding the selection of eating outlets among youth guests, individuals staying at hard budget and budget accommodations tend to visit fast food/ self-service outlets and sandwich bars/bakeries. For those from mid-sector hotels, they are inclined to eat at restaurants (see Table 2). The perceptual map derived from the correspondence analysis delineates some differences among the three groups of respondents (see Fig. 2).

Seemingly, the youth guests of hard budget accommodation are likely to eat their meals in the bedroom as a way of saving their travel budgets. For those from budget accommodations, they demonstrate a preference to visit cafeterias. Lastly, the guests staying at mid-sector accommodations like to have their meals at full-service restaurants.

Choice of Evening Activities

In reference to attending evening activities, the youth staying at hard budget properties show they have a strong inclination to walk (see Table 3). The guests from budget and mid-sector accommodations appear to share similar

Table 2. Selecting Eating Outlets among Youth Patrons Staying in a Different Type of Lodging Facility.

	Hard Budget		Budget		Mid-Sector	
	%	Rank	%	Rank	%	Rank
1. Fast food/self-self food outlets	23.5	1	23.5	2	6.0	6
2. Sanwich bars/bakeries	21.4	2	23.8	1	8.8	4
3. Restaurants	15.0	3	20.5	3	42.1	1
4. Cafes/coffee-shop	10.8	6	11.7	4	13.5	3
5. Cafeterias	7.21	7	10.6	5	6.1	5
6. In the bedroom	10.9	5	5.2	6	5.4	7
7. Hotel restaurants	11.3	4	4.7	7	18.1	2

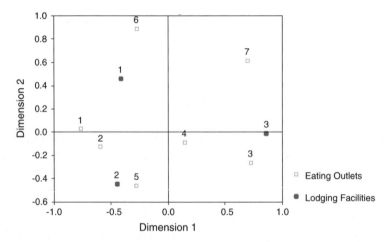

Fig. 2. Selecting Eating Outlets among Youth Patrons. Note: (a) Regarding Lodging Facilities: 1 = Hard Budget; 2 = Budget; 3 = Mid-Sector. (b). Regarding Eating Outlets: 1 = Fast Food/Self-Self Food Outlets; 2 = Sandwich Bars/Bakeries; 3 = Restaurants; 4 = Cafes/Coffee-Shop; 5 = Cafeterias; 6 = In the Bedroom; 7 = Hotel Restaurants.

activity preferences including attending cultural activities, visiting restaurants, and discos/bars (see Table 3).

The second correspondence analysis unveils other distinct variations in regard to attending evening activities (see Fig. 3). The resultant data indicate that in addition to walking, simply staying in their rooms could be an

Table 3. Attending Evening Activities among Youth Patrons Staying in a Different Type of Lodging Facility.

	Hard Budget		Budget		Mid-Sector	
	%	Rank	%	Rank	%	Rank
1. Staying at accommodation	16.0	4	6.8	7	7.9	5
2. Sports activities	3.1	7	10.9	5	4.1	6
3. Cultural activities	17.3	3	23.1	2	23.4	1
4. Walk	23.3	1	12.0	4	14.6	4
5. Cyber cafes	5.1	6	6.9	6	2.2	7
6. Gaming rooms	2.3	8	2.6	8	1.6	8
7. Restaurant	11.3	5	13.1	3	26.6	2
8. Discos/bars	21.6	2	24.6	1	19.6	3

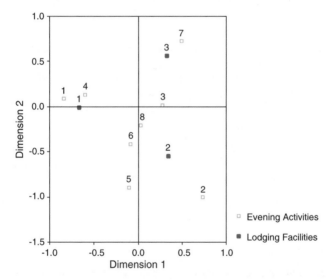

Fig. 3. Attending Evening Activities among Youth Patrons Note: (a) Regarding Lodging Facilities: 1 = Hard Budget; 2 = Budget; 3 = Mid-Sector. (b) Regarding Evening Activities: 1 = Staying at Accommodation; 2 = Sports Activities; 3 = Cultural Activities; 4 = Walk; 5 = Cyber Cafes; 6 = Gaming Rooms; 7 = Restaurant; 8 = Discos/Bars.

alternative for the guests of hard budget accommodation. Further, the study finds that guests staying at budget hotels are likely to visit discos/bars and gaming rooms. Alternatively, they might visit cyber cafes, cultural events, and do sports activities. The above results further confirm that the guests staying at budget and mid-sector accommodations have a large desire to spend money in their evening activities.

Length of Stay

Regarding the length of stay among the respondents, the average stay is around six to seven days. Moreover, no significant difference in the duration of stay is found (see Table 4). As for the perceived prices of accommodations among youth visitors, hard budget and budget accommodation appear to be considered as affordable.

For mid-sector hotel guests, the perception is rather mixed; about half of the respondents think that the hotel is expensive while almost 49% of the respondents regard it as affordable (see Table 5). The price of some hard budget accommodations (28.2%) is considered as cheap, compared to that of budget (9.3%) and mid-sector (3.3%) accommodations. The above findings further imply that hard budget and budget accommodations in Switzerland are in general affordable for a week-long vacation.

Table 4. Duration of Stay among Youth Patrons Staying in a Different Type of Lodging Facility.

	Hard Budget	Budget	Mid-Sector	F	Sig.
Mean	6.98	7.18	6.24	0.196	0.822
S.D.	18.8	13.9	4.9		

Table 5. Differences in Perceived Prices of Accommodations among Youth Patrons Staying in a Different Type of Lodging Facility.

	Hard Budget %	Budget %	Mid-Sector %
Expensive	24.0	25.7	49.7
Affordable	47.8	65.0	47.0
Cheap	28.2	9.3	3.3

CONCLUSIONS

The study evaluated youth tourists' trip preferences and their perceptions of accommodation in Switzerland among visitors staying at three different types of properties (i.e. hard budget, budget, and mid-sector). Not surprisingly, the price is the vital factor determining the reasons for selecting accommodation for those staying at hard budget properties. Proximity to points of interest represents the main reasons for choosing budget and mid-sector accommodations. When examining the differences in preference to eating outlets, the respondents from mid-sector lodging facilities have a notable demand for full-service restaurants while other groups of visitors prefer to visit self-service eateries. The study further finds that the youth guests of hard budget properties are not keen to attend evening activities which the guests have to pay for. Most guests of hard budget and budget properties regard the cost of the accommodations they stayed at as affordable while the youth visitors of mid-sector properties believed them to be expensive.

It is important to recognize a limitation of the study. The study uses the types of properties as the comparison criteria. However, regarding the room rate, the variations between the properties in different categories may not be so distinct. For example, some hard budget accommodations might charge the similar rate as budget ones; some budget facilities might have similar rates as three-star hotels, which fall into mid-sector hotel category in the current study. Therefore, the proprieties the respondent stayed at might not truly represent the travel expenditures of respondents. However, using property type as a comparison standard could be a helpful tactic of market segmentation.

It is enlightening to note that proximity to points of interest is a critical decision factor in selecting budget and mid-sector accommodations. It is noted that the properties adjacent to the entertainment centers tend to be more expensive. Since attractive price is one of the major concerns for youth tourists in hotel selection, those budget and mid-sector properties away from the points of interest might have a good chance to attract the youth tourist. For those properties that have a disadvantage of location, the availability of transportation services could be important in enticing the demand of youth tourists. For example, providing a shuttle bus to tourist spots helps alleviate the concerns of accessibility.

It appears that the guests from hard budget properties have a limited travel budget, which influences their choice of activities and the selection of eating outlets. Due to the exploratory nature of the current study, some predilections for food consumption are not examined in detail. These issues could be further investigated by using a qualitative approach to help extract more choice attributes. In terms of lessons for the industry, for practitioners from hard budget properties, it is important to center on the guests' budget concern. For example, printing brochures covering free-of-charge activities and providing self-service kitchens.

The perception of room rate of hard budget and budget Swiss accommodations seems positive while the price perceptions of mid-sector properties appears to be negative. For youth tourists, the hotels of three to five stars might not be ideal accommodations for a week-long trip, although they might be considered as great bargain from the aspects of service offerings. The limited budget is the main issue of youth tourists regarding activities taken and accommodation stayed. Consequently, it may be difficult to further augment the number of youth tourists staying at mid-sector Swiss properties. Since hard budget properties are the traditional accommodations attracting youth tourists, the new market potential may depend upon the development of budget properties.

The study finds that about half of the respondents regard this type of property expensive while the other half believes it to be affordable. For those having the negative price perception, the practitioners may consider deploying new marketing strategies that could modify the perception of price in order to boost demand.

As stated in the introductory remarks, the youth travel market has consistently been underestimated in terms of numbers and not fully understood in terms of potential. It is hoped that this study provides a clearer snap shot of the possibilities within the youth tourism sector for industry and that measures are taken to make the Swiss hospitality industry more able to exploit these opportunities. Lastly, it is to be remembered that the experiences of the youth tourists of today provide an important base for the travel decisions of future generations (Richards & Wilson, 2003).

REFERENCES

Australia Now. (1998). Australia, Labour Special Article – the youth labour market. Available at: http://www.abs.gov.au/Ausstats/abs@nsf/Lookup/, 14.01.2003.

Carr, N. (1998). The young tourist: A case of neglected research. *Progress in Tourism and Hospitality Research, 4*, 307–318.

Carr, N. (2002). A comparative analysis of the behaviour of domestic and international young tourists. *Tourism Management, 3*, 321–325.

Chen, J. S. (2001). Measuring tourism impacts from urban residents' perspectives. *Journal of Hospitality and Tourism Research, 25*(3), 235–250.

Chen, J. S., & Gursoy, D. (2000). Cross-cultural comparison of the information sources used by first-time and repeat travelers and its marketing implications. *International Journal of Hospitality Management, 19*(2), 119–203.

Chen, J. S., & Uysal, M. (2002). Market positioning analysis: A hybrid approach. *Annals of Tourism Research, 29*(4), 987–1003.

Harris Interactive.com. (2003). US online youth spend $164 billion annually. Available at: http://www.harrisinteractive.com/news/allnewsbydate.asp?NewsID = 143, 14.01.2003.

Horak, S., & Weber, S. (2000). Youth tourism in Europe: Problems and prospects. *Tourism Recreation Research, 25*(3), 37–44.

Malhotra, N. K. (1996). *Marketing research: An applied orientation.* Upper Saddle River, NJ: Prentice-Hall.

Mintel International Group. (2004). *The Youth Travel Market.* London: Author.

Richards, G., & Wilson, J. (2003). New horizons in independent youth and student travel. In: A report to the international student travel confederation (ISTC) and the association of tourism and leisure education (ATLAS). Amsterdam: International Student Travel Confederation.

Rozycki, P., & Winiarski, R. (2005). Social factors influencing tourist activity among youths. *Tourism Review, 60*(1), 20–25.

Sellars, A. (1998). The influence of dance music on the UK youth tourism market. *Tourism Management, 19*(6), 611–615.

Student Youth Travel Association. (2004). *Canadian youth travel market exceeds $12 billion in Canada.* Ontario: Author.

World conference concludes youth tourism underestimated. (1992). World conference concludes youth tourism underestimated. *The Vancouver Sun,* February 1, p. E.3.

RESEARCH NOTES

TRENDS IN TOURISM ACCOMMODATION INVESTMENT IN AUSTRALIA

Mainul Haque

ABSTRACT

The accommodation of the Australian Tourism industry and contributes around $2.9 billion to the tourism gross value employs 18% of all tourism employees annually. Despite this important economic contribution, there is a general lack of information on the investment trends in this sector. This paper highlights the past investment trends and factors that have affected those investment decisions during the last three decades, and provides the estimates of the future investment. Forecast shows that over the next 10 years around 52,800 new rooms will be required to meet the expected tourism demand by 2013 and around $5.3 billion new investment will be required to construct those extra facilities. The historical patterns of investment in the sector suggest that this expected requirement for new investment is readily achievable.

INTRODUCTION

Australia's vast geography and wide spread human settlements across its' majestic land required people to travel for business and other purposes since

Advances in Hospitality and Leisure, Volume 2, 215–238
Copyright © 2006 by Elsevier Ltd.
All rights of reproduction in any form reserved
ISSN: 1745-3542/doi:10.1016/S1745-3542(05)02011-4

the early days of the colonial settlements. Accommodation had to be provided for the miners, shearers, construction workers who built the roads and railways as well as for the public servants who had to travel across the vast land of this country for business and other purposes. In those early days the tourism accommodation was mostly in the form of pubs, inns or motels. However, as the population and their income grew, people's need for travel, travel patterns and their taste for holiday and accommodation needs also changed over time.

The industry responded to this changing demand by providing increased and diversified accommodation facilities, ranging from budget motel to high quality and international standard luxury hotels and resorts. Today the accommodation industry encompasses a range of accommodation styles such as hotels, motels, resorts, serviced apartments, bread and breakfasts, farm stays and caravan parks. The sector has also become an important component of Australia's $73 billion tourism industry – $7.2 billion in accommodation services is consumed by tourists each year. The latest Australian Tourism Satellite Account (Australian Bureau of Statistics (ABS), 2004a) shows that in 2003–2004 the accommodation sector's gross value added reached $2.9 billion, a 21% increase on the $2.4 billion figure in 1997–1998. The accommodation sector is also a large provider of tourism jobs and employed 94,200 people or around 18% of all tourism employees during 2003–2004. This employment represents around 1% of Australia's total workforce.

Despite this important economic contribution, there is a general lack of information on the investment trends in this important sector of the tourism industry. The objectives of this paper are to:

• review the past investment trends and factors that have affected those investment decisions during the last three decades from 1970 to 2003; and
• provides an estimate of future accommodation investment needs for the next 10 years to meet the likely future demand.

It is expected that findings of this paper will help inform debate about the future investment needs of the accommodation sector.

The paper is organised as follows. The next section reviews the past investment trends in the Australian accommodation sector and factors that have influenced those investment decisions during the last three decades from 1970 to 2000. Followed by a discussion on current performance of the accommodation market focusing on demand and supply issues and how they have influenced investment decisions during the last three years from 2001 to 2003. Finally, a model to predict the likely future demand for hotel, motel and guesthouse accommodation and likely investment required to construct those facilities for the next 10 years are discussed. The methodology and assumptions behind the model are also discussed in this section.

INVESTMENTS DURING THE LAST THREE DECADES

The level of investment and the stock of tourism accommodation has increased significantly during the last three decades, mainly due to significant increase in international tourism. Australia now has a diverse stock of accommodation facilities ranging from caravan parks and country town motels to high quality international standard hotels and resorts in cities and regions across the country. However the transition from heavy reliance on domestic visitor to a rising international visitor has not been very smooth due to fluctuation in international arrivals, which in turn has affected tourism demand and investment intention.

Accommodation investment in this paper has been measured by the value of accommodation commencements published by the Australian Bureau of Statistics (2004b). Fig. 1 shows the annual average growth rates of the value of non-residential building and accommodation commencements during the last three decades. The accommodation commencements involve buildings primarily providing short-term or temporary accommodation and include serviced apartments, hotels, motels, cabins, youth hostels and lodges. The value of accommodation commencements includes all new and refurbished accommodation facilities in Australia.

Data shows that the growth in the value of accommodation commencements has greatly outgrown the total non-residential building commencements during the past two decades (Fig. 1). The annual average growth rate

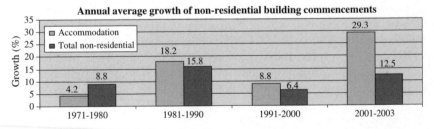

Fig. 1.   Annual Average Growth Rates of the Value of Building Commencements, 1971–2003.

of the value of accommodation commencements during the 1970s was 4.2%, compared to 8.8% for total non-residential buildings. During the building boom of the 1980s the accommodation commencements growth was 18.2%, compared to 15.8% for total non-residential building.

Despite the external shocks and the reported over supply of accommodation that has been affecting the tourism industry since 2001, the annual average growth of the value of accommodation commencements has been double that of total non-residential buildings during the last three years, with the value of accommodation commencements increasing from $500 million in 2001 to around $900 million in 2003. It should be noted that the last three years data may not be a good comparison with the commencement growth of earlier decades. This high growth rate could be a temporary phenomenon and over the long run (i.e. during the next 10 years) the annual average growth rate of the value of accommodation commencement could return to its historical average rate of around 10% per annum.

Investment Trends During 1970–2000

Investment decisions are often based on a number of economic and non-economic factors such as expected rate of returns, level of current and future expected demand, and other external economic conditions such as changes in interest rates, exchange rate fluctuations and likely domestic and world economic growth, all of which will have an impact on tourism demand and investment decisions. This part examines some of these factors that have affected tourism investment during the last 30 years.

Commencements During the 1970s
Fig. 2 shows the trends in the value of accommodation and total non-residential building commencements from 1970 to 2003. It shows that over most of this period, accommodation building commencements have been volatile, but have moved in a similar pattern to the rest of the non-residential building sector. The value of accommodation commencements during the 1970s was relatively less stable compared to the total non-residential building sector and declined from $112 million in 1970 to a low of $58 million in 1975 (down by around 47%) before rising to around $106 million in 1979 (Fig. 2).

Commencements During the 1980s
Value of accommodation commencements increased by around 600% during 1980s, up from only $240 million in 1981 to an all time high of around

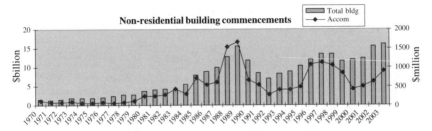

Fig. 2. Trends in Non-Residential Building Commencements, 1970–2003.

$1.7 billion in 1989 (Fig. 2). As mentioned earlier, the annual average growth rates of the value of accommodation commencements during this decade was 18.2%, compared to 15.8% for total non-residential building commencements. Several economic and non-economic factors affected this phenomenal growth of building commencement during this period. Some of the economic factors were:

- The deregulation of Australian banking sector in 1985 substantially increased competition in the sector.[1] A number of overseas banks received license to operate in Australia and many State banks, previously involved mainly with residential property market, expanded their scope to increase their market shares. All of these developments had an impact on increasing the availability and reducing the cost of investment funds.
- Depreciation of the Australian dollar, especially in relation to the Japanese Yen, attracted a significant amount of Japanese investment to Australia. The Japanese investors were the major contributors to development and investment in Australian hotels during the 1980s. For example, Japanese investment increased from around $1.2 billion in 1986 to more than $3.5 billion in 1989, an impressive growth of more than 190% during this short period. During the 1980s Japan was also the largest foreign investor nation in Australia and accounted for more than 70% of all foreign investment in tourism.
- Expected net income from increased property investment that was influenced by a buoyant Australian economy and increased tourism demand through a steady rise of international and domestic visitors. For example the number of international visitors to Australia increased by more than 25% during 1985–1989 (Fig. 3), and the hotel occupancy rates increased by 8 percentage points from 1983 to 1988 (Fig. 4).
- The expectation of substantial capital gains as asset prices were rising, specially after the 1987 stock market crash that led many investors to

Fig. 3. International Visitor arrival Growth, 1985–2003.

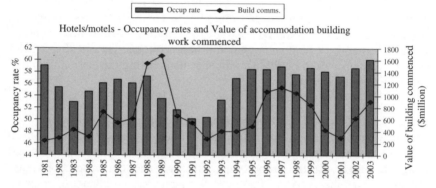

Fig. 4. Occupancy Rates and Value of Accommodation Building Commencements.

move their funds away from shares to property market, including the accommodation sector. This led to increases in property prices and the expectation of further increases attracted more investment.

Investors commencing construction during this period would have been influenced by these factors. In addition to the above-mentioned economic factors, other events that affected tourism demand and investment growth in Australia during the 1980s were:

• Significant relaxations in foreign investment policy in Australia. In 1986 the Australian Government made a number of changes to its foreign investment policy in Australia. For example, the net benefits test and the Australian equity requirements for takeovers and new businesses in tourism sector were suspended. Foreign investment proposals were to be automatically approved unless they were deemed contrary to the national interest.

• Expected tourism growth, both international and domestic, due to the Australian Bicentennial celebrations and the Brisbane World Expo in 1988.

All of these factors positively influenced investment decision during the 1980s with the value of accommodation commencements reaching an all time high of $1.7 billion in 1989. Total foreign investment in tourism also increased by more than 300%, up from $1.2 billion in 1986 to around $5 billion in 1989. Japan was the main source of investment and provided more than $3.5 billion or 70% of total foreign investment in 1989. Other source countries in 1989 were Singapore (6%), Malaysia (2%), United States of America (3%), Hong Kong (8%), United Kingdom (2%) and New Zealand (1%).

Commencements During the 1990s
Tourism investment decisions during this decade were influenced by a number of factors and they include:

• reduced growth of international visitors, compared with the period up to 1988–1989;
• the economic recession of the early 1990s;
• the adverse effects of first Gulf war on international travel;
• the aftermath of high interest rates on debt laden businesses in Australia;
• the reduction in level of foreign investment, specially Japanese investment as Japanese financial institution came under pressure from falling property and equity prices in Japan;
• sale of existing accommodation properties, mainly to Asian investors from Singapore, Malaysia and Hong Kong, at prices below replacement value during early part of 1990s; and
• Sydney winning the right to host the 2000 Olympic and Paralympic Games.

Following the 1980s property boom, the value of accommodation commencements declined considerably in the late 1980s, mainly due to a substantial rise in interest rates (interest rate in Australia reached a high of around 17% in 1989) and a significant drop in international visitor arrivals. Overseas visitor arrivals growth declined from a high of around 25% per annum in 1986 to a negative 8% in 1990, due to the domestic pilots strike in 1989, as shown in Fig. 3 (international tourism arrivals to Australia were booming in 1980s peaking at 25% per annum growth between 1986 and 1989). These two factors, coupled with the economic recession in early 1990s had a negative impact on overall tourism demand and reflected in lower occupancy and room rates, as shown in Fig. 4.

This softening of demand and the devastating effect of the high-interest rates of the late 1980s resulted in large numbers of insolvencies and receiverships, involving both hotel management companies and individual hotel operators in Australia. Furthermore, the availability of accommodation properties at prices considerably below their replacement costs in early 1990s also led investors to reappraise their investment intentions during this period. The result was a significant fall in the value of accommodation commencements from the high of around $1.7 billion in 1989 to only $270 million in 1992 (Fig. 4).

Accommodation building commencements started to rise in 1993 when the International Olympic Committee announced Sydney as the wining city to host the 2000 Olympics. The gradual recovery of the economy and the expectation of Olympic generated demand started to be reflected in an increase in the value of commencements, from $270 million in 1992 to more than $400 million in 1993 and reached a pre-Olympic peak of $1.2 billion in 1997 (a 340% increase between 1992 and 1997).

The gradual recovery of the domestic economy and the expected gain from the 2000 Olympic Games also attracted an influx of foreign investment (Fig. 5). For example, in 1993–1994 total foreign investment in tourism increased by more than 180% to around $4.2 billion, compared to $1.5 billion in 1992–1993. This was the second highest increase in foreign investment in tourism, after the record high of around $5 billion in 1988–1989 (i.e. during Australia's Bicentennial celebrations and the Brisbane World Expo). Investment from Asian countries such as Singapore (up by 8000%), Malaysia (up by 1800%) and Hong Kong (up by 30%) increased significantly over the year. These investors were attracted not only by the prospect of the Olympic gains but also picked up significant bargains during the aftermath of high interest rates of late 1980s (the interest rate peaked at around 17% in 1989), when many hotels were sold at bargain prices.

Although there was a drop in overseas investment in 1994–1995, Australia's stable socio-political environment and strong economic growth

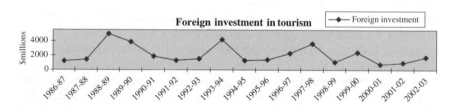

Fig. 5.   Foreign Investment in the Tourism sector, 1986–2003.

continued to attract overseas investors. Total foreign investment in tourism increased from $1.3 billion in 1994–1995 to around $3.6 billion in 1997–1998 (up by 176%). Largest growths in foreign investments were from the United States of America (up 200%), Germany (up 200%), France (up 650%), Singapore (up 22%), Malaysia (up 75%), New Zealand (225%) and United Kingdom (up 1200%). However, investment from Hong Kong declined by 69% and there was no investment from Japan during this period.

The Asian currency crisis in late 1997 affected the investment climate in the region and reduced the inflow of foreign funds to Australian tourism industry. Total foreign investment declined by around 70%, from $3.6 billion in 1997–1998 to only $1.1 billion in 1998–1999. Investment from all countries declined during this year.

Following the Asian currency crises there was significant excess capacity in the industry. This was further compounded by low visitor growth. International arrivals declined by around 3.5% and domestic visitor growth declined by 1.1% in 1999. The low demand and availability of excess supply led to a fall in accommodation investment in late 1990s. Value of accommodation commencements declined from the pre-Olympic boom of $1.2 billion in 1997 to only around $425 million in 2000 (down by 66%).

Patterns in Regional Investment in 1990s

The pattern of accommodation building commencements has varied considerably between the States and Territories. Historically the most populous States of New South Wales, Queensland and Victoria attracted the bulk of commencements. However with the growth of niche and regional tourism, the smaller States and Territories have been attracting a significant portion of total accommodation commencements more recently.

As shown in Table 1, the share of the value of total accommodation commencements has remained unchanged for the ACT, NSW and Victoria during the pre-Olympic (1990–2000) and post-Olympic (2001–2003) periods, but declined considerably in Queensland. Smaller States such as South Australia and Western Australia have attracted a significant share of total commencements although there have been modest increases in Tasmania and in Northern Territory. The changing building commencements trend indicates changes in travellers' taste over the period and the need to provide more boutique and exotic accommodation facilities in regional areas. The 5 star rated luxury safari camp *longitude 131* in Uluru, that was build in 2002 with around $10 million, is an example of this kind of investment in regional Australia.

Table 1. Shares of the Value of Accommodation Commencements by States – 1990–2003.

States	Share of Total Non-Residential Building Commencements During 1990–2000 (%)	Share of Total Non-Residential Building Commencements During 2001–2003 (%)
NSW	37	36
VIC	19	19
QLD	31	20
SA	2	6
WA	7	13
TAS	1	2
NT	2	3
ACT	1	1
Total	100	100

Current State of Investment in Accommodation

In order to speculate the emerging trends for future tourist accommodation investment, one needs to reflect on what is happening now and what has occurred more recently. The previous section reviewed the investment trends during the last three decades. In this section, the paper reviews the current investment trends covering the post-Olympic period and the recent events that have affected tourism demand and investment.

The industry has been severely affected by a number of external shocks during the past few years. For example the collapse of Ansett Airlines, the events of September 11 in 2001, the Bali bombing in 2002, the effect of SARS and the Iraq war in 2003. All of these events have had some degree of negative impact on tourism growth and accommodation demand in Australia.

Australia has experienced negative growth of inbound arrivals during the last three (2001–2003) years (Fig. 4). Following the strong positive growth up until 2001, international visitor nights have declined by 0.1% in 2002 and by 2.6% in 2003. Expenditure by international visitors also declined by 3.7% in 2003, after recording a positive growth in 2002. Overseas arrivals growth has been improving recently (Fig. 6) with total arrivals reaching an all time high of 5.1 million visitors in the 12 months to July 2004 (surpassing the previous high of 5.06 million visitors in the 12 months to August 2001, which included the 2000 Olympic period).

The trend in domestic tourism has been flat in recent years. Although there has been some quarterly increases, total domestic visitor nights have

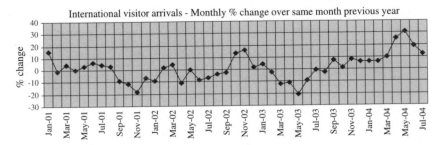

Fig. 6. Monthly Change in Overseas Arrivals to Australia, January 2001–May 2004.

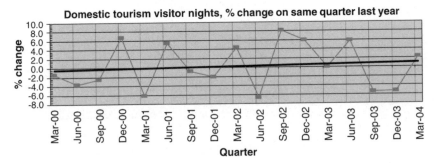

Fig. 7. Changes in Domestic Visitor Nights, March 2000–March 2004.

recorded negative growth in all but one year during the last four years from 2000 to 2003 (Fig. 7). In 2003, total domestic visitor nights declined by 1.5%, with business travellers (down by 6.9%) and holidaymakers (down by 2.5%) recording the strongest declines. Similarly domestic visitor expenditure has also been fluctuating and declined by 1% in 2003. In the case of hotel occupancy rates, there has been some volatility. After a fall in occupancy rates following the Sydney 2000 Olympic Games, latest figures show that the room occupancy rates have begun to rise again – albeit slowly (Fig. 3).

This fluctuating demand has affected the performance of the accommodation sector. Data shows that key performance indicators of the accommodation sector have grown relatively mildly during the post-Olympic period (2001–2003), compared to the pre-Olympic period (1998–2000), as shown in Fig. 8.

Fig. 8 shows that although total guest arrivals and room occupancy have grown stronger during the last three years, but room nights occupied and

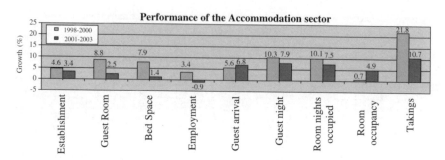

Fig. 8. Performance of the Accommodation during Pre- and Post-Olympic (1998–2000 and 2001–2003) Periods.

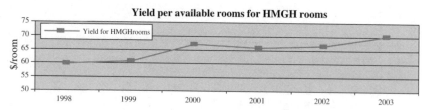

Fig. 9. Yield Per Available Room for the HMGH; 1998–2003.

total takings have grown slower in recent years, compared to pre-Olympic period. This indicates substantial discounting in room rates in the industry during the turbulent periods over the last three years.

For investment decision-making, an investor would be interested in growth of yield per room, as opposed to growth in takings per room. Fig. 9 shows changes in yield per available room for the hotel, motel and guesthouse with 15 or more rooms for the 1998–2003 period. The yield is defined as the average takings per available room. During the last six years the yield per available room for the hotels, motels and guesthouses (HMGH) sector has increased by around 17%, from around $60 per available room in 1998 to around $70 per available room in 2003.

Although the nominal value of the yield per room has grown considerably over the last few years (Fig. 9), but an investor would be more interested in real yield per room for investment decision. Table 2 shows a comparison of the annual average growth of yield per available room and the Consumer Price Index (CPI) during the pre-Olympic and post-Olympic period. This comparison gives an indication of growth in real yield (i.e. the difference between the nominal yield and the CPI).

Table 2. Annual Average Growth of Yield Per Available Room and the CPI, 1998–2003.

Annual Average Growth by Category	1998–2003(%)	1998–2000(%)	2001–2003(%)
Hotel, motel and guest houses	3.0	5.8	3.1
Consumer price index (financial year)	2.8	1.8	2.9
Real yield per available room in HMGH sector	0.2	4.0	0.2

Table 2 shows the comparison of the annual average growth of CPI and the yield per available room for the HMGH sector. The annual average rate of growth of yield per available room has been around 3% during 1998–2003, compared to 2.8% growth of CPI. This implies that the growth of real yield per available room has been positive, and grown by an annual average of around 0.2% during the last six years.

The growth in real yield, however, has been very strong during the pre-Olympic period (1998–2000), as shown in column 2. This indicates relatively higher demand for accommodation and higher room rates during the Olympic period by domestic and international visitors.

Despite various external shocks that have affected the tourism industry in recent years, the annual average real yield per available room has increased by around 0.2% per year during the last three years (2001–2003).

Thus, despite the external shocks and negative visitor growth during the last three years, real yield per available room has been growing positively, albeit slowly. As a result, accommodation building commencements have been growing. For example the value of total accommodation commencement has increased by around 80%, compared to 28% growth for the total non-residential building commencements between 2001 and 2003.

Table 3 shows the growth in value of accommodation commencements during the pre and post-Olympic periods by States and the Territories. Column 1 of Table 3 shows growth of the value of commencement from 1997 to 2000. The significant negative growth during this pre-Olympic period is due to the fact that value of building commencements peaked in 1997 and dropped to its lowest in 2000, when most of the Olympic related construction activities were completed. Column 2 of Table 3 shows the growth of the value of commencement from 2001 to 2003. It shows that commencements have increased in all States, except South Australia and the two Territories. Commencements in Tasmania have been increasing in both periods.

Accommodation commencements have also been growing relatively stronger than the non-residential building sector during the last three years

Table 3. Growth in Value of Accommodation Commencements by States, 1998–2003.

States	Commencement Growth from 1997–2000(%)	Commencement Growth from 2001–2003(%)
NSW	−75	122
VIC	−70	27
QLD	−48	94
SA	−16	−40
WA	−65	209
TAS	106	282
NT	−18	−56
ACT	256	−88
Total	−63	80

from 2001 to 2003. Value of accommodation building commencements has increased by an annual average of 29.3% per year, compared to 12.5% for total non-residential building commencement during 2001–2003 (Fig. 1).

Along with building commencements, foreign investment in tourism has also increased from $780 million in 2001 to over $1.7 billion in 2003 (up by around 118%). During this period investment increased mainly from Japan (up by more than 1000%), United Sates of America (up by more than 100%), and Singapore (up by 18%). However, foreign investment declined from New Zealand (down by 100%), United Kingdom (down by 75%) and France (down by 90%) during the last three years to 2003.

Sydney 2003 Rugby World Cup, Australia's stable macroeconomic settings along with its strong economic growth, strong consumer confidence, and positive growth of visitor nights and room occupancy rates are some of the factors that have contributed to this continuing growth of investment in the accommodation sector in Australia.

Future Investment Needs

Investment is one of the essential components for continuing growth of tourism. How fast the tourism industry grows can also be estimated, in addition to visitor growth, by the rate at which investment takes place. Tourism investment is undertaken by both private and public sectors to construct facilities that would benefit the industry. Public sector investment in the industry could include construction of infrastructure facilities such as roads, bridges, port facilities and airports. Private sector investment could include construction of accommodation facilities, golf courses, resorts and the like. For the purpose of this paper the investment forecasts have been limited to focusing on the hotel, motel and guesthouse sector.

THE MODEL

There are not many studies that attempted to predict long-term supply need for accommodation and the required investment, particularly for Australia. Previous studies include the report *The Sydney and Environs Accommodation Supply and Demand Study*, prepared for the New South Wales Tourism Olympic Forum (Olympic Forum 1994 (2001)) and a report by the Productivity Commission (1996). The methodologies used in these studies are similar to Choy (1985). These studies assumed long-run occupancy rate, and constant growth rate to forecast accommodation needs in Sydney. However, these studies only predicted the expected room requirements and did not quantify amount of likely investment required to construct those expected rooms.

The accommodation investment forecast model developed in this paper uses similar methodologies but extends the model to include the room construction cost to predict the likely annual investment requirement for the industry. The model is produced through four-stage equations, as shown. We know that a typical room occupancy rate is a function of the room nights occupied over the number of rooms and the number of days in the period. In mathematical form the room occupancy rate equation is:

$$OC_{it} = RNO_{it}/R_{it}T \tag{1}$$

where OC_t denotes room occupancy rates; RNO_t denotes room night occupied; R_t is the number of rooms; and T is total number of days in the period that is required to calculate the occupancy rates, t is time and i the number of observations that runs from 1 to nth observation.

Solving for total number of rooms we get:

$$\text{or} \sum_{i=1}^{n} R_{it} = \sum_{i=1}^{n} RNO_{it}/OC_{it}T \tag{2}$$

where R_t denotes number of rooms in period t. In addition to rooms, a typical hotel also requires construction of ancillary facilities such as shower, toilet, gymnasium, restaurant/bar or coffee house, lounge, foyers, corridors, staircase etc. Incorporating these extra facilities the total equivalent room space equation is:

$$\sum_{i=1}^{n} Rm_{it} = \sum_{i=1}^{n} R_{it}(1 + \omega_{it}) \tag{3}$$

where Rm is the total number of equivalent room space and ω the extra floor space required per room.

Construction of an accommodation establishment involves fixed cost as well as variable costs per room. For the purpose of this exercise it has been assumed that total construction cost (both fixed and variable) increases in line with the non-residential building construction price index over time. Thus the investment equation becomes:

$$\sum_{i=1}^{n} I_{it+1} = \sum_{i=1}^{n} Rm_{it}\lambda_{it}(1 + \delta_{it+n}) \tag{4}$$

where I denotes total investment, λ construction cost per room and δ non-residential building construction price index, t is time period, and n runs from year zero to infinity.

Scope of the Study and Data Sources

As mentioned earlier, this paper focuses on the accommodation sector investment only. The scope of this paper has further been restricted to the long-term investment forecast of HMGH, due to limitations in visitor night and construction cost data.

Visitor Nights Data

The Tourism Forecasting Council (TFC) (2004) produces long-term forecasts of visitor nights in HMGH. But for the purpose of modelling we need room nights occupied data. The TFC's forecast of visitor nights data has been used to predict the room nights occupied in HMGH over the forecast period.

Construction Cost Data

The construction cost of accommodation facilities varies according to the star grading, location and quality of room inclusions. For example, the quality of fittings and fixtures (e.g. washing sink, taps, toilet facilities and carpet in the room) in a 5 star rated facilities will be of higher quality, compared to a lower graded 4 or 3 star hotel.

Hotel construction cost will also vary according to room size. Higher grade facilities are normally required to construct larger rooms which invariably increases the construction cost due to extra floor space, shower, toilet and other extra amenities such as restaurants and bar, gymnasium, larger corridor, foyer etc, compared to a lower grade hotel.

In recent years 4 star rooms have contributed the bulk of total hotel, motel and serviced apartment supply. For example 4 star rooms constituted 44% of this supply, compared to 33% in 3 star and only 11% in 5 star categories during December quarter 2003. But due to the lack of construction cost data for 4 star rooms, the investment forecasts in this paper used 3 star construction cost data. For example Davis Langdon Australasia (DLA) (2004) publishes hotel construction cost data by major Australian cities for 3 and 5 star grade hotels, but not 4 star hotel rooms. It has not been possible to source the construction cost data from other sources.

Estimation Methodology

The forecasts produced in this paper are based on an analysis of demand, and current and likely future supply responses. Historical supply and demand relationships have been reviewed from the data collected from the ABS and the TFC. The raw data have been analysed to identify changes in demand and supply and the necessary investment required to meet that demand in the outer years.

The demand forecasts are primarily based on the annual international and domestic visitor nights for HMGH forecasts produced by the TFC. The visitor nights data have been used to estimate the room nights occupied (measure of demand) data for the HMGH sector. The visitor nights data has been sourced from the TFC and the room nights occupied data for HMGH establishments with 15 rooms or more has been sourced from the *Tourist Accommodation* published by the Australian Bureau of Statistics (2004b).

Historical analysis shows that on average, the visitor nights data have been 2.8 times greater than the room nights occupied in the HMGH during the last six years from 1998 to 2003. The exception was in 2001 when this ratio was 2.9, due to a 1.45% decline in room nights occupied. The average number of persons per occupied room in the HMGH sector has been around 1.8 during this period. During the same period the occupancy rates in the HMGH have ranged from 56.5% to 58.2% per year and the six years average has been around 57.5%. It is important to note that this period (1998–2003) covers the Olympic generated extra visitor growth as well as the post-Olympic downturn due to various external instabilities that affected tourism growth and the accommodation demand.

Assumption 1. Based on this past trend it has been assumed that during the forecast period: (a) average number of persons per occupied room in the HMGH sector will continue to be around 1.8 persons; (b) the visitor nights will continue to be 2.8 times greater than the room nights occupied in HMGH; and (c) the average equilibrium occupancy rates in the HMGH sector will be 57.5%.

Based on the above assumptions, the number of room nights occupied and the required room supply has been estimated for the period to 2013 (Eq. 2).

The approach to construction costs has been to standardise this to a 3 star hotel with standard room fittings and services. Industry analysts have advised that normally a 3 star hotel will have around 30 square meters gross floor area per room. Analysts also advised that on average an additional 25%–30% of extra floor space per room is required for amenities such as restaurants and bar, gymnasium, corridor, foyer, stairs etc. Thus the equivalent floor space required for a 3 star hotel will be around 37.5 square meters (30 square meter floor space per room, plus 7.5 square meter equivalent floor space per room for extra amenities as mentioned above).

The construction costs data has been sourced from Davis Langdon Australasia (2004) using estimates for the 3 star grade and then averaged from data on major Australian cities. DLA also publishes nation wide average per square meter hotel construction cost data for engineering services such as mechanical, electrical, fire, transportation and hydraulics. These two sets of data (construction and engineering services) have been combined to derive per square meter construction cost data for the investment forecast (Eq. 4).

Data provided by DLA shows that the nationwide average construction cost for a 3 star hotel room during 2003 was around $2615 per square meter. Thus the average construction cost for a 3 star hotel is assumed to be around $78,450 per room. This measure of costs is the nominal value of future building construction costs for the HMGH sector. Also this estimated cost per room does not include the land cost.

Hotel construction costs are expected to increase over time due to changes in material prices, inflation and other price pressures. The ABS publishes the construction industries *Producers Price Indexes* data (Australian Bureau of Statistics, 2004c) which includes a non-residential building (e.g. hotels, shops, buildings, hospitals, schools, etc.) construction index. This index has been used to account for future growth in hotel construction costs (Eq. 4).

During the last six years the non-residential building construction cost index has increased by an annual average of around 2.5%.

Assumption 2. Based on the above it has been assumed that for a 3-star hotel room;

(a) will have 30 square meters floor space and will cost around $2615 per square meters and construction cost will be around $78,450 per room;
(b) each room will require the equivalent of an additional 25% or 7.5 square meters space per room for extra amenities and will cost an additional $19,612 per room to construct those extra equivalent floor space; and
(c) building construction index will continue to grow by an annual average of around 2.5% per year.

RESULTS AND DISCUSSIONS

This section discusses the forecast produced by the model, based on the forgoing assumptions, and any investment policy considerations that might be required to meet the expected demand for rooms for the period to 2013. As mentioned earlier, the room supply forecast produced in this paper will assist the industry in better investment decision-making and will assist in developing a sustainable and profitable accommodation market in Australia.

Accommodation Demand

The expected growth in tourism from domestic and international sources has important implications for the stock of short-term accommodation in HMGH. As mentioned earlier, the Tourism Forecasting Council (2004) forecasts of visitor nights data has been used to estimate the demand for room nights occupied in the HMGH sector by the domestic and international visitors by 2013. According to estimate, total room nights occupied in the HMGH sector is expected to grow by annual average 2.6% per year, from 35 millions in 2003 to around 46 million by 2013 (Fig. 10).

Stock Requirement by 2013

The expected number of room nights occupied by international and domestic visitors has been used to help estimate the level of room stock required by 2013. The room supply requirements have been estimated

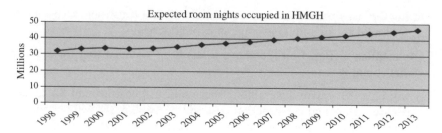

Fig. 10. Expected Room Nights Occupied in the HMGH Sector by 2013.

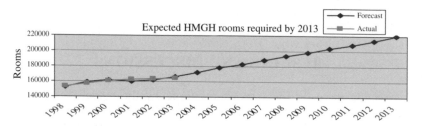

Fig. 11. Expected Total Rooms Required in HMGH Sector by 2013.

assuming an average equilibrium occupancy rate of 57.5% for the HMGH sector. This equilibrium rate is based on the last six years average occupancy rate for the HMGH sector.

The model has been used to predict the past values and future expected room supply for the sector. Estimated and actual values of HMGH room supply have been plotted in Fig. 11 to see the goodness of fit of the model. Values for the 1998–2003 period are actual room supply and the model has been used to predict the likely room supply for 2004–2013 period.

The estimates show that in the long run, HMGH room supply is expected to grow by an annual average of 2.6% per year (during 2004–2013), to a total stock of around 220,000 rooms by 2013. This equates to a total of around 52,800 extra HMGH rooms by 2013. This is equivalent to some 211 new HMGH facilities at an average of 250 rooms (Fig. 12).

Estimate shows that the annual average growth rate of actual and estimated room numbers during the 1998–2003 period is similar at around 1.3% per year, which indicates soundness of the model (as mentioned earlier the model has been used to predict past values of room supply as well). The stability of the model is also reinforced by the fact that the actual and

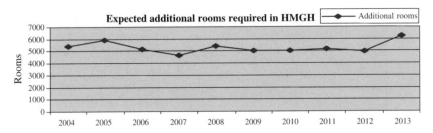

Fig. 12. Additional Expected HMGH Rooms Required by 2013.

estimated number of rooms for the 1998–2003 period is very close and provides a good fit for the model (Fig. 11).

The above forecast assumes a constant growth of demand for room and a steady rate of room yield. The tourism industry is vulnerable to external shocks, as happened during the Asian Financial Crises, the SARS and the Boxing Day Tsunami in 2004; it is plausible that the growth rates could vary from year to year. However, it is expected that in the long run, the growth rates will return to its historic average. Accommodation businesses are also expected to adjust their investment decisions in the event of higher than the expected demand or yield. If occupancy rate, room demand or yield increases by more than the assumed rate (used in the model), then obviously the industry will need to supply more than the predicted 52,800 rooms to meet the extra demand and vice versa. However, due to the lag between hotel construction and hotel opening, one would expect a rise in room rate in the short-run, until the market clears.

Investment

The results presented in Figs. 11 and 12 show significant investment in new stock is required to meet the expected demand generated by the international and domestic visitors. Fig. 13 shows the new investment requirement to meet the expected demand for rooms by 2013. As mentioned earlier, during the next 10 years a total of 52,800 new HMGH rooms will be required by 2013. In terms of investment levels (Eq. 4), this new infrastructure equates to around $5.3 billion of new plant, based on the average construction cost of $78,450 per room for a 3 star graded facility. On average, around $530 million per year of new investment is expected in the HMGH sector over the next 10 years. Investment forecast produced in this paper relates to construction of new HMGH rooms only and does not consider refurbishments of existing facilities.

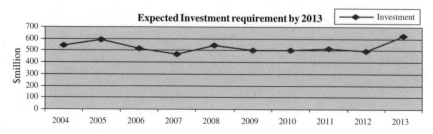

Fig. 13. Expected Investment Required in HMGH Sector by 2013.

The Australian Bureau of Statistics (2004d) publishes data on the value of building work done in hotels and similar establishments. These establishments include HMGH, serviced apartments, boarding houses, cabins, youth hostels, lodges, migrant hostels and other temporary accommodation facilities (the ABS does not publish any separate figure for the HMGH sector). Total value of new investment in constructing these facilities ranged from $483 million in 2000–2001 to $1.2 billion in 1998–1999 and averaged around $879 million per year over the last seven years from 1996–1997 to 2002–2003. Assuming the value of building work done in hotels and similar establishments continue to grow by $879 million per year and the value of new investment in HMGH sector grows by around $530 million per year (Fig. 13), then we can expect to see an average of around $349 million per year new investment to construct accommodation facilities such as serviced apartments, boarding houses, cabins, youth hostels and lodges (but excluding HMGH sector).

In addition to demand, investment decision will also be influenced by current and expected profitability of the hotel. The hotel profitability on other hand will be dependent on many factors including demand, yield, cost and availability of finance, operating cost and so on.[2] The annual profits could vary from year to year, but in long the run the, hotels are expected to earn the normal rate of return from their investment. The actual rate of return could be higher than the normal rate of return, if the accommodation demand grows more strongly than expected, and not enough rooms are available. In this situation the investors will need to supply more rooms and the likely investment could be higher than $5.3 billion that has been forecasted by the model.

CONCLUSION

For a long time the TFC has been providing authoritative forecast of tourism demand in Australia, but there has been a general shortfall of supply side forecast. This paper has developed a model to predict future supply requirement and the likely investment required to construct those extra rooms. The approach taken in this paper in forecasting the room supply is similar to other studies, but this model incorporates the likely construction cost. The forecasts suggest that over the next 10 years around 52,800 new HMGH rooms will be required to meet the expected tourism demand by 2013, and around $5.3 billion in new investment will be required to construct these extra facilities.

Hotels are long-lived assets and investors need to take a long-term view in allocating their resources. The model developed in this paper is simple and user friendly and could be a useful tool for industry planning and development. The industry planners and developers will be able to use this model to predict the likely capital requirement to construct the expected rooms in any given period. This information will be useful for forward planning and budgeting, especially in the accommodation sector where there is a time lag between construction commencement and the availability of room supply.

The accommodation investment in Australia is generally driven by the private sector with little or no influence from the Government. The Government aims to provide a stable macroeconomic environment (e.g. low inflation, low interest, good economic growth etc.) that underpins a favourable investment climate. Using these measures the Australian economy has performed very well over the last decade (Australian Treasury, 2004). The Government however, has provided active support to promote domestic and international tourism. For example in the recent Tourism White Paper (2003) the Government has provided more than $235 million to support the tourism industry in Australia. This assistance and the on-going promotion of the country by Tourism Australia[3] aims to increase international visitors to Australia from 5.2 million in 2004 to 9.3 million in 2014. These visitors will need to be provided with additional facilities, including the likely extra rooms. Based on past trends in accommodation investment, it appears that current macroeconomic and tourism policy settings will be sufficient to deliver the required level of investment in the accommodation sector.

NOTES

1. Between 1983 and 1985, the then Treasurer the Hon Paul Keating deregulated the Australian monetary system by (a) floating the Australian dollar in December 1983; (b) granting 40 new foreign exchange licences in June 1984; and (c) granting 16 banking licences to 16 foreign banks in February 1985.

2. The model developed in this paper focuses on the likely room requirement and the expected construction cost and has not addressed the profitability issues. For excellent discussion on this issue see Carey (1992) and Choy (1985).
3. Tourism Australia is Australia's statutory body responsible for the promotion of domestic and international tourism in Australia. Further information on this agency is available from http://www.tourism.australia.com.

ACKNOWLEDGEMENTS

I would like to thank two anonymous referees and Michael Shiel for their comments on an earlier version of this paper. Also grateful thanks to my colleague Stan Fleetwood who has helped in many ways during the preparation of this paper. Views expressed in this paper are my own and does not necessarily reflect the views of my employer and the Government.

REFERENCES

Australian Bureau of Statistics. (2004a). *Australian tourism satellite account*. Canberra, Australia: Australian Government Publishing Service.
Australian Bureau of Statistics. (2004b). *Tourist accommodation, Australia*. Australia: Australian Government Publishing Service.
Australian Bureau of Statistics. (2004c). *Producer price indexes*. Australia: Australian Government Publishing Service.
Australian Bureau of Statistics. (2004d). *Building activity*. Canberra, Australia: Australian Government Publishing Service.
Australian Treasury. (2004). *Australia's medium-term challenges*. Canberra, Australia: Australian Government.
Carey, K. (1992). Optimal hotel capacity: The case of Barbados. *Social and Economic Studies*, *41*(2), 103–126.
Choy, D. J. L. (1985). Forecasting hotel-industry performance. *Tourism Management*, *6*(1), 4–7.
Davis Langdon Australasia. (2004). *Property and construction industry handbook 2004*. Sydney: Davis Langdon Australia.
Olympic Forum 1994. (2001). *Sydney and Environs – accommodation demand and supply study 1994–2000*. Sydney: Tourism New South Wales.
Productivity Commission. (1996). *A model of investment in the Sydney 4 & 5 star hotel market*. Canberra, Australia: Australian Government Publishing Service.
Tourism Forecasting Council. (2004). *Forecast*. Sydney: Tourism Australia.
Tourism White Paper. (2003). *Tourism white paper: A medium to long term strategy for tourism*. Canberra, Australia: Australian Government Publishing Service.

INTERNATIONAL VISITORS' PERCEPTIONS OF OKLAHOMA

Suosheng Wang

ABSTRACT

Oklahoma's attractions have not caught much attention from either the international tourists or tourism researchers. In order to promote international tourism and make effective marketing strategy, it is important for Oklahoma to be well informed of visitors' perceptions prior to any actual campaigns. A survey was conducted at Oklahoma's twelve Welcome Centers in 2002 and 202 valid questionnaires were returned. Based on the survey, Oklahoma's underlying attraction dimensions were examined and the dimensions that determined Oklahoma's overall attractiveness were identified. Implications of this study were further discussed and recommended.

INTRODUCTION

One of tourism's characteristics is its invisibility. Tourists who want to visit a destination cannot test the product in advance, but have to rely on the image created and transmitted by the destination. Hence, destination image is the most important aspect of a tourist attraction from a marketing point of view, and measuring and managing this image becomes a major priority for destination marketers and researchers. In order to remain competitive,

Advances in Hospitality and Leisure, Volume 2, 239–253
Copyright © 2006 by Elsevier Ltd.
All rights of reproduction in any form reserved
ISSN: 1745-3542/doi:10.1016/S1745-3542(05)02012-6

destination marketers must be able to understand how tourists perceive the products of the destination.

Oklahoma is a moderately attractive destination in the United States as can be seen from the number of tourism arrivals. There is no doubt that Oklahoma is not as popular as other states such as California and Florida in attracting either domestic or international tourists. For instance, the number of Oklahoma's annual international tourist arrivals was less than 10,000 in 2002. Nonetheless, tourism has become Oklahoma's third largest industry, which contributed $3.6 billion to the state's economy annually. Being aware of the importance of the tourism industry and its great potential in the future, Oklahoma State launched a state-wide tourism awareness campaign – 'Tourism, Oklahoma's Newest Cash Crop' (Marks, 2002). The purpose of this campaign was to increase the awareness of Oklahoma's tourism among its economic leaders and people, and to enhance its competitive edge and destination image in both the domestic and international travel markets.

Destinations need to project their distinctive images in order to enhance tourism appeal. According to Gartner (1996), understanding images held by target markets is essential for marketers to avoid moving the image into a position held by an able and strong competitor. However, a search of previous studies shows that none of the destination image studies has ever discussed the state of Oklahoma. Without identification of its image, destination's marketing would be aimless, resulting in a waste of limited human and financial resources. According to Wang, Qu, and Ap (2005), a smaller destination without a recognized distinctive image would find it harder to compete with its overwhelmingly big neighbor destination. Oklahoma's big neighbor is Texas, which has undoubtedly attracted most of the international visitors in this area. Obviously, one of the essential tasks facing Oklahoma's tourism marketers is to identify and distinguish its destination image prior to actual marketing campaigns. Otherwise, one risk is that all its marketing efforts could be in vain.

In order to better understand Oklahoma' attractions as perceived by the international visitors, with the support and assistance of Oklahoma's Tourism and Recreation Department (OTRD), a survey was conducted at Oklahoma's 12 Welcome Centers in 2002. The purpose of this survey was to explore and examine Oklahoma's attractions from the perspective of international visitors. Specifically, one objective was to explore and examine Oklahoma's underlying destination dimensions; the second objective was to identify and discuss the important destination dimensions in determining Oklahoma's overall attractiveness.

This study started with a brief literature review of the previous studies on destination attractions and images, the methodology applied in this study, and then followed by the results of the survey and discussions of the findings.

LITERATURE REVIEW

Crompton (1979) defined image as the sum of beliefs, impressions, ideas, and perceptions that people hold of objects, behavior, and events. Given the importance of destination image study, this topic has been widely discussed in previous studies (Gunn, 1972; Crompton, 1979; Lew, 1987; Embacher & Buttle, 1989; Reilly, 1990; Schiffman & Kanuk, 1994; Gartner, 1996). For instance, Gunn (1972) defined images as being formed either on an induced or organic level. He argued that organic images are formed as a result of exposure to newspaper reports, magazine articles, TV reports, and other non-tourism specific information sources, while induced image formation is a function of the marketing and promotion efforts of a destination area. While little can be done to influence organic image, marketers can induce an image by investment in promotion (Gunn, 1988). Phelps (1986) contended that images are formed on two levels, primary and secondary. Secondary image formation results from any information received from another source. Primary image formation results from actual visitation. Fakeye and Crompton (1991) further pointed out that destination image is conceptualized as evolving from an organic image, through an induced image, to a complex image. According to Gartner (1996), "destination images are made up of three distinctly different but hierarchical interrelated components: cognitive, affective, and conative. The interrelationship of these components ultimately determines predisposition for visitation" (p. 457).

To completely measure destination image, Echtner and Ritchie (1993) suggested that several components must be captured. These include attribute-based images, holistic impressions, and functional, psychological, unique, and common characteristics. Images of the tourism product and the destination are composed of the perceptions of individual attributes (such as climate, accommodation facilities, friendliness of the people) as well as more holistic impressions (mental pictures of imagery) of the place. Destination image characteristics can be classified as functional (e.g., climate, prices, roads, nightlife, mental picture of physical characteristics) and psychological (e.g., friendly people, generally safe, general feeling and impression of the atmosphere of the place). Furthermore, the images of destination range from those based on "common" functional and psychological traits to those based on more distinctive or "unique" features or feelings.

The attributes of destination image that had been used in previous studies were derived and summarized by Echtner and Ritchie (1991), who grouped the attributes used by various researchers into categories. They found that the more frequently used attributes were: scenery/natural attractions; friendliness/receptiveness; costs/price levels; climate, tourist sites/activities; nightlife; and entertainment. Echtner and Ritchie further pointed out that the attribute lists may be incomplete by failing to incorporate all of the relevant functional and psychological characteristics of the destination image. To combat this problem, Echtner and Ritchie suggested that fairly extensive research should be conducted in the primary stage of scale construction. In terms of destination's overall attractiveness, Chen and Hsu (2000) argued that, "although previous studies have developed critical attributes tied to tourists' destination images, leading attributes that would help tourism scholars and practitioners measure the total attractiveness of a destination are still unknown"(p. 411).

Literature review indicates that destination marketers and researchers should not only study destination images based on visitors' agreement ratings, but also further explore the relative importance of the attractions in determining the destination's overall attractiveness. For example, this study focused on examining Oklahoma's destination attraction attributes, but it would also be interesting to see whether visitors' agreement ratings of Oklahoma's destination attributes would be an accurate measurement of its overall attractiveness. Such an understanding is essential to practitioners since it will reveal the most important attraction dimensions, which should be emphasized in the actual tourism marketing activities.

Destination images have been utilized as a mechanism of predicting the strengths and weaknesses of the destination. To evaluate the market potential of Oklahoma, this research examines tourists' perceptions of Oklahoma.

RESEARCH METHOD

This study used a descriptive research method, aiming to explore and identify the attraction dimensions of Oklahoma as perceived by the international visitors.

A survey questionnaire was developed for this study. In creating a list of destination attributes for the survey, previous destination image studies

(Echtner & Ritchie, 1991; Phelps, 1986; Gartner, 1989) were referenced. Related publications and promotional brochures on Oklahoma's tourism attractions were reviewed. An interview was conducted with some of OTRD marketers and researchers in charge of Oklahoma's tourism promotion. As a result, 27 items were selected to depict Oklahoma's destination attractions. Respondents were asked to rate their level of agreement to the destination attraction statements using a 5-point Likert scale ranging from "strongly disagree – (1)" to "strongly agree – (5)". In terms of measuring Oklahoma's overall attractiveness, two items with 5-point Likert scale were used as indicators of the overall attractiveness. The two indicators were 'what do you think of the likelihood of visiting Oklahoma in your future trips?' and 'Do you think that Oklahoma is a recommendable destination to your relatives and friends for their future trips?'

A pilot test was conducted to examine the content validity and reliability of the questionnaire before the survey was undertaken. Consequently, a total of 20 samples were collected. A reliability analysis (Cronbach's alpha) was performed to test the reliability and internal consistency of each of the attributes measured. The Cronbach alpha is 0.79, which is considered acceptable as a good indication of reliability. The questionnaire was developed in English, and then translated into German, French, and Spanish.

OTRD offered a substantial support to the survey especially in facilitating the translation, printing, and distribution of the questionnaires. An orientation meeting was held at the OTRD building attended by the OTRD tourism marketing managers in charge of the Welcome Centers. A detailed instruction was discussed and formulated in the meeting as a guidance for distributing the questionnaires. Since not many visitors came to visit Oklahoma especially after the 9-11 incident, a convenience sampling was employed and the questionnaires were distributed at all the 12 Welcome Centers. At each Welcome Center, all visitors were asked to sign up, and those who registered as foreigners were approached by the staff to see whether they were willing to fill out the questionnaire. The survey started from August 2002 and was eventually concluded at the end of November. Eight hundred questionnaires were distributed to the international visitors and 238 completed questionnaires were returned, representing a response rate of 29.75%. Among them, 202 questionnaires (25.25%) were found to be useful for data analyses.

Data was entered into the Statistical Package for Social Sciences Windows Version 10.0 (SPSS) program and analyzed accordingly. A frequency analysis was conducted for the questions in the questionnaire to examine the distribution of the responses. Mean ratings were computed for the perceived destination attributes. Factor analysis was used to group the destination into a smaller set of dimensions. The appropriateness of factor analysis was assessed by Bartlett's sphericity test, measures of sampling adequacy (MSA), partial correlation among variables, and Cronbach's reliability alpha. The criteria for the number of factors to be extracted were based on eigenvalue, percentage of variance, significance of factor loading, scree plot, and assessment of the structure. Only factors with eigenvalue greater than 1 were considered significant. Multiple regression analysis was employed to determine the impact of destination dimensions on the overall destination attractiveness. Destination dimensions, which were extracted from factor analysis, were used as independent variables, while Oklahoma's overall attractiveness was treated as the dependent variable.

RESULTS

Respondents' Profile

Respondents' demographic profile is presented in Table 1. Table 1 shows that the majority of respondents are males (61.5%), with females representing 38.5% of the sample. In terms of age, the main age groups are those between 41 and 50 years (22.2%), 31–40 years (20.2%), and 51–60 years (19.7%). The majority of respondents are first-time visitors (61.2%). And most of them are pleasure tourists (55.8%) and VFR (visiting friends and relatives – 18.6%).

Table 1. Demographic Profiles of Respondents ($n = 202$).

Age Group	Frequency	Percent	Countries	Frequency	Percent	Gender	Frequency	Percent
20 or below	9	4.5	Germany	55	29.1	Male	120	61.5
21–30	39	19.7	Canada	30	15.9	Female	75	38.5
31–40	40	20.2	UK	18	9.5			
41–50	44	22.3	Mexico	16	8.5			
51–60	39	19.7	France	8	4.2			
61 or above	27	13.6	Netherlands	8	4.2			
			Others	54	28.6			

Perceived Destination Attributes

The perceived destination attribute ratings of Oklahoma's attractions are listed in Table 2. The top two attributes with the highest mean scores are related with local residents' attitudes toward international visitors. Other attributes with high mean scores include "interesting native American history", "attractive pristine wilderness/fascinating wildlife", "a taste of the cowboy life and culture", and "beautiful state parks/lakes". The attributes with low mean scores are "moderate climate", "adventurous activities, such as hunting, rock climbing", "wonderful golfing", "convenient local transportation", and "interesting nightlife".

Table 2. Mean Ratings of the Perceived Destination Attributes.

Attributes	*N*	Mean	S.D.
Helpful local residents	197	4.30	0.787
Friendly local residents	199	4.24	0.841
Interesting native American history	200	4.17	0.796
Attractive pristine wilderness/fascinating wildlife	195	4.01	0.843
A taste of the cowboy life and culture	197	4.00	0.789
Beautiful state parks/lakes	197	4.00	0.721
Attractive country and western music	188	3.95	0.755
Beautiful western arts and crafts	197	3.94	0.799
Spectacular scenery	201	3.93	0.894
Interesting museums	194	3.88	0.843
Lots of recreational facilities/activities	194	3.85	0.780
Appetizing local food/cuisines	193	3.80	0.740
Great variety of shopping goods	195	3.76	0.859
Appealing American Indian activities	194	3.76	0.747
Interesting festivals/activities	195	3.74	0.900
Wide variety of accommodations	194	3.71	0.788
A land of startling contrast	196	3.68	0.819
Easy accessibility	197	3.64	0.860
Alluring water activities	193	3.60	0.805
Unspoiled eco-systems	187	3.50	0.772
Moderate prices	194	3.49	0.803
Tranquil environment	196	3.46	0.957
Adventurous activities, such as hunting, rock climbing	190	3.38	0.759
Wonderful golfing	190	3.35	0.813
Moderate climate	193	3.25	0.866
Interesting nightlife	192	3.18	0.795
Convenient local transportation	191	3.16	0.989

Note: Scale: 1 = strongly disagree; 2 = disagree; 3 = neutral; 4 = agree; 5 = strongly agree.

Destination's Underlying Dimensions

The results of factor analysis are presented in Table 3. For the 27 destination items, the test statistic for sphericity is large (2767.344) and statistically significant at 0.001. The Kaiser-Meyer-Olkin (KMO) measure of
sampling adequacy of these variables is 0.827, which according to Kaiser
(1974), is meritorious. The communality ranges from 0.57 to 0.88, sug-
gesting that the variance of the original values is reasonably explained by
the common factors. As a result, six dimensions comprising 26 saliently
loaded items emerge from the analysis. The six factors explained 70.08% of
the variance with eigenvalues ranging from 1.18 to 9.60. The Cronbach's
alphas for the six factors range from 0.81 to 0.89, all highly above the
minimum value of 0.50, which is considered acceptable for research in its
exploratory stages (Nunnally, 1978). The Scree Test also suggests that six
factors would be appropriate. Component correlation matrix indicates that
most of the factors are moderately correlated with each other. Because of
this, an oblique rotation will produce a better estimate of the true factors
and a better simple structure than will an orthogonal rotation. This verifies
the adequacy and necessity of applying the oblique rotation for the factor
analysis.

As indicated in Table 3, Factor 1 consists of five items, which are mainly
describing Oklahoma's fundamental conditions for traveling such as transportation, accessibility, price, and climate. It was labeled "Convenience
of Traveling". Factor 2 consists of four items, all closely related with
Oklahoma's cultural and historical attractions, hence named "Cultural
Attractions". Factor 3 is represented by five factors depicting Oklahoma's
natural resources, and it was labeled "Natural Attractions". Factor 4 is
converged by five items symbolizing Oklahoma's attractiveness in recreation and outdoor activities. This factor was named "Outdoor Recreational
Activities". The five items formulating Factor 5 introduce Oklahoma's
accommodations, shopping, and nightlife, thus named "Accommodation/
shopping/nightlife".

The summated scales of the six factors reveal that, Factor 6, "Local
Attitudes", has the highest mean score of 4.27. The second highly rated
factor is Factor 4, "Outdoor Recreational Activities", followed by Factor 3,
"Natural Attractions"(3.82), Factor 5, "Accommodation, Shopping, and
Nightlife"(3.63), and Factor 2, "Cultural Attractions"(3.56). The factor
with the lowest mean score is Factor 1, "Convenience of Traveling"(3.37).

Table 3. Oklahoma's Destination Attraction Dimensions.

Item Statement							Communality
	Structure Matrix Factor Loadings						
Factors	1	2	3	4	5	6	
Factor 1 – Convenience of traveling							
Convenient local transportation	0.834						0.77
Moderate prices	0.832						0.73
Easy accessibility	0.828						0.70
Tranquil environment	0.779						0.65
Moderate climate	0.720						0.71
Factor 2 – Cultural attractions							
Interesting museums		0.832					0.78
Interesting native American History		0.825					0.71
Beautiful western arts and crafts		0.779					0.66
A taste of the cowboy life and culture		0.710					0.57
Factor 3 – Natural attractions							
Attractive pristine wilderness/ fascinating wildlife			0.734				0.75
A land of startling contrast/unusual geological formations			0.733				0.65
Spectacular scenery			0.708				0.74
Unspoiled eco- systems			0.694				0.59
Beautiful state parks/lakes			0.680				0.65
Factor 4 – Outdoor recreational activities							
Alluring water activities, e.g., fishing, canoeing, camping				0.856			0.79
Wonderful golfing				0.784			0.70
Adventurous activities, such as hunting, rock climbing				0.739			0.79

Table 3. (Continued)

Item Statement	Structure Matrix Factor Loadings						Communality
Appealing American Indian activities	0.653						0.65
Lots of recreational facilities/ activities	0.594						0.57
Factor 5 – Accommodation/shopping/nightlife, etc.							
Wide variety of accommodations		0.810					0.76
Appetizing local food/cuisines		0.775					0.76
Great variety of shopping goods		0.663					0.64
Interesting festivals/ activities		0.648					0.57
Interesting nightlife		0.612					0.60
Factor 6 – local attitudes							
Friendly local residents						0.927	0.88
Helpful local residents						0.920	0.87
Eigenvalue	9.60	2.48	2.20	1.53	1.23	1.18	
Variance (percent)	36.91	9.55	8.46	5.89	4.72	4.54	
Cumulative variance (percent)	36.91	46.47	54.93	60.82	65.54	70.08	
Cronbach's alpha	0.85	0.84	0.81	0.81	0.82	0.89	
Summated mean	3.37	3.56	3.82	4.0	3.63	4.27	
Number of items (total = 26)	5	4	5	5	5	2	

Note: Extraction method: Principal Component Analysis; Rotation method: Promax with Kaiser Normalization.

Dimensions Leading to Destination's Overall Attractiveness

The two items, "respondents' likelihood to revisit Oklahoma" and "respondents' likelihood to recommend Oklahoma to their friends", were converged to represent Oklahoma's overall attractiveness and treated as the dependent variable in the Multiple Regression analysis. Reliability analysis was employed to see if these two items were internally consistent (0.754). The summated mean of these two items was 4.0. All the attraction dimensions extracted from the Factor Analysis were entered as independent variables. The Multiple Regression analysis was conducted, with stepwise

Table 4. Predicting Oklahoma's Overall Attractiveness with Destination Attraction Dimensions.

Variable	B	Beta	t	Sig.	VIF
(Constant)	0.161		0.672	0.502	
X_2	0.237	0.209	3.880	0.000	1.358
X_3	0.444	0.415	7.096	0.000	1.604
X_4	0.320	0.320	6.003	0.000	1.328

	Sum of Squares	df	Mean Square	F	Sig.
Regression	43.461	3	14.487	90.389	0.000
Residual	31.574	197	0.160		
Total	75.036	200			

method to examine the relationships between the independent variables and the dependent variable. Results were shown in Table 4.

The regression equation model indicates a good adjusted R^2 of 0.573, which means that 57.3% of the dependent variable's variations can be explained by the independent variables in the model. The F-ratio of 90.389 is significant (*Prob.* <0.001), indicating that result of the equation model could hardly occur by chance. The degree of variable collinearity is considered acceptable with the variance inflation (VIF) less than 10, and the condition indices less than 30 (Belsley, 1991). T-statistic test was used for testing whether the independent variables contribute meaningful information to the predictions of the dependent variable. If t-value of an independent variable is found to be significant at the level of 0.05, that variable is then included in the model. Validation of the model was pre-tested by splitting the sample into one estimation sample and one validation sample. This process shows that the equation model and adjusted R^2 are quite similar, hence verifying that the model is quite robust.

By following such a procedure, three independent variables were found to be significant in predicting the dependent variable, i.e., Factor 2, "Cultural Attractions", Factor 3, "Natural Attractions", and Factor 4, "Outdoor Recreational Activities". Other factors were excluded from the equation model. The standardized regression coefficient "Beta" indicates the rank order of importance of the predictor variables. Based on the Beta (standardized coefficients), we can detect which factor has relatively more explanatory power in predicting the dependent variable. Thus, it is found that the most important factor is Factor 3, "Natural Attractions" (*Beta* = 0.415), followed by Factor 4, "Outdoor Recreational Activities" ($Beta = 0.320$), and then Factor 2, "Cultural Attractions" (0.237).

DISCUSSION AND CONCLUSION

This study examined Oklahoma's destination attributes and explored its attraction dimensions as well as the relationships between the attraction dimensions and Oklahoma's overall attractiveness.

In terms of Oklahoma's attraction attributes, it was found that the items reflecting the friendliness of local residents were most highly rated by the respondents. Previous studies showed that local people's attitude is important in attracting tourists but need to be handled moderately. On one hand, residents' negative reaction toward tourists could sharply decrease travelers' satisfaction and severely damage a community's image (Pearce, 1980). On the other hand, tourists may have their vacation spoiled or enhanced by local attitudes (Knox, 1982). Oklahoma's tourism marketers should take the advantage of local community's support of tourism to enhance its overall image. Other favorably perceived destination attributes included items related with the native American attractions, Indian traditions and cowboy life style. This echoed the efforts made by OTRD to promote Oklahoma as a "Native American" state. One caution in promoting this image, however, is that whether and to what extent the international visitors chose to visit this country because of America's native attractions. This slogan might be interesting to the domestic visitors and easy for Oklahoma to distinguish itself from the other states, but might not be very attractive to the international visitors.

Comparatively, Oklahoma's nightlife was not highly rated by the respondents, neither were its local transportation or climate. Most international visitors treated Oklahoma as an en route destination, and the length of stay in the state was relatively short which might not have left tourists much time to explore its nightlife. In terms of transportation, Oklahoma is a state located in the central area of America, with no international airports linking with major tourist-generating countries. Considering that accessibility is a fundamental component in making a successful destination, the lack of gateway airport is one of Oklahoma's major disadvantages in developing and promoting international tourism. As for climate, Oklahoma's climate is dry and is extremely hot in summer, tourists will not favor its climate especially when they visit in summer time. Golfing, which was regarded as one of Oklahoma's highlights in attracting leisure and sport tourists failed in capturing international visitors' attention. One reason for this could be that Oklahoma may have only made limited efforts in promoting its attractions in the international travel markets as compared with other states.

Oklahoma's six underlying attraction dimensions were gleaned from the selected destination attributes depicting Oklahoma's various kinds of attractions. The dimension of "local attitudes" received the highest rating score, followed by "Outdoor Recreational Activities" and "Natural Attractions". The dimension of "Cultural Attractions" which though had been emphasized by Oklahoma's tourism marketers as an important factor in promoting and attracting visitors, was not very favorably perceived. In other words, international visitors might consider Oklahoma's cultural attractions as attractive as its scenery attractions and outdoor recreational activities. This indicates that, even if Oklahoma's appeal in culture might be considered unique in comparison with the attractions of the other states, it may still fail in attracting visitors if they do not hold a strong perception of the unique image. This is because each destination may project distinctive images as a reflection of the uniqueness of their specific local environment, culture, and economy (Stabler, 1988; Gregory, 1989; Shaw & Williams, 1994), but visitors prefer destinations with strong and salient images (Woodside & Lysonski, 1989). One suggestion for Oklahoma's tourism marketers is to put some emphasis on and give more exposure to the promotions of its cultural attractions in the international travel market, meanwhile, reinforce its culture-related tour products.

In terms of the relationships between the destination dimensions and Oklahoma's overall attractiveness, this study identified three important dimensions significantly contributing to Oklahoma's overall attractiveness. In order of importance, these dimensions include "Natural Attractions", "Outdoor Recreational Activities", and "Cultural Attractions". One implication is that Oklahoma's tourism marketers could enhance its overall attractiveness by emphasizing its marketing efforts mainly on these important dimensions. Further observation showed that, though "local attitudes" was rated the highest in terms Oklahoma's attractions, this dimension had no significant impact on determining Oklahoma's overall attractiveness. In other words, the highly rated destination attraction dimension was not the leading factor assessing Oklahoma's overall destination attractiveness. This indicates that agreement ratings of destination dimensions may not be an accurate measurement of destination's overall attractiveness. This finding supports the previous argument made by Chen and Hsu (2000). A practical significance of this study is that, destination marketers should not only be keen on promoting the destination's highly rated attractions, more importantly, they should further identify and emphasize on the important dimension(s) which is actually salient in enhancing the destination's overall attractiveness.

In summary, Oklahoma has hardly caught researchers' much attention in examining its destination attractions before. This study acted as an initial effort in analyzing its destination image and attractions from the perspective of international visitors. It is hoped that the findings of this study would help the local tourism marketers better understand the features of Oklahoma's destination attractions and thus make more effective marketing strategies in promoting Oklahoma's tourism to the international travel markets. Further research is recommended to focus on the major specific market segments as visitors from different countries may perceive the same destination differently. Besides, one thing needs to be cautious in terms of the interpretation of this study, i.e., due to the small number of international visitors coming to Oklahoma, a convenience sample was used for the data collection, thus potential bias could be possible, which should be taken into consideration when referring the findings of this study for any generalization purposes.

REFERENCES

Belsley, D. A. (1991). *Conditioning diagnostics: Co-linearity and weak data in regression.* New York: Wiley.

Chen, J. S., & Hsu, C. H. C. (2000). Measurement of Korean tourists' perceived images of overseas destinations. *Journal of Travel Research, 38*(4), 411–416.

Crompton, J. L. (1979). An assessment of the image of Mexico as a vacation destination and the influence of geographical location upon that image. *Journal of Travel Research, 17*(4), 18–23.

Echtner, C. M., & Ritchie, J. R. B. (1991). The meaning and measurement of destination image. *The Journal of Tourism Studies, 2*(2), 2–12.

Echtner, C. M., & Ritchie, J. R. B. (1993). The measurement of destination image: An empirical assessment. *Journal of Travel Research, 31*(4), 3–13.

Embacher, J., & Buttle, F. (1989). A Repertory Grid Analysis of Austria's Image as a Summer Vacation Destination. *Journal of Travel Research, 27*(3), 3–7.

Fakeye, P. C., & Crompton, J. L. (1991). Image differences between prospective, first-time, and repeat tourists to the lower Rio Grande valley. *Journal of Travel Research, 30*(2), 10–16.

Gartner, W. C. (1989). Tourism image: Attribute measurement of state tourism products using multidimensional scaling techniques. *Journal of Travel Research, 28*(2), 16–20.

Gartner, W. C. (1996). *Tourism development – principles, processes and policies.* New York: Van Nostrand Reinhold.

Gregory, D. (1989). Area differentiation and post-modern human geography. In: D. Gregory & R. Walford (Eds), *Horizons in human geography* (pp. 67–96). New Jersey: Barnes and Noble.

Gunn, C. A. (1972). *Vacationscape: Designing tourist regions.* Austin: University of Texas.

Gunn, C. A. (1988). *Tourism planning* (2nd ed.). New York: Taylor & Francis.

Kaiser, H. F. (1974). An index of factorial simplicity. *Psychometrika, 39,* 31–36.

Knox, J. M. (1982). Resident visitor interaction: A review of the literature and general policy alternatives. In: F. Rajotte (Ed.), *The impact of tourism development in the Pacific* (pp. 76–107). Peterborough, Ontario: Trent University.

Lew, A. A. (1987). A framework of tourist attraction research. *Annals of Tourism Research, 14,* 553–575.

Marks, K. (2002). *Travel and tourism.* http://www.otrd.state.ok.us/travel_and tourism.htm, 1/11/2002.

Nunnally, J. C. (1978). *Psychometric theory* (2nd ed). New York: McGraw-Hill.

Pearce, P. L. (1980). Perceived changes in holiday destinations. *Annals of Tourism Research, 9,* 145–164.

Phelps, A. (1986). Holiday destination image – the problem of assessment: An example developed in Menorca. *Tourism Management,* September, pp. 168–180.

Reilly, M. D. (1990). Free elicitation of descriptive adjectives for tourism image assessment. *Journal of Travel Research, 28*(4), 21–26.

Schiffman, L., & Kanuk, L. (1994). *Consumer behavior* (5th ed.). New Jersey: Prentice-Hall.

Shaw, G., & Williams, A. M. (1994). *Critical issues in tourism: A geographical perspective.* Oxford: Blackwell.

Stabler, M. J. (1988). The image of destination regions: Theoretical and empirical aspects. In: B. Goodall & G. Ashworth (Eds), *Marketing in the tourism industry: The promotion of destination regions* (pp. 133–161). New York: Croom Helm.

Wang, S., Qu, H., & Ap, J. (2005). Images of the Pearl river delta travel destinations in China. *Tourism Review International, 8*(4), 339–349.

Woodside, A. G., & Lysonski, S. (1989). A general model of traveler destination choice. *Journal of Travel Research, 17,* 8–14.

THE EFFECTS OF AIRFARES AND FOREIGN EXCHANGE RATES ON GLOBAL TOURISM

Henry G. Iroegbu

ABSTRACT

This article assessed the effects of airfares and foreign exchange rates on Global Tourism demand. It identified three categories from the assessment – The Market Segment Effect; The Substitution Effect; and The Facilitation Effect. The tourism literature is rich with vast studies on the effects of various components of tourism prices on international tourism, but lacking in comprehensive categorization of the identified effects. Such assessment would enable tourism destination planners and service providers to be able to focus on identified specific issues and finding their pertinent solutions. It has been determined that while there might be identified profound effects, their solutions are not applicable to all tourism destinations or services.

INTRODUCTION

Global tourism is on the verge of recovery from the negative impact of turbulent international events, such as the September 11, 2001 terrorist attack in US and the Severe Acute Resperatory Syndrome (SARS) virus. A

Advances in Hospitality and Leisure, Volume 2, 255–263
ISSN: 1745-3542/doi:10.1016/S1745-3542(05)02013-8

British research group – Mintel has projected a strong increase in global tourism in the foreseeable future.

The three major tourist-originating countries – Germany, Britain, and the United States are predicted to have a combined number of 240 million of their residents as international tourists by 2005. This is a 30% increase from approximately 185 million of their outbound international tourist in 1999. The strong growth in international tourism demand is projected up to 2015. Germany is anticipated to hold on as the greatest generator of international tourists in 2015. The forecast shows Britain to become the second largest producer of overseas visitors, passing United States, which would descend to the third international tourists generating country.

The tourism industry has emerged as one of the largest and fastest growing industries in the global economy (Eadington & Redman, 1991). It is a silent export that contributes approximately 5.5% of the world gross output, 7.3% of capital investment, and 11.1% of world taxes (World Travel and Tourism Council, 1992). It has become the economic power source of many countries and has facilitated the development of infrastructure and improvement in employment levels in developing countries.

For a tourist destination to remain competitive, it must have the ability to attract its share of the international tourism market. As Stevens (1992, p. 46) noted, "competitiveness is an encompassing concept whose bottom-line indicator is value for money." The purpose of this article is to assess the effects of airfares and foreign exchange rates on global tourism demand. This will help to understand tourists' behavior in deciding a destination choice.

Although tourism literature has detailed studies on the effects of various components of tourism prices on International tourism, none has assessed them into comprehensive categories. Such assessment would enable tourism destination planners and service providers to be able to focus on identified specific issues and finding their appropriate solutions, rather than tackling broad issues with generalized ineffective solutions. Thus, this article establishes a conceptual categorization of the identified effects of tourism prices in the literature, with emphasis on the effects of airlines and foreign exchange rates on global tourism demand.

Morley (1994a) expressed the notion of multidimensional facets of tourism prices with much of tourists' expenses being on fares, accommodation, food, sightseeing, gifts, etc. However, international tourists base their travel decisions on notable major tourism prices, such as airfares (Morley, 1994a) and exchange rates (Witt & Martin, 1987), which are more salient in long-distance traveling.

Demand theory hypothesizes that the demand for travel is an inverse function of relative prices. That is, the greater (lower) the cost of living in the destination country relative to the origin country, the lower (greater) the tourism demand, every other thing being equal (Lee, Var, & Blaine, 1996). Generally, economic delineation projects the demand for a product as a function of both its price as well as the pattern of its demand curve (Dolan, 1980).

A good understanding of the implications of a destination's tourism prices on international tourism demand is very essential for a successful tourism development. Changes in price usually cause changes in demand, just as changes in demand would also induce changes in price. Therefore, there is an interrelationship between prices of attractions in a destination and the demand of the destination's tourist attractions. Crouch (1992) stated that residents of a destination country, in spite of their inclinations to domestic tourism, normally dominate the total demand for items such as food, accommodation, car rental, and souvenirs. With such accord, tourism demand is assumed to be a function of price, but does not often affect tourism price (Anastasopoulou, 1984; Artus, 1972; Fujii & Mak, 1981; Little, 1990).

Crouch (1992) illustrated this point by explaining that the validity of the assumption of a perfectly elastic supply curve declines in destinations where international tourists' receipts are the main source of revenue for economy. In summing it, Crouch (1994) stated that in the context of international travel, the cost of the trip comprises of foreign exchange rates, price of primary tourist services and secondary goods and services in the destinations, the cost of transportation between the originating country and country of destination, and the absolute effect of exchange rate fluctuations on tourists' purchasing power.

DEMAND ELASTICITY FOR TOURISM SERVICES

Neo-classical economists advocate the concepts of classic economic theory, which projects the income of tourists and the price of goods and services relative to the price of substitutes as the essential factors of international tourism demand (Stronge & Redman, 1982). Barry and O' Hagan (1972) determined three aspects of tourism price: costs of living at the destination; transportation costs; and exchange rates.

The price elasticity of demand is a measurement of the percentage change in demand relative to the percentage change in price. Mak (1988) also suggested that demand is termed elastic if an increase in the price of lodging/

tourism service induces a noticeable decrease in the amount of lodging/ tourism service demanded. On the other hand, demand is inelastic if an increase in the price of the lodging/tourism service induces a minor decrease in the amount of lodging service demanded.

AIRFARES

The rapid growth of low-cost air carriers has rejuvenated the increase in demand of global tourism (eturbo News, 2003). The direct relationship between airfares and tourism demand was identified by Abeyratyne (1993), which stressed Burkhart and Medlick (1974, p. 3) proposition that "the most important attribute of tourism is that it is inextricably linked to transport, as the latter is the necessary precondition of tourism." Naturally, travelers prefer traveling by the cheapest fare, any cut in transportation cost would generate more tourist traffic in most of the cases (Abeyratyne, 1993).

Stronge (1982) found airfare to be significant and with price elasticity that increases with increase in distance traveled. The summer 1993 enormous airfare discounts resulted to a record number of sold tickets. The discounts coupled with stronger US foreign exchange in 1993 brought a surge in outbound tourism by US tourists (Robertshaw, 1993). Underwood (1994), emphasized the trickle effect prompted by low airfares on other tourism-oriented products, such as hotels and car rentals. Thus, according to Underwood, low airfares usually entice travelers, who become captured guests to higher-than-expected hotel and car rental rates.

In establishing the effect of airfares on international tourism demand, Morley (1994a) determined a significant negative effect on tourists' destination choice associated with airfare increases. The study found hotel tariffs and exchange rates to have impacts that are lesser than the airfare impact. It also discovered that larger parties are more price-sensitive and increased airfare affects destination choice of frequent tourists and larger families, thus the impact of higher airfares induces relative preference by potential tourists for closer and cheaper destinations (Morley, 1994b).

FOREIGN EXCHANGE RATE

The volatility of international tourism flow is usually difficult to forecast. This is due to susceptibility of international tourism to vital factors, such as variations in exchange rate, relative inflation of tourist goods and services, and turbulent global events (Witt, Newbould, & Watkins, 1992). Exchange rates apparently project the purchasing power of tourists who are more knowledgeable about fluctuations in foreign exchange rates than about detailed prices at their destinations (Witt & Martin, 1987).

Various theoretical and empirical aspects have been used to determine the influence of exchange rate on foreign travel demand. Theories such as the theory of purchasing power parity infer that holding transportation costs and trade barriers constant, long-run exchange rates should signify the absolute costs of living between countries (Gordon, 1981). The proposition by Gray (1966) propagated the notion that most travelers are not aware of prices in advance and thus, basing their expense estimates on the rate of exchange. Therefore, any depreciation in a destination exchange rate would induce a rise in its international tourism demand.

While some studies such as Loeb (1982); Quason and Var (1982); and Truett and Truett (1987) found exchange rate to be statistically insignificant in determining international tourism demand, other studies such as Artus (1972); Uysal and Crompton (1984); Little (1990); and Rosensweig (1986) found it to be statistically significant. Lee et al. (1996) used econometric models to determine that the effect of exchange rates on international demand on South Korean tourism varies from different origin countries. In the eight origin countries studied, namely: Japan; USA; Taiwan; Hong Kong; UK; West Germany; Philippines; and Canada, Lee et al. (1996) determined positive coefficient signs for exchange rate variables for all of them except UK with a negative coefficient, which was not significant.

Lee et al. (1996) determined elasticity for Korean tourism based on foreign exchange variable, ranging from a low of 0.08 (for Japanese tourists) to a high of 5.34 (for Canadian tourists). Tourists from Canada, Philippines, US, and Hong Kong appeared to be very responsive to exchange rate changes. The study established that while the exchange rate variable was statistically significant in the case of Japan, the elasticity estimate indicates that Japanese tourists were not sensitive to exchange rates.

Qui and Zhang's (1995) Canadian study identified that exchange rate is significant for international tourists from United Kingdom, France, and West Germany. Witt and Martin (1987) suggested that exchange rates are likely to play a proxy role as tourists are more knowledgeable and capable of informing themselves about exchange rates than about detailed prices at their destinations.

In a study to determine the effect of devaluation on Mexico's receipts and expenditures for tourism, Fish and Gibbon (1991) found that in 1977, a year after the first devaluation occurred, the country's nominal tourism receipts increased from 836 million U.S. dollars in 1976 to 967 million U.S. dollars in 1977. In terms of real dollar value of the pesos that world tourists spent in Mexico, receipts increased by 1224.6%. Mexican tourist expenditures increased by only 69.5% over the same period. Except for 1983, real receipts increased in every year, both before and after devaluation (Fish & Gibbons, 1988). The study confirmed that the effect of peso devaluation on Mexico's international tourist demand depends on the reaction of both international and Mexican travelers to the devaluation/appreciated value of the peso.

On the Canadian issue, exchange rate is known to have hurt Canadian tourism in 1989 and 1990 when the Canadian dollar rose to a 10-year high of 1.12 Canadian dollar to 1 US dollar. The US visitors, who saw their purchasing power decline from 20% to 12%, suspended traveling to Canada. The US market was estimated to have been off by 20% (Lyke, 1990). Canadian hoteliers attributed the low demand by US tourists to the weak US dollar exchange rate to the strong Canadian dollar (Lyke, 1990). Montreal and Toronto, the two Canadian cities that have heavily tapped the northeastern US market for tourists in the last decade, were the ones that felt the exchange rate crunch the most.

Montreal saw occupancy levels during 1989 drop 4.2%; they were off another 3.6% for the early part of 1990. Toronto was down 1% in 1989 and occupancy was slightly up for 1990 entering the summer season (Lyke, 1990) (see Table 1). The city of Vancouver was able to survive the crunch due to its popularity with Asian tourists. It saw an increase of 3% in its average occupancy levels in 1989, with room rates soaring from 74 dollars to 82 dollars. These observations were also determined by Qui and Zhangs' (1995) finding that, the US international tourists are sensitive to increase in Canadian exchange rates.

Morley (1994b) also confirmed that tourists put more emphasis on exchange rates than on hotel tariffs, since changes in exchange rate usually have direct impact on hotel tariffs and destination prices that have to be paid in the local currency.

Table 1.   Occupancies in Canada (% change in occupancy rate).

City	1989 vs. 1988
Montreal	−4.2%
Vancouver	+3.0
Toronto	−1.0
Calgary	−2.0

Source: Lyke (1990).

CONCLUSIONS AND SUMMARY

The effect of airfares and foreign exchange rates on international tourism demand reflects the volatility and sensitivity of international tourism. The review of literature on international tourism demand shows determinant interaction between the tourism factors (airfares and foreign exchange rates) and international tourism demand. As Fig. 1 depicts, an increase in the rate of foreign exchange of a destination country, and an upward surge of air-fares to that destination would result in a decrease in international tourism demand of that particular tourist destination.

Morley (1994a) substantiated this negative relationship when its findings determined a significant negative effect on tourists' destination choice associated to airfare increases. Also, the study found that exchange rates and hotel tariffs have lesser impacts than the airfare impact. Such airfare impacts are found to affect larger parties, larger families, and frequent tourists who evidently prefer closer and cheaper destinations to destinations with high exchange rates and increase airfares. This perspective of tourists' characteristics is categorized as: First category, "The Market Segment Effect."

As Gray (1966) determined, most travelers are rarely aware of prices in advance and often budget their expense estimates on the rate of exchange. From an economic perspective as established by "demand theory," any depreciation in a destination exchange rate would contribute to a rise in its international tourism demand. Other studies such as Abeyratyne (1993), have determined that when prices fluctuate, tourists' spend their money where it acquires more satisfying utilities, which is just another way of saying that tourists are very sensitive to tourism prices in various tourism markets. This tourists' characteristic is categorized as: Second category, "The Substitution Effect."

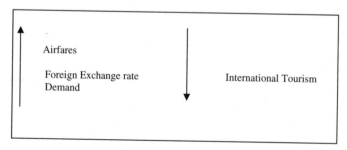

Fig. 1. Determinant Interaction Effect (Negative Relationship).

The elasticity of the price factors–airfares and foreign exchange rates vary from the different tourism-originating countries. The degree of sensitivity of international tourists to the impact of changes of the above factors on international tourism demand depends on the level of responsiveness of tourists from each originating country. Thus, the effects of the above tourism price factors are not generally applicable. They have differing degrees of impacts on international tourists from various originating countries. Also, Robertshaw (1993) established lower airfares facilitate more overseas trips and Gordon (1981) proposition of "purchasing power parity" enhances tourist flow from originating countries with stronger foreign exchange rate to country of destinations with relative weaker foreign exchange rates. This concept of tourists' behavior is categorized as: Third category, "The Facilitation Effect."

An understanding of the assessed effects on international tourism would enable tourist developers, planners, service providers, channel distributors, governments, and other practitioners to be able to identify issues that are specifically challenging to their individual operations. A good grasp on the issues would enable them to focus on pertinent resolutions to the identified specific issues.

REFERENCES

Abeyratyne, R. I. R. (1993). Air transport tax and its consequences on tourism. *Annals of Tourism Research, 20*, 450–460.

Anastasopoulou, P. G. (1984). *Independencies in international travel: The role of relative prices. A case study of the Mediterranean region.* Ph.D. dissertation. New York, NY: New School for Social Research.

Artus, J. R. (1972). An economic analysis of international travel. *IMF Staff Papers, 19*(3), 579–613.

Barry, K., & O'Hagan, J. (1972). An econometric study of British tourist expenditure in Ireland. *Economic and Social Review, 3*(2), 143–161.

Burkhart, A. J., & Medlick, S. (1974). *Tourism: Past, present and future.* London: Heinemann Connecticut Reporter.

Crouch, G. I. (1992). Effect of income and price on international tourism. *Annals of Tourism Research, 19*, 643–664.

Crouch, G. I. (1994). Price elasticities in international tourism. *Hospitality Research Journal, 17*(3), 27–39.

Dolan, E. G. (1980). *Basic economics.* Illinois: The Dryden Press.

Eadington, W. R., & Redman, M. (1991). Economics and tourism. *Annals of Tourism Research, 18*, 41–54.

eturbo News (2003). *Global tourism to pick up.* http://www.eturbonews.com/edition/04AUG2003, p.2

Fish, M., & Gibbon, J. D. (1991). Mexico's devaluations and changes in net foreign exchange receipts form tourism. *International Journal of Hospitality Management, 10*(1), 73–80.

Fujii, E., & Mak, J. (1981). Forecasting travel demand when the explanatory variables are highly correlated. *Journal of Travel Research, 18*(4), 31–34.

Gordon, R. J. (1981). *Macroeconomics* (2nd ed.). Boston: Little, B.

Gray, H. P. (1966). The demand for international travel by the United States and Canada. *International Economic Review, 7*, 83–92.

Lee, C., Var, T., & Blaine, T. W. (1996). Determinants of inbound tourist expenditures. *Annals of Tourism Research, 23*(3), 527–542.

Little, J. S. (1990). International travel in the U.S. balance of payments. *New England Economic Review*(May/June), 42–55.

Loeb, P. D. (1982). International travel to the United States: An econometric evaluation. *Annals of Tourism Research, 9*(1), 7–20.

Lyke, R. (1990). Exchange rates hurts Canadian tourism. *Hotel and Motel Management, 24*, 2.

Mak, J. (1988). Taxing hotel room rentals in the US. *Journal of Travel Research, 27*(1), 10–15.

Morley, C. L. (1994a). Discrete choice analysis of the impact of tourism prices. *Journal of Travel Research, 33*(2), 8–14.

Morley, C. L. (1994b). Experimental destination choice analysis. *Annals of Tourism Research, 21*(4), 780–791.

Quason, J., & Var, T. (1982). A tourism demand function for the Okanagan, B.C. *Tourism Management, 3*, 108–115.

Qui, H., & Zhang, J. (1995). Determinants of tourist arrivals and expenditures in Canada. *Journal of Travel Research, 33*(2), 43–49.

Robertshaw, N. (1993). How long '93's airfares will go is anyone's guess (Airline fares for tourists from Memphis, Tennessee). *Memphis Business Journal, 14*(48), 35.

Rosensweig, J. A. (1986). Exchange rates and competition for tourists. *New England Economic Review*(July/August), 57–67.

Stevens, B. F. (1992). Price value perceptions of travelers. *Journal of Travel Research, 31*(2), 44–48.

Stronge, W. B. (1982). The overseas demand for tourism in the United States. *The Review of Regional Studies, 12*(3), 40–53.

Stronge, W. B., & Redman, M. (1982). US tourism in Mexico: An empirical analysis. *Annals of Tourism Research, 9*, 21–35.

Truett, D. B., & Truett, L. J. (1987). The response of tourism to international economic condition: Greece, Mexico, and Spain. *The Journal of Developing Areas, 21*(2), 177–190.

Underwood, E. (1994). One hand feeds the other: Low airfares, high hotel and car rental rates, overview of travel industry. *Mediaweek, 4*(40), 138–141.

Uysal, M., & Crompton, J. (1984). Determinants of demand for international tourist flows to Turkey. *Tourism Management, 5*, 288–297.

Witt, S. F., & Martin, C. A. (1987). Econometric models for forecasting international tourism demand. *Journal of Travel Research, 25*(1), 23–30.

Witt, S. F., Newbould, G. D., & Watkins, A. J. (1992). Forecasting domestic tourism demand: Application for Las Vegas arrivals data. *Journal of Travel Research, 31*(2), 36–40.

World Travel and Tourism Council. (1992). *Travel and tourism in the world economy*. London: World Travel and Tourism Council.

CUSTOMERS' PREFERENCES TO HEALTHY MEALS

Willy Legrand and Philip Sloan

ABSTRACT

Today's restaurant customer is tempted with an unprecedented array of culinary delights coming from all around the planet. Consumers have been increasingly concerned about personal well-being and are better equipped to gain knowledge about health and nutrition through abundant information in print and other media such as the Internet. This study strives to discover what German restaurant goers really consider to be healthy. Due to the paucity of literature on healthy meals, this research attempts to initiate exploratory investigations testing a new psychological construct of healthy meals by using college students as the study population. This study finds that low-fat and non-genetically modified ingredients are the main concerns when respondents select a healthy meal. In addition, gender and eating habits affect the perceptions of healthy meals. Lastly, drawing from the key findings, suggestions for future research are proposed.

INTRODUCTION

The food service industry is an enigma. Eating out is a popular activity amongst Europeans. If the industry performs badly, it has the potential of harming consumers through food poisoning and other eating-related

Advances in Hospitality and Leisure, Volume 2, 265–273
ISSN: 1745-3542/doi:10.1016/S1745-3542(05)02014-X

diseases (Sloan, 2004). Foodborne disease is a growing health predicament in Europe and Worldwide (Clayton, Griffith, & Price, 2003). Research shows that consumers believe that food has become, over the last 20 years, less safe, less tasty, less healthy and more expensive (Verdurme, Gellynck, & Viaene, 2002). However, if the industry acts wisely, it can significantly increase the health and well-being of a nation.

Driven by health and environmental concerns ranging from aging baby boomers seeking more healthful choices to intense media scrutiny over the use of pesticides, herbicides, antibiotics and hormones in our food supply, Western consumers are increasingly turning to healthy food choices. Several trends have combined to fuel the surge in such consumerism. The price of many health food products – from free-range eggs to organic tomatoes – is now competitive with conventional alternatives, and consumers can find an increasing number in the choice of healthy products in more stores than ever before.

Consumers have also been alarmed by increasing reports of mercury in fish, antibiotics in meat and poultry and hormone-mimicking chemicals in shampoos and cosmetics. In a survey carried out in the U.S.A. on 2,000 adults by the American Natural Marketing Institute (NMI, 2003) it was found that 88% agreed that "it was important for companies to not just be profitable, but to be mindful of their impact on the environment and society". More than 70% of those surveyed said that knowing a company is aware of its impact on the environment and society in general makes them more likely to buy its products or services.

Statistics from the European Health Food Industry show that while sales of healthy food products such as food supplements and organic foods are expanding by between 10% and 20% per year (Hollingsworth, 2000), ironically so too are belt lines. In recent studies conducted by the European Union more than 40% of the adult population is overweight in Germany, which has the largest organic food market in Europe with over US$1.6 billion (Wier & Calverley, 2002), 15% of both France and the U.K. populations are clinically obese. These percentages are the highest since records began in the early 1960s.

Figures from the American Heart Association show that 96 million American adults have high cholesterol, 70 million suffer from digestive upsets and 60 million are at risk from blocked arteries and triglycerides. The Healthy Eating Index, developed by the United States Department of Agriculture, is based on various aspects of a healthy diet, such as total fat, saturated fat, cholesterol, sodium, variety and the food pyramid elements. The index, designed to provide a measure of overall dietary quality, classifies the majority of Americans (74% of the population) as "needing improvement" (Basiotis, Carlson, Gerrior, Juan, & Lino, 2002). Nevertheless, interest at consumer level is confirmed by the Organic Trade Association (OTA, 2004) data showing that the U.S. organic industry grew 20% to reach $10.8 billion in consumer sales in 2003 and that 44% of organic foods sold came from supermarket and grocery stores (Perlik, 2005). Sales of organic food in the U.K. topped £1 billion for the first time in 2003 (Soil Association's Organic Food and Farming Report, 2003), making the U.K. the third biggest outlet for organic food in the world. Three out of four babies eat organic food on a regular basis and organic baby food now accounts for nearly half of all baby food sold. Overall, sales of organic food and drink are growing twice as fast as the conventional grocery market, at over 10% a year. The second biggest organic market in the world is Germany with retail sales of £1.6 billion in 2003.

The public is showing more interest in healthy food options served in restaurants; it was found that 44% of people questioned would like to eat healthy and organic meals when eating out (Soil Association's Organic Food and Farming Report, 2003). Evidence of changes to a more healthy food are appearing as restaurant operators are tackling the health-oriented market, targeting not only the fitness-oriented person but also the larger population. Examples to be found include; menu items listing their respective calorie contents, information concerning the sourcing or origin of menu ingredients. 'Natural' and 'organic' are words often used to describe or depict the method of growing or origin of ingredients and there is a present trend describing steaks or other meat items as being 'hormone- and antibiotic-free'.

According to the Reed Research Group's organic food study conducted for Restaurant & Institutions trade magazine, Chefs are keen on obtaining 'organic' products due to two main factors: there is a perceived improvement in quality and freshness of organic products and increasing customer demand for these products (Perlik, 2005). In addition to privately owned catering establishments, many mid range and fast food restaurants are adapting their menus to the new demands. New chain restaurants in North America offering healthy food are gaining success such as Health Express, Healthy Bites Grill and World Wrapps. The Ritz in London became the capital's first hotel to offer diners-certified organic meals. A range of organic dishes are offered on the hotel's summer à la carte menu including noisettes of lamb Edward VII, grilled fillet of Angus beef with sauce Bearnaise, Caesar salad with bacon lardons and tian of provencal vegetables with vine tomato coulis.

Other issues that trigger the eating sensitivities of consumers are genetically modified (GM) foods (Verdurme & Viaene, 2003), such as the tomato
paste now widely used, chemical pesticides and herbicides on our breakfast
cereals and battery farming. In the U.K. over 150 million farm animals are
reared, many of whom are kept in confined conditions which are distressing
to the animals and which also encourage the spread of disease like Bovine
Spongiform Encephalopathy (BSE). It is argued that many consumers associate organic to animal-friendly products (Harper & Makatouni, 2002).
Behind the "back to nature" trend is an increasing level of affluence that
makes more costly alternatives more affordable to sectors of the European
public. While the nutritional content of organic food is not much different
from that of a traditional food, some consumers prefer and are able to
afford organic products (Fillion & Arazi, 2002).

Among certain population groups, these foods are viewed as both healthy
and high in status, appealing to both health- and status-conscious consumers (Zanoli & Naspetti, 2002). Traditional health food consumers are usually
those whose purchases are governed by their beliefs and lifestyles. As the
market sector expands, other consumer segments are developing such as
aging baby boomers, university students and others who view health food as
a tasty or chic alternative to conventional food. In a survey conducted in
Canada on organic food consumers, it was found that in reality those who
purchase organic food are not that different to the Canadian population as a
whole (Environics International Ltd, 2001). 18% of Canadians purchased
organic food regularly and a total of 71% (approximately 21.8 million) of
Canadians have at least tried organic foods, whereas only 26% (approximately 8 million) have never purchased any organic food. Of special interest
are the 12 million Canadians (30% of the population) who purchase organic
foods fairly often (i.e. more than one to two times per year). Of these, 60%
are females and are slightly more likely to be in the 25–34 age group than in
the over 55 age group. In the U.S.A., Perlik (2005) reports that college-age
customers tend to incorporate organic and natural ingredients into their
eating lifestyle rather sooner and faster than the general population. In all
cases, consumer interest in organic food has grown in many industrialised
countries but organic consumption constitutes only a small percentage,
1.5–2% of the entire food consumption (Wier & Calverley, 2002). In a
similar way "exotic" ingredients are perceived by many to be healthy and
are finding their way increasingly onto restaurant menus. Culinary diversity
is highly compatible with the healthy food trend. Many ethnic varieties, such
as Mediterranean and Asian cuisine, are considered inherently healthy.

Consequently, it is considered that food and eating implies tradition, roots and cultural connotations. Barasi in Human Nutrition mentions that each individual experiences eating in a different way and therefore, the concept of nutrition will differ greatly. Barasi (1997) states that "some may see eating as a mean of warding off hunger and others as a pleasurable experience in its own right and something to anticipate and plan [which] represent the two extremes implied by the saying 'eat to live' and 'live to eat'". Either way, nutrition plays an important role in defining healthy eating. Nutritionists have developed various tools to pinpoint and define healthy food. Herbert and Kasdan (1995) observed that a nutritious diet incorporates the "3–5–7 of good nutrition: 3 keywords (moderation, variety and balance), 5 basic food groups and 7 dietary guidelines". The five food groups (cereal, vegetable, fruit, fruit, milk and meat products) make up the food guide pyramid created by the U.S. Department of Agriculture (USDA) and the U.S. Department of Health and Human Services. However, many consider the food guide pyramid is outdated and does not guide people towards healthy eating. Nutrition experts at the Harvard School of Public Health created the Healthy Eating Pyramid to overcome the flaws of the traditional USDA pyramid. Although the Healthy Eating Pyramid includes the traditional five food groups, it divides grains between whole and white, adds plant oils, incorporates a multiple vitamin group and includes alcohol consumption guidelines. Furthermore, the new pyramid "sits on a foundation of daily exercise and weight control [as] these two related elements strongly influence (…) chances of staying healthy" (Harvard School of Public Health, 2004).

The pyramid does not cover issues surrounding the methods of production and the preparation of the foodstuff for consumption. The methods of growing the recommended daily two to three servings of fruit as well as the cooking techniques utilised for the recommended daily servings of poultry or the dressing that accompanies the salad may have an equal if not greater impact on the overall nutritional benefit of the meal. One major side effect of this media glut of information is the apparent scepticism of consumers.

More specifically, consumers seem to have become jaded about reports regarding health claims, particularly those that are negative. Eggs and butter have alternatively fallen out of and back into favour. Chocolate, wine and now red meat all have experienced similar swings in study-based health claims.

In 2002, the *Archives of Internal Medicine* published a study on the health benefits of eating white meat as opposed to red. It concluded that lean red meat is interchangeable with lean chicken and fish, with regard to their influence on blood cholesterol levels. Beef processors, supermarkets and the media were quick to pick up on this new research on "health food" characteristics of steaks and other cuts of beef. After 20 years of hearing that a limited intake of red meat is necessary to maintain a heart-healthy diet, consumers are now met with yet another seeming contradiction. It is hoped that the resultant data will provide concrete suggestions for further research on the issues surrounding healthy eating.

METHOD AND FINDINGS

To meet the goal of the study, the research deployed a series of surveys on college students with study questionnaires including the measurement of demographic traits, perceptions of healthy meals and lifestyle assessment. The draft questionnaire was developed through two qualitative methods entailing focus group surveys and a panel of experts. In the focus group survey, 65 attributes pertaining to the perceptions of healthy meals were recorded. However, after the initial screening from an expert panel 17 perception attributes were retained in the questionnaire. A pilot study was then conducted to examine the reliability and validity of the questionnaire. One perception question was eliminated due to a low reliability loading. In the final survey stage, the questionnaires were collected from 235 college students living in the cities of Cologne, Bonn and the surroundings.

The study first examined the perceptions of healthy eating by analysing the mean of perceptual attributes. Subsequently, a series of t-tests were conducted to detect if gender, eating habit and lifestyle affect the perceptions of healthy eating. Lastly, a logistic regression analysis was deployed to determine which healthy eating attributes are likely to affect respondents' restaurant selection.

Table 1 presents the rankings of agreement regarding the perceptions of healthy eating. The concept of a healthy meal is measured by 16 perceptual attributes, only four attributes do not meet the agreement of the respondents. These four perceptual attributes are tied to the presentation and tastes of the food. The "low-in-fat" attribute is the most agreeable image of healthy meals while "non-GM ingredients" is also considered as a critical criterion in selecting healthy meals. Surprisingly, "low in salt" is not highly regarded as a determinant of healthy meals.

Regarding the socio-demographic and lifestyle factors influencing the perceptions of healthy meals, the results are presented in Table 2. Males and females show differences in the perceptions of "low-in-fat", "high-in-fibre",

Table 1. The Perceptions of Healthy Meals ($N = 235$).

Attributes	Means	Rankings
Low in fat	3.97	1
No genetically modified ingredients	3.93	2
High in fibre	3.78	3
Low in sugar	3.68	4
Fish from a natural origin	3.64	5
Vegetable with an organic label	3.56	6
Pork of an organic origin	3.50	7
Poultry of an organic origin	3.50	7
Beef of an organic origin	3.49	9
Low in calories	3.33	10
Low in salt	3.29	11
With fresh ingredients	3.26	12
Gourmet	2.10	13
Good taste	1.68	14
Well presented	1.67	15
Good smell	1.51	16

Table 2. Differences in the Perceptions of Healthy Meals.

	Level of Significance
Gender (male vs. female)	
Low in fat	0.000
High in fibre	0.021
Non-(GM) ingredients	0.033
Eating habit (healthy vs. non-healthy)	
Low in sugar	0.003
Non-(GM) ingredients	0.019
Vegetarian (yes vs. no)	
Good smell	0.001
Search information from the Internet (use vs. no)	
Low in sugar	0.002
Good taste	0.012

and "GM ingredients". Females are more likely to look into the above three items in choosing a healthy meal. Additionally, individuals having good eating habits are unlikely to regard low-in-sugar and non-GM ingredients as the important criteria. Vegetarians agree that any meal, which smells good, is healthy. Those using the Internet to search for health information are likely to see "low in sugar" as an important preference to healthy meals

Table 3.   The Perceptual Attributes Affecting the Choice of Restaurants.

Attributes	B	Sig.
Low in sugar	1.23	0.000
Non-(GM) ingredients	0.483	0.022

while the non-users tend to treat the good taste of meals as a preference to healthy meals.

With a logistic regression analysis, the important attributes affecting the choice of restaurants are derived (see Table 3). The study finds that "low in sugar" and "non-GM ingredients" affect respondents' selection of restaurants whenever they search for healthy meals. Of these two, low in sugar had more effect on respondents' choice of restaurants.

CONCLUSION

The current research finds that fat, sugar, fiber and GM ingredients are the important criteria in the choice of healthy meals among German college students. However, gender and eating habits could be the factors explaining the perceptual differences. Specifically, low-sugar and non-GM ingredients are the two important criteria that affect students' selection of restaurants serving health meals.

It is interesting to note that the level of fat is one of the top considerations of healthy meals. However, promoting the idea of low-fat consumption could be misleading since certain types of fat benefit personal health. It is plausible that researchers could centre on the development of persuasive communication strategies, which better educate restaurant goers in appropriate fat consumption. Furthermore, GM ingredients affect meal choices. However, the definitions of GM foods are confusing. Further studies could consider developing the standards of GM meals that would give better assistance to consumers when making meal choices.

REFERENCES

Barasi, M. E. (1997). *Human nutrition: A health perspective.* London: Arnold.
Basiotis, P. P., Carlson, A., Gerrior, S. A., Juan, W. Y., & Lino, M. (2002). *The healthy eating index: 1999–2000.* U.S. Department of Agriculture, Center for Nutrition Policy and Promotion, CNPP-12.

Clayton, D. A., Griffith, C., & Price, P. E. (2003). An investigation of the factors underlying consumers' implementation of specific food safety practices. *British Food Journal, 105*(7), 434–453.

Environics International Ltd. (2001). *Food issues monitor survey 2001.* Retrieved July 16, 2005, from http://www.environics.net/eil/

Fillion, L., & Arazi, S. (2002). Does organic food taste better? A claims substation approach. *Nutrition & Food Science, 32*(4), 153–157.

Harper, G. C., & Makatouni, A. (2002). Consumer perception of organic production and farm animal welfare. *British Food Journal, 104*(3), 287–299.

Harvard School of Public Health. (2004). *Food pyramids: What should you really eat?* Retrieved July 12, 2005, from http://www.hsph.harvard.edu/nutritionsource/pyramids.html

Herbert, V., & Kasdan, T. S. (1995). What is a healthy food plan? In: V. Herbert & G. J. Subak-Sharpe (Eds), *Total nutrition: The only guide you'll ever need* (pp. 3–16). New York: St. Martin's Griffin.

Hollingsworth, P. (2000). Marketing trends fuelling healthful foods success. *Food Technology, 54*(10), 53–58.

Natural Marketing Institute (NMI). (2003). *Health and wellness trends report.* Retrieved July 15, 2005, from http://www.nmisolutions.com/r_hwt.html

Organic Trade Association (OTA). (2004). *The OTA 2004 manufacturer survey overview.* Retrieved July 12, 2005, from http://www.ota.com/pics/documents/2004SurveyOverview.pdf

Perlik, A. (Ed.) (2005). Organics' chemistry. *Restaurant & Institutions,* February 15, pp. 38–42.

Sloan, D. (Ed.) (2004). *Culinary taste: Consumer behaviour in the international restaurant sector.* Oxford: Elsevier Butterworth-Heinemann.

Soil Association's Organic Food and Farming Report. (2003). Retrieved July 16, 2005, from http://www.soilassociation.org/farmingreport

Verdurme, A., Gellynck, X., & Viaene, J. (2002). Are organic food consumers opposed to GM food consumers? *British Food Journal, 104*(8), 610–623.

Verdurme, A., & Viaene, J. (2003). Exploring and modelling consumer attitudes towards genetically modified food. *Qualitative Market Research: An International Journal, 6*(2), 95–110.

Wier, M., & Calverley, C. (2002). Market potential for organic foods in Europe. *British Food Journal, 104*(1), 45–62.

Zanoli, R., & Naspetti, S. (2002). Consumer motivations in the purchase of organic food: A means-end approach. *British Food Journal, 104*(8), 643–653.

AN INVESTIGATION
OF PERCEIVED JUSTICES
AND CUSTOMER SATISFACTION

Denver E. Severt

ABSTRACT

Service research including justice has ignored the full range of service outcomes possible and has only been conducted when a service failure has occurred. This study allows for a full spectrum of service outcomes including service success, service failure, and service recovery. This study used the survey method to collect data to measure the relationship of justice constructs (i.e., interactional, distributive, and procedural justice) to overall justice and customer satisfaction. The researcher used a convenience sample-survey method. Graduate students in a service class collected 50 useable questionnaires for the pilot study. The researcher and two graduate students collected 302 useable questionnaires in an airport for the main study. Path analysis results showed that interactional, distributive, and procedural justice, all had direct effects and a significant positive relationship to overall justice and customer satisfaction, and overall justice had a direct and significant positive relationship to customer satisfaction.

Advances in Hospitality and Leisure, Volume 2, 275–290
Copyright © 2006 by Elsevier Ltd.
ISSN: 1745-3542/doi:10.1016/S1745-3542(05)02015-1

INTRODUCTION

Published research regarding the role of justice in achieving or failing to achieve customer satisfaction focuses only on service recovery after a service failure (Tax, Brown, & Chandrashekaran, 1998), overlooking the full spectrum of service encounter outcomes including service success, service recovery, and service failure (Smith & Bolton, 1998). This void leaves businesses and researchers with insufficient information concerning the relationships between the justice experienced in a service encounter and the customer's satisfaction level. This study aimed to fill some of that gap by asking the following question: What are the relationships of interactional, distributive, and procedural justice to overall justice and to customer satisfaction?

Interactional, distributive, and procedural justice, measure service encounter fairness associated with the people, output, and process involved, respectively. These constructs are based on perceptions of justice or fairness (Greenberg, 1990a) and have been confirmed (Bies & Moag, 1986). Tax et al. (1998) highlighted the importance of considering the effects of the interaction of the three constructs on customer satisfaction. This researcher has joined the current cadre of researchers in partitioning justice into interactional, distributive, and procedural justice, which is an adaptation of Greenberg's taxonomy of justice that divided procedural justice into systems and informational justice and distributive justice into configural and interpersonal justice (Cropanzano, 1992).

Interactional Justice

Interactional justice arises from the interpersonal part of a transaction (Greenberg, 1990b). It is an intangible part of the service encounter experience composed of fairness judgments related to the attributes of honesty (Goodwin & Ross, 1989), politeness (Clemmer, 1988; Goodwin & Ross, 1989), effort (Folkes, 1984; Mohr & Bitner, 1995), empathy (Parasuraman, Zeithaml, & Berry, 1988), and explanation (Bies & Shapiro, 1987). Defined by Tax et al. (1998) as the perceived fairness in interactions between people when the guest is present in the service delivery system or while the service is being carried out, interactional justice has also been defined as the quality of interaction between two parties involved in a conflict (Bies & Moag, 1986). It has been shown to affect the quality of service delivered (Grant, Shani, & Krishnan, 1994).

Distributive Justice

Distributive justice is the perceived fairness of the tangible outcome of the service encounter (Hocut, Chakraborty, & Mowen, 1997). Equity (Goodwin & Ross, 1992), equality (Greenberg, 1990a), and need (Deutsch, 1985) have been used in defining it. Problems with measuring distributive justice arise because equity, equality, and need are not easy for the customer to distinguish and it is difficult for the service personnel and customers to assess input and output value (Deutsch, 1985). The distributive justice equity model has been tested extensively in sociological and organizational behavior research (Greenberg, 1990a). Distributive justice has been used many times to explain justice or fairness (Tax, 1993). Researchers favor use of the distributive-justice model when inputs and outputs are easily measured.

Procedural Justice

Procedural justice is process fairness. Service recovery literature has defined procedural justice as the organization's step-by-step actions in solving problems (Lind & Tyler, 1988). Tax and Brown (1998) called procedural justice, the adequacy of the criteria or procedure used in decision making. In assessing procedures, the customer makes a subjective comparison of the processes used to handle a transaction, service recovery, or injustice. In order of importance, the attributes of procedural justice are (1) assuming responsibility, (2) timing and speed, (3) convenience, (4) follow-up, (5) process control, (6) flexibility, and (7) knowledge of the process (Tax et al., 1998).

Customer Satisfaction

Customer satisfaction continues to be one of the topics that companies research most. Consequently, theorists are continuing to explore new models and methods that may unlock meaningful information about customer satisfaction. Marketing researchers have not yet agreed on one global definition for customer satisfaction. Although the constructs have been thoroughly explored, one theoretical model has not and likely will not be accepted due to the complex process involved in arriving at a customer's judgment of satisfaction or dissatisfaction. This researcher defines customer satisfaction and dissatisfaction as the consumer's judgments regarding a firm's success or failure in meeting expectations, with met expectations resulting in satisfaction and unmet expectations resulting in dissatisfaction (Oliver, 1980).

Consumer satisfaction research started as early as the 1960s (Cardozo, 1965). The literature suggests that customer satisfaction is a by-product of the confirmation or positive disconfirmation of expectations and that customer dissatisfaction is a by-product of negative disconfirmation of expectations (Day, 1984; Oliver, 1980).

Based on the past mentioned literature and relationships, this research poses the following hypotheses: interactional, distributive, and procedural justice are positively related to (a) overall justice and (b) customer satisfaction.

METHOD

A pilot study was done to verify the reliability of the scale items, a pretest was conducted, and then a main study questionnaire was collected. This study used a recall research design. Respondents were asked to recall a service encounter and answer a questionnaire about the encounter. The customer who consumes services is the unit of measure. The customer-offered-face validity was used because the customer participated in the service encounter.

The customer is a justifiable unit of measure for the following reasons: (1) Service models have identified customers as partial employees (Mills, 1990) and have shown that customer and employee perceptions of service transactions are correlated (Schneider, 1980).(2) The customer is similar to the units employed in other empirical services marketing studies (Bitner, Booms, & Mohr, 1994; Maxham, 1998; Smith, 1998; Swanson, 1998; Tax et al., 1998).

The following steps were taken by the researcher to prepare the questionnaire and collect the data for this research: First, a pretest of the questionnaire was done to verify face validity. Second, a pilot study was done to verify the reliability of the scale items. Third, the main study questionnaires were collected. This study used a quantitative recall research design. Respondents were asked to recall a service encounter and answer a questionnaire about the encounter.

Path analysis was conducted for the hypotheses to determine the direct and indirect effects of interactional, distributive, and procedural justice on overall justice and customer satisfaction. The research questions meet the path analysis stipulation of having one dependent and multiple independent variables. Although there are inherent complexities in dividing overall justice into the three categories of interactional justice, distributive justice, and procedural justice, it is meaningful to understand more about each construct both for research models and for practical advice for managers. The quantitative results highlight this. For example, the correlation between interactional and procedural justice was high and the correlations between distributive justice and procedural and interactional justice were high. This multicollinearity threatens the validity of path models (Pedhazur, 1992); nonetheless, researchers agree that other than allowing for as large a sample size as possible, there are few simple solutions to this research dilemma.

A χ^2 test of significance was applied to the data for each hypothesis to determine significance ($p \leq 0.05$) and to verify whether the sign of the path coefficient for each justice variable was the same as the sign of the overall justice and customer satisfaction coefficients. After collecting data, the researcher tested the path assumptions, i.e., statistical relationship, normality, equal variance of customer satisfaction, and lack of correlation of error (Hair, Anderson, Tatham, & Black, 1992).

RESULTS

The survey's demographic descriptive statistics are presented in Table 1. Of the 302 respondents, 52% were male and 48% were female. Eighteen percent of survey respondents were 22 years of age and under, 34% were between 23 and 33, 26% were between 34 and 44, 15% were between 45 and 54, 5% were between 55 and 64, and 2% were 65 or over. Respondents reported their ethnic backgrounds as 10% African-American, 17% Asian, 3% Hispanic, 67% White, and 3% other. Marital status showed 31% were single, 9% were divorced, and 60% were married; none were widowed. The education reported by respondents showed 2% had some or no high school, 13% were high school graduates, 36% had some college, 23% were college graduates, 12% had some graduate school, and 14% had a graduate or professional degree.

Sixty percent of respondents recalled satisfying service encounters and 40% recalled dissatisfying service encounters. The majority of identified service providers were restaurants (26%), retail stores (20%), airports (17%), automotive repair shops (12.3%), and hotels (6.5%). The remaining identified business types (18.2%) involved funeral home, lawn mower repair, ticket purchase, grocery shopping, telephone, housing, hospital, doctor,

Table 1. Demographic Statistics for the Main Study ($n = 302$).

Characteristics	Frequency	Percent
Gender		
Male	145	48
Female	154	52
Age		
22 and under	55	18
23–33	102	34
34–44	77	26
45–54	45	15
55–64	13	5
65 and over	7	2
Ethnicity		
African-American	31	10
Asian	50	17
Hispanic	8	3
White	201	67
Other	8	3
Marital status		
Single	91	31
Divorced	28	9
Married	181	60
Widowed	0	0
Education		
Some or no high school	4	2
High school graduate	38	13
Some college	106	36
College graduate	69	23
Some graduate study	36	12
Graduate/professional	41	14

home repair, insurance, cleaning company, theater, local government, child care, hair, library, dry cleaner, bank, postal, and electricity services. Approximately 20% of respondents did not report the specific type of service business involved in their recalled encounter.

After purification of the scale items resulting from the pilot study, all measurement scales for use in the main study had CAs greater than 0.90 (Table 1), i.e., prior experience, 0.96; interactional justice, 0.95; distributive justice, 0.95; procedural justice, 0.96; overall justice, 0.94; and customer satisfaction, 0.97 (see Table 2).

Table 2.   Statistics and Reliability Estimates for Main Study Scales
($n = 302$).

Scale Item[a]		Mean	Standard Deviation	Cronbach's Alpha
Prior experience	1	3.1026	2.0081	0.96
	2	4.9073	1.9744	
	3	4.9371	1.9663	
Interactional justice	1	3.2748	2.2606	0.95
	2	2.7252	1.9360	
	3	2.8775	1.9887	
	4	3.1457	2.0456	
	5	3.2417	1.9828	
	6	2.9470	1.9624	
	7	3.1523	2.0965	
Distributive justice	1	2.7152	2.0161	0.95
	2	2.7815	1.8095	
	3	2.9735	2.0716	
	4	3.1391	2.2100	
	5	3.1391	2.2055	
	6	3.1060	2.2550	
Procedural justice	1	3.0397	1.9728	0.96
	2	3.1258	2.0225	
	3	3.0828	1.9740	
	4	3.0960	2.0380	
	5	3.1656	2.0163	
	6	3.0563	1.9834	
	7	2.9801	2.0749	
	8	3.3675	2.2056	
	9	4.7053	2.3032	
Overall justice	1	3.0033	2.1834	0.94
	2	3.2384	2.2075	
	3	3.2483	2.2430	
Customer satisfaction	1	3.0795	2.2175	0.97
	2	3.0033	2.0838	
	3	3.1556	2.2276	
	4	3.1623	2.2077	
	5	4.7550	2.3384	
	6	3.1192	2.2157	

[a]Measured on a 7-point Likert scale.

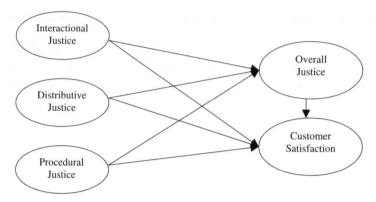

Fig. 1. Path Model of Justice and Customer Satisfaction.

Consumers' conclusions regarding interactional, distributive, and procedural justice were hypothesized to influence perceptions of overall justice and customer satisfaction. In accordance with the path analysis approach (Anderson & Gerbing, 1988), the constructs were specified in a structural model (Fig. 1) to examine the hypothesized relationships. Because equity theory holds that justice is a function of the ratio of inputs to outputs (Adams, 1965) and that consumers judge inputs or justice types before deciding overall justice, the model begins with interactional, distributive, and procedural justice and shows the justice constructs as distinct. It does not show directional effects among the three justice variables because such directional effects were not analyzed in this study.

To assess the model, path coefficients (direct effects) and explained variance (R^2) for the justice constructs were examined. Following the suggestions of Hoyle and Panter (1995), the model fit was determined by several goodness-of-fit statistics, including χ^2, root-mean-square residual (RMR), goodness-of-fit index (GFI), adjusted goodness-of-fit-index (AGFI), and comparative fit index (CFI). The χ^2 is the usual method for testing the closeness of fit between the unrestricted sample covariance and the restricted covariance matrix. RMR is a kind of an average of the fitted residuals. GFI is a standardized overall measure of fit based on properties of the observed and reproduced values of the covariance matrix. AGFI is the GFI adjusted for the number of the model degrees of freedom. CFI is an incremental fit index that is robust across various sample sizes. The model yielded a χ^2 estimate of 0, goodness-of-fit and adjusted goodness-of-fit indices of 0.99 and 0.89, respectively, a CFI reading of 1, and an RMR of

Table 3.   Path Analysis Results for Interactional, Distributive, Procedural Justice, Overall Justice, and Customer Satisfaction.

Model Path	Path Coefficient	t Value*
Overall justice ($R^2 = 0.75$)		
Interactional justice	0.23	3.23
Distributive justice	0.48	7.57
Procedural justice	0.31	3.80
Customer satisfaction ($R^2 = 0.84$)		
Interactional sustice	0.26	4.55
Distributive sustice	0.18	3.25
Procedural justice	0.27	4.20
Overall justice	0.35	7.76

*Significant at $p < 0.05$.

0.037. The model $p = 1$. The fit between the data and the model was supported in all instances.

Hypothesis 1. Interactional justice is positively related to (a) overall justice and (b) customer satisfaction.

Path analysis results (Table 3) showed interactional justice to have a significant effect on both overall justice and customer satisfaction. The path coefficients of 0.23 and 0.26 for overall justice and customer satisfaction and the corresponding t values of 3.23 and 4.55, respectively, were significant at $p < 0.05$ level and supported both hypotheses (Table 3).

As perceived personal interactions were favorable during the service encounter, there was a positive direct effect on overall justice and customer satisfaction. Direct effects (the path coefficient) result from interactional justice acting alone; indirect effects are mediated by distributive or procedural justice (Table 4). The total effect of interactional justice, the sum of its combined direct and indirect effects, was also positive.

Hypothesis 2. Distributive justice is positively related to (a) overall justice and (b) customer satisfaction.

Path analysis (see Tables 3 and 4) showed a significant effect of distributive justice on overall justice and customer satisfaction. Distributive justice had a larger effect than interactional or procedural justice on overall justice, with a path coefficient of 0.48 ($t = 7.57$, significant at the $p < 0.05$ level). For customer satisfaction, distributive justice had a path coefficient of 0.18 ($t = 3.25$, significant at the $p < 0.05$ level). The strong direct effect of

Table 4. Effects of Justice on Customer Satisfaction.

	Effect					
	Overall justice			Customer satisfaction		
Justice	Direct	Indirect[a]	Total	Direct	Indirect[a]	Total
Interactional	0.23	N/A	0.23	0.26	0.06	0.32
Interactional justice	0.23	N/A	0.23	0.26	0.06	0.32
Distributive	0.48	N/A	0.48	0.18	0.07	0.25
Procedural	0.31	N/A	0.31	0.27	0.07	0.34
Overall				0.35	N/A	0.35

[a]N/A indicates the effect was not examined in this study.

0.48 on overall justice showed distributive justice had the greatest effect on overall justice. Distributive justice also showed a significant yet smaller direct effect of 0.18 on customer satisfaction. The data supported both the procedural justice hypotheses.

Hypothesis 3. Procedural justice is positively related to overall justice and customer satisfaction.

Path analysis results (see Tables 3 and 4) supported the effect of procedural justice on overall justice and customer satisfaction. For overall justice, procedural justice had a path coefficient of 0.31 and a corresponding t value of 3.80 with significance at the $p < 0.05$ level. For customer satisfaction, procedural justice showed a path coefficient of 0.27, and a corresponding t value of 4.20 significant at the $p < 0.05$ level. The data supported the hypothesized positive relationship of procedural justice to overall justice and customer satisfaction.

Decomposition of path analysis revealed direct and significant positive effects on overall justice by interactional, distributive, and procedural justice. Distributive justice was shown to have the largest direct influence on overall justice. Procedural justice showed the next largest influence. Interactional justice showed the least influence. Interactional, distributive, and procedural justice demonstrated an $R^2 = 0.75$ of overall justice (see Table 4), implying a robust model. Robustness was similarly indicated by interactional, distributive, procedural, and overall justice accounting for 84% of the variance in customer satisfaction levels.

Study results showed significant direct and indirect effects of interactional justice on overall justice and customer satisfaction. Across recalled service encounters, high perceptions of interactional justice yielded high perceptions of overall justice and customer satisfaction. The results, which are supported by earlier studies that reached similar conclusions regarding higher levels of interactional justice leading to higher levels of customer satisfaction, confirm the importance of just interpersonal treatment in achieving customer satisfaction during the service encounter.

DISCUSSION AND CONCLUSIONS

What is the Relationship of Interactional Justice to Overall Justice and Customer Satisfaction?

Interactional justice has primarily been explored in customer satisfaction studies when service failure has occurred. This study, which benefits greatly from prior research, is of recalled service encounters across the spectrum of outcomes and offers a more comprehensive view of interactional justice in service transactions. Interactional justice arises from the interpersonal part of a transaction (Greenberg, 1990b). It is an intangible part of the service encounter experience composed of justice judgments related to the attributes of honesty (Goodwin & Ross, 1989), politeness (Clemmer, 1988; Goodwin & Ross, 1989), effort (Folkes, 1984; Mohr & Bitner, 1995), empathy (Parasuraman et al., 1988), and explanation (Bies & Shapiro, 1987; Bitner et al., 1994). Defined by Tax et al. (1998) and this author as the perceived fairness in interactions between people when the guest is present in the service delivery system or while the service is being carried out, interactional justice has also been defined as the quality of interaction between two parties involved in a conflict (Bies & Moag, 1986).

Interactional justice has been shown to affect the quality of service delivered (Grant et al., 1994). Bitner et al. (1990) discovered that 43% of poor outcomes in service transactions are due to front-line employees' responses to a service failure. Unacceptable answers about service failures from others in the business accounted for 51% of poor outcomes (Hocut et al., 1997). Marketing studies that have employed the notion of interactional justice in customer satisfaction research (Blodgett, Wakefield, & Barnes, 1995; Blodgett & Tax, 1993; Goodwin & Ross, 1989, 1992; Oliver & Swan, 1989; Smith & Bolton, 1998; Smith, Bolton, & Wagner, 1999; Tax et al., 1998) support interactional justice as a significant predictor of customer satisfaction with service recovery efforts. Smith (1998) operationalized interactional justice as the presence or absence of an apology after a service failure and during a service recovery attempt. It has been noted that many

times the interpersonal treatment experienced appears to remain in salient
memory longer than the other details of a service encounter.

What is the Relationship of Distributive Justice to Overall Justice and Customer Satisfaction?

Study results showed significant direct and indirect effects of distributive
justice on overall justice and customer satisfaction. In fact, distributive justice showed the largest total effect and highest predictive power on overall
justice and was significantly related to customer satisfaction. These results
have been confirmed by previous theoretical and empirical research, including Smith's (1998) experimental study that found customer satisfaction
was higher with higher perceptions of distributive justice.

Distributive justice is the perceived fairness of the tangible outcome of the
service encounter (Hocut et al., 1997). Equity (Goodwin & Ross, 1992;
Oliver & DeSarbo, 1988; Oliver & Swan, 1989), equality (Greenberg, 1990a),
and need (Deutsch, 1985) have been used in defining it. Problems with
measuring distributive justice arise because equity, equality, and need are
not easy for the customer to distinguish, and it is difficult for the service
personnel and customers to assess input and output value (Deutsch, 1985).

Distributive justice is important to overall justice because it is likely that
many guests form an overall perception of their service encounter based on
the value received compared to the value expected. Clientele who receive an
acceptable outcome may overlook many wrongs during the service encounter and deem the service appropriate. Distributive justice can reduce the
impact of interactional and procedural injustices when the ultimate distribution is acceptable to the guest. If the multiple attribute notion of perceptions of justice and customer satisfaction is espoused, it is still likely that
achieving favorable distributive justice or product output will produce more
favorable perceptions of interactional and procedural justice and, therefore,
higher levels of overall justice and customer satisfaction.

Researchers tend to measure distributive justice when inputs and outputs
are easily quantified, which was not always the case in the reported recalled
encounters. Nonetheless, respondents identified a level of distributive justice. The distributive justice equity model has been tested extensively in
sociological and organizational behavior research. Distributive justice has
been used many times to explain justice or fairness (Tax, 1993). Empirical
equity research has supported the role of distributive justice in service
recovery (Blodgett et al., 1995; Blodgett & Tax, 1993; Goodwin & Ross,

1989, 1992; Spreng, Harrell, & MacKoy, 1995). Distributive justice is achieved in a service failure and recovery when the customer receives at least what they would have received before the service failure occurred. This has been referred to as restoration to at least value level (Adams, 1965) and as atonement (Bell & Zemke, 1987). Reimbursement, replacement, repair, correction, and credit are attributes of attempts to recover from distributive injustice (Tax et al., 1998).

Implications
The high predictive power of distributive justice for overall justice and its significant effect on customer satisfaction imply that service personnel should be trained to ensure that the guests' needs and expectations are fairly met. The service personnel must recognize distributive injustice and know what to do to restore justice when a customer's expectations are not met. Clientele must be happy with the quantity and quality of the goods and services rendered. In order for companies to ensure that the product delivered is what the patron expects, employees and managers must be aware of product offerings and product promises and be trained to look for and correct deviations before and as they occur. Front-line employees who are empowered by specific procedural guidelines to restore distributive justice are most likely to achieve the overall justice that enhances the chances of customer satisfaction.

What is the Relationship of Procedural Justice to Overall Justice and Customer Satisfaction?

Study results showed procedural justice had significant effects on overall justice and customer satisfaction. These results were presaged by previous theoretical and empirical research, including Smith's (1998) finding that customer satisfaction was higher when perceptions of procedural justice in a service recovery were higher.

Procedural justice, or process fairness, has been defined in service recovery literature as the organization's step-by-step actions in solving problems (Lind & Tyler, 1988). Tax and Brown (1998) called procedural justice the adequacy of the criteria or procedure used in decision making. In assessing procedures, the customer makes a subjective comparison of the processes used to handle a transaction.

Services marketing studies have used procedural justice to measure fairness. Burroughs (1982) and Greenberg and McCarty (1990) used it to analyze pay equity in an organization setting. Bies and Shapiro (1987) applied it to human resource practices. Goodwin and Ross (1989, 1992) used the consumer's opportunity to participate by offering opinions to measure procedural justice. Procedural justice, which has proven difficult to manipulate in experimental situations, has been studied in research that used retrospective self-reports focused on service failures and recoveries (Goodwin & Ross, 1992).

Assuring procedural justice across service outcomes is essential to achieving good customer satisfaction assessments. Therefore, business owners and managers will want to include procedural justice when designing systems and when training front-line staff and all personnel who interact with customers. The attributes of procedural justice should be considered when designing a service-delivery system. A training program that considers customers' perceptions of procedural justice must take into account the attributes of procedural justice identified by Tax et al. (1998). In order of importance, they are (1) assuming responsibility, (2) timing and speed, (3) convenience, (4) follow-up, (5) process control, (6) flexibility, and (7) knowledge of the process.

Finally, more studies are called for which can partition satisfaction down further into those satisfied and those dissatisfied and to look further into the dynamic relationships between justice and satisfaction. More of these studies should consider the full range of service encounter outcomes such as this research as opposed to only measuring justice in the realm of service failure. Additionally, while recent work has been conducted in an experimental setting and an applied setting (Matilla & Cranage, 2005), more work is needed in both experimental and applied settings to capture the rich data and to lend support to advances in theory that can be gained from customer reports of service encounters.

REFERENCES

Adams, J. S. (1965). Inequity in social exchange. *Advances in Experimental Social Psychology, 2*, 267–299.

Anderson, J., & Gerbing, D. (1988). Structural equation modeling in practice: A review and recommended two-step approach. *Psychological Bulletin, 103*(3), 411–423.

Bell, C. R., & Zemke, R. (1987). Service breakdown: The road to recovery. *Management Review, 1*(1), 32–35.

Bies, R. J., & Moag, J. S. (1986). Interactional communication criteria of fairness. In: R. J. Lewicki, B. H. Sheppard & M. H. Bazerman (Eds), *Research in organizational behavior* (pp. 23–38). Greenwich, CT: JAI Press.

Bies, R. J., & Shapiro, D. L. (1987). Interactional fairness judgments: The influence of causal accounts. *Social Justice Research, 1*, 199–218.

Bitner, M. J., Booms, B. H., & Mohr, L. A. (1994). Critical service encounters: The employees viewpoint. *Journal of Marketing, 58*(October), 95–106.

Blodgett, J. G., & Tax, S. S. (1993). The effects of distributive and interactional justice on complainants repatronage intentions and negative word-of-mouth intentions. *Journal of Satisfaction, Dissatisfaction and Complaining Behavior, 6*, 100–110.

Blodgett, J. G., Wakefield, K. L., & Barnes, J. (1995). The effects of customer service on consumer complaining behavior. *Journal of Services Marketing, 9*(4), 31–42.

Burroughs, J. D. (1982). Pay secrecy and performance: The psychological research. *Compensation Review, 14*, 44–54.

Cardozo, R. N. (1965). An experimental study of customer effort, expectation, and satisfaction. *Journal of Marketing Research, 2*(August), 244–249.

Clemmer, E. C. (1988). *The role of fairness in customer satisfaction with services.* Ph.D. dissertation, University of Maryland.

Cropanzano, R. (1992). Justice in the workplace: Approaching fairness, *Human resource management.* NJ: Hillsdale.

Day, R. S. (1984). Toward a process model of consumer satisfaction. In: H. Hunt (Ed.), *Conceptualization and measurement of consumer satisfaction and dissatisfaction* (pp. 201–222). Cambridge, MA: Marketing Science Institute.

Deutsch, J. (1985). *Distributive justice: A social–psychological perspective.* New Haven, CT: Yale University Press.

Folkes, V. S. (1984). Consumer reactions to product failure: An attributional approach. *Journal of Consumer Research, 10*(March), 398–409.

Goodwin, C., & Ross, I. (1989). Salient dimensions of perceived fairness in resolution of service complaints. *Journal of Business Research, 25*, 149–163.

Goodwin, C., & Ross, I. (1992). Consumer responses to service failures: Influence of procedural and interactional fairness perceptions. *Journal of Business Research, 25*, 149–163.

Grant, R. W., Shani, R., & Krishnan, R. (1994). TQM's challenge to management theory and practice. *Sloan Management Review, 36*(1), 25–35.

Greenberg, J. (1990a). Organizational justice: Yesterday, today, and tomorrow. *Journal of Management, 16*(2), 399–432.

Greenberg, J. (1990b). Looking fair versus being fair: Managing impressions of organizational justice. *Research in Organizational Behavior, 12*, 11–157.

Greenberg, J., & McCarty, C. L. (1990). Comparable worth: A matter of justice. In: G. R. Ferris & K. M. Rowlands (Eds), *Research in personnel and human resource management,* (Vol. 8, pp. 111–157). Greenwich, CT: Jai Press.

Hair, J., Anderson, G., Tatham, B., & Black, E. (1992). *Multivariate data analysis: With readings.* New York: MacMillan Publishing Company.

Hocut, M. A., Chakraborty, G., & Mowen, J. C. (1997). The impact of perceived justice on customer satisfaction and intention to complain in a service recovery. *Advances in Consumer Research, 24*, 457–463.

Hoyle, R. H., & Panter, A. T. (1995). Writing about structural equation models. In: R. H. Hoyle (Ed.), *Structural equation modeling: Concept, issues, and applications* (pp. 158–176). Thousand Oaks, CA: Sage.

Lind, E. A., & Tyler, T. R. (1988). *The social psychology of procedural justice.* New York: Plenum Press.

Matilla, A., & Cranage, D. (2005). Service recover and pre-emptive strategies for service failure both lead to customer satisfaction and loyalty – but for different reasons. *Journal of Hospitality and Leisure Marketing, 13*(3), 159–179.

Maxham, J. (1998). *Service failure and recovery.* Ph.D. dissertation, Louisiana State University.

Mills, P. K. (1990). On the quality of services in encounters: An agency perspective. *Journal of Marketing, 58*(July), 20–38.

Mohr, L. A., & Bitner, M. J. (1995). The role of employee effort in satisfaction with service transactions. *Journal of Business Research, 32,* 239–252.

Oliver, R. L. (1980). A cognitive model of the antecedents and consequences of satisfaction decisions. *Journal of Marketing Research, 14*(March), 495–507.

Oliver, R. L., & DeSarbo, W. S. (1988). Response determinants in satisfaction judgments. *Journal of Consumer Research, 14*(March), 495–507.

Oliver, R. L., & Swan, J. E. (1989). Consumer perceptions of interpersonal equity and satisfaction in transactions: A field survey approach. *Journal of Marketing, 53*(April), 21–35.

Parasuraman, A., Zeithaml, V. A., & Berry, L. L. (1988). SERVQUAL: A multiple item scale for measuring consumer perceptions of service quality. *Journal of Retailing, 64*(Spring), 12–40.

Pedhazur, E. J. (1992). *Multiple regression in behavioral research.* New York: Holt, Rinehart & Winston.

Schneider, B. (1980). The service organization: Climate is crucial. *Organizational Dynamics, 9*(autumn), 52–65.

Smith, A. (1998). *A model of customer satisfaction with service encounters involving failure and recovery.* Ph.D. dissertation, University of Maryland.

Smith, A., & Bolton, R. (1998). An experimental investigation of customer reactions to service failure and recovery encounters, paradox or peril? *Journal of Service Research, 1*(1), 65–81.

Smith, A., Bolton, R., & Wagner, J. (1999). A model of customer satisfaction with service encounters involving failure and recovery. *Journal of Marketing Research, 36*(August), 356–372.

Spreng, R. A., Harrell, G. D., & MacKoy, R. (1995). Service recovery: Impact on satisfaction and intentions. *Journal of Services Marketing, 9*(1), 15–23.

Swanson, S. (1998). *Service failure and recovery.* Ph.D. dissertation, University of Kentucky.

Tax, S. (1993). *The role of perceived justice in complaint resolutions: Implications for services and relationship marketing.* Ph.D. dissertation, Arizona State University.

Tax, S., & Brown, S. (1998). Recovering and learning from service failure. *Sloan Management Review, 40*(1), 75–88.

Tax, S., Brown, S., & Chandrashekaran, M. (1998). Customer evaluations of service complaint experiences: Implications for relationship marketing. *Journal of Marketing, 62,* 60–76.

SUBJECT INDEX

291

SET UP A CONTINUATION ORDER TODAY!

Did you know that you can set up a continuation order on all Elsevier-JAI series and have each new volume sent directly to you upon publication? For details on how to set up a **continuation order**, contact your nearest regional sales office listed below.

To view related series in Business & Management, please visit:

www.elsevier.com/businessandmanagement

30% Discount for Authors on All Books!

A 30% discount is available to Elsevier book and journal contributors on all books (*except multi-volume reference works*).

To claim your discount, full payment is required with your order, which must be sent directly to the publisher at the nearest regional sales office above.